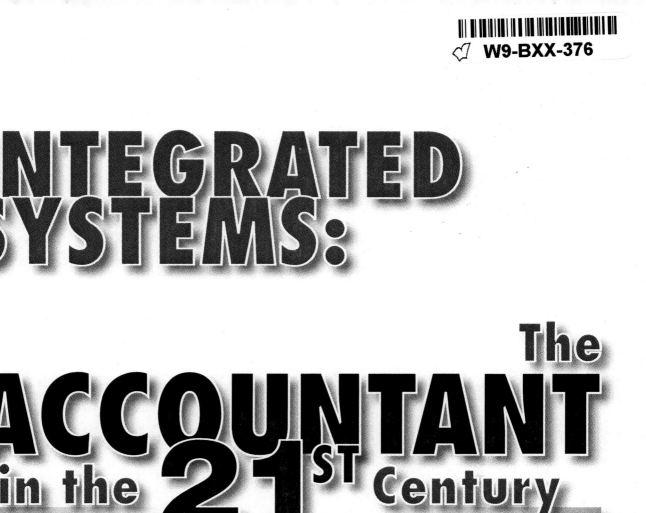

INTEGRATED SYSTEMS:
The ACCOUNTANT in the 21ST Century

Merle Martin
Professor of Accounting Information Systems
California State University, Sacramento

Monica Lam
Professor of Accounting Information Systems
California State University, Sacramento

Victor Dossey
Director of Enterprise Architecture
Getronics North America

PEARSON

Custom
Publishing

Printed in the United States of America

10 9 8 7 6 5 4 3 2 1

ISBN 0-536-85839-X

2004160491

KK

Please visit our web site at *www.pearsoncustom.com*

PEARSON CUSTOM PUBLISHING
75 Arlington Street, Suite 300, Boston, MA 02116
A Pearson Education Company

forward

"What a strange machine man is.
You fill him with bread, wine,
fish and radishes, and out come
sighs, laughter, and dreams."

— Nikos Kazantzakis

Have you ever started reading the Forward to a book and found it to be so dry that you didn't even want to start reading Chapter 1? Well, to ensure that this won't happen with this textbook, we'll begin this book with an Aggie fable.

They finally had completed their arduous journey over the yellow brick road to Emerald City – Dorothy, the Tin Man, the Scarecrow, the Cowardly Lion, and, of course, the little dog Toto. They were brusquely ushered into a huge, dim-lit chamber that seemed quite empty. They looked all about the room looking for some signs of life. Finally Dorothy, in a quivering voice, said, "Hello – Mr. Wizard – are you here?"

Then lightening bolts crashed throughout the room, accompanied by great gusts of wind that almost disassembled the Scarecrow. Strobe lights pulsed erratically with random splashes of every color. Suddenly there appeared before them a 16-foot holograph of Bill Gates bellowing in a rumbling voice, "Who dares to enter the presence of the great and powerful Wizard of Oz?"

They all cowered and trembled at this frightful scene – that is, all but the darling dog Toto. He started barking ferociously at the Microsoft giant. Then Toto turned and scooted to a curtain barely visible at one corner of the room. He stood at the curtain, yipping in a ceaseless staccato. Finally, Dorothy and the others (all except, of course, the Cowardly Lion) cautiously approached the curtain that was commanding Toto's anger. Dorothy carefully pulled back a curtain edge. She was stunned by what she saw.

There was a short, plump, elderly man wearing glasses and a green eyeshade which partially covered his shiny, bald head. He was jumping back and forth while pulling switches and pushing buttons at a very large electronic console. He continued this for several moments until he spotted Dorothy looking at him in astonishment. The man jumped back and said in a shaky voice, "Oh, my goodness! Oh, my goodness! I've been busted!"

Later, they all sat together sipping cappuccinos and nibbling on Oreo cookies. Dorothy and her entourage listened intently as the wizard began to tell his story. "I used to be an accountant in Kansas. I followed all the rules carefully and only shredded documents when I was told to do so. I always did what everyone else told me to do. When they changed the rules, I dutifully altered the way I was doing things. I was a loyal ledger soldier. But nobody seemed to respect me. I was merely a tiny cog in the complex machinery of the accounting gods."

The wizard took a sip from his cappuccino, swallowed whole two Oreo cookies, and then continued. "One day I decided that I had had enough. I was no longer going to be a reactive pawn that let others dictate its path though life's contest. I was going to take control of my destiny

– to be proactive and make others react to me. I started studying technology, focusing on emerging technologies that few people knew about yet. I learned to use these new wonderments before others even knew they existed. I searched the Internet and managed to steal the identity of some magician named Merlin. Then I moved to Oz and here I am – the great and powerful Wizard of Oz, also known as the Cybersavvy Accountant."

Everyone was impressed except for Toto, who was busy gnawing at the wizard's ankles. Dorothy never returned to Kansas. Life was too exciting in Oz.

The moral of this fable is that *you can bark at technology all that you want, but that won't scare it away*. This textbook is about the Oz-like business world that has been thrust upon us all too suddenly, it seems. Specifically, the pages that follow focus on the effects of current and emerging technologies on the accounting profession. It is our contention that the field of accounting need not change drastically to counter a new cyber business world. Instead, we must target our proven skill sets, knowledge and professionalism to this new world. Our purpose here is as much to incite new thinking about our profession as it is to impart knowledge.

We have used a very pragmatic approach. The authors have over 40 years of consulting and practitioner experience in designing, deploying and managing accounting and other business technology systems. Many of the examples used in this book emanate from that practical experience. We must, however, offer one warning. It seems that, whenever anyone in the business technology field returns from a coffee break, events and systems have changed rapidly. Any book describing such business technology undergoes the risk of not including the latest fads or innovations. We have striven to minimize references to specific hardware and software brands and types in order to minimize this risk.

This textbook is designed as adjunct material to a first course in Accounting Information Systems (AIS), as a resource for a second undergraduate AIS course, or as a resource for Accountancy graduate courses. It also can be used in courses stressing accountant Continuing Professional Education credit. We assume that the reader will have had preliminary instruction in computer principles and basic AIS knowledge.

We wish to thank Dr. Suzanne Ogilby of California State University, Sacramento for her technical assistance on portions of this book. We also want to thank Cindra Shields (Spokane, WA.) for her presentation and graphic design.

Merle Martin
Monica Lam
Victor Dossey

SHORT TABLE OF CONTENTS

Chapter	Topic	Page

EXPANDED TABLE OF CONTENTS

CHAPTER 1 new accounting forces

> "Tradition: a clock that tells what time it was."
>
> — *Elbert Hubbard*

Have you ever wondered what type of idiot would leave his or her cell phone on during a Star Wars movie? Do you ever get annoyed when someone at the next table in a restaurant is talking on a cell phone so loudly that you can't carry on a decent conversation with your attractive meal-mate? Have you ever waited 15 minutes on the telephone while the automated answering system tries to find you a human operator? One has to wonder whether modern communication technologies are more trouble than they're worth. But this is not a new dilemma as illustrated by this true story of over a hundred years ago.

By nature Edgar Degas, the French painter and sculptor, was conservative. He didn't take kindly to "new fangled" inventions. His friend the etcher Jean-Louis Forain, however, believed in progress. He and Degas had frequent arguments about the advantages and disadvantages of human progress.

Forain had installed that new invention, the telephone. He arranged to have a friend phone him during a meal to which Forain had invited Degas. The phone rang; Forain rushed to answer it. After a short conversation, he returned to the table beaming with pride at his new machine. Degas merely scowled and said in a voice dripping with scorn, "So that's the telephone. It rings and you run."

Nothing's changed! The same skepticism could exist today, except that now we are using cell phones. We stop concentrating on our driving along a crowded highway because our cell phone is ringing and we *must* answer it. We slavishly respond to our cell phones in the middle of a meeting, a movie, or even a classroom lecture. At least Jean-Louis' phone was confined to his residence. Our cell phones command us wherever we may be.

We invent technology, but technology also invents us. As business people and as members of society, we often must change what we are doing and how we are doing it in response to new technologies. For example, we invented the automobile but, in fact, the automobile also invented us. 25 percent of the United States economy is tied up with the automotive business, counting not only the manufacture of automobiles, but the roads and services needed to accommodate them. Our economy has changed significantly as a result of our invention of the automobile.

Today it is our new invention - the Internet – which is changing the ways we work and conduct our lives. For example, because of Internet marketing, a rapidly growing number of consumers no longer will accept products which are designed for everybody ("one size fits all"). They demand that their computers, automobiles and even education be customized to fit their specific needs. In addition, these consumers expect to receive their customized products or services quickly; they no longer are tolerant of delivery times in weeks but insist on delivery times in days or even less. Waiting in line for a product or service is becoming an obsolete tradition. We invented the Internet. Now the Internet is inventing a new way of life for us, both personally and professionally.

Our technology and business landscapes are changing at an extraordinary pace. There has been more technological progress in the last 25 years than in the previous two centuries (Kurzwell). For example, the Internet became a major economic force in just four years; this is but a fraction of the time that it took for the radio, personal computers, or television. Microsoft didn't even include the Internet as a part of its strategic planning until 1996. This rapid pace of change means that we must change our professional practices faster than ever before in order to adapt to new technologies and new ways of doing business. This is true for accounting as well as for other business professions. Our accounting standards are steeped in business traditions and models which technology is changing. So must we change our accounting roles and focus – we must be reinvented by the technology which is pulling us forward.

This chapter discusses the problems created for the accounting profession by the intersection of rapidly changing business models and technological deployment of these models. We explore what will be the role of the 21st century accountant in the sequence of (a) the Increase in Business Complexity, (b) the Heterogeneous Business Landscape, (c) the Changing Accounting Profession, and (d) Accounting and Technology

RELEVANCE OF THIS CHAPTER TO ACCOUNTING

What an exciting time it is to be an accountant! Yet a skeptic might say, "Exciting? Are you crazy! The reputation of our profession is at an all-time low, the numbers of accounting students is dwindling, and I have to be technologically retrained every time I return from a coffee break. Exciting", that skeptic might continue, "I think it's scary!" While these concerns may be legitimate, skeptics must keep in mind that all meaningful change comes with growing pains which sometimes can be rather severe but are survivable. If our accounting profession does not change as rapidly as does the world around us, then professional accountants may become the dinosaurs that other professions have accused us of being.

There are certain traits that distinguish accounting from other business fields. The professional accountant knows the total business structure, requires proof of performance, possesses analytical and critical thinking skills, and has a deep-seated sense of what should be ethical and professional behavior. These traits will lend themselves well to what will be needed in a rapidly changing, at times chaotic business future. Accountants can play major roles in shaping and redirecting the business models of this future. These traits will be essential in the years to come only if the professional accountant is willing to apply them to newly emerging technologies and business models rather than focusing on traditional models. There is a bright future for the accounting professional but there are some hurdles that must be overcome.

THE INCREASE IN BUSINESS COMPLEXITY

Our business setting is becoming more complex. This presents significant problems for accountants who must oversee day to day business dealings. This increasing complexity results from rapid technological growth and increased complexity of business dealings.

Rapid Technological Growth: Technology is growing at an exponential rate. *Exponential Growth* is an increase in the rate by which something is growing. For example, suppose that a business's earnings increase eight percent the first year, ten percent the second year, and 13 percent the third year. This is exponential earnings growth because, not only is the amount of earnings increasing, but the *rate* of that increase also is increasing. Technology innovation has been increasing exponentially since the beginning of the 20th century. Some futurists predict that this exponential growth rate will not flatten but will continue to rise indefinitely.

Whether this proves to be true or not, we can certainly expect technology to rise dramatically during the next 10 to 15 years. We also contend that there is an accompanying exponential curve that will rise as fast as the technology phenomenon. Business dealings are becoming more and more complex.

Business Processing Complexity: The complexity of business dealings is increasing in two ways. First, the number of business relationships is increasing exponentially. Second, the typical business transaction is becoming more complex.

Increase in Number of Business Relationships: There is a phenomenon referred to as the ***Network Effect:*** the exponential increase in network complexity given only a linear increase in network size (Glover et al, 2001). Let's use the example of Dell Computers to illustrate this effect. Dell used to have a one-on-one relationship with each customer (Figure 1-1A). Therefore, there were only two transaction paths (messages) involved: Dell to the customer and the customer to Dell.

Now Dell hands off its manufactured computers to UPS to deliver to the customer. A third party now has been added to this business dealing. Because of this, there now are six message paths that can be used: Dell to the customer and back, Dell to UPS and back, and UPS to the customer and back (Figure 1-1B).

The number of trading partners in the Dell system has increased from two to three, or 33 percent. Yet Dell message possibilities (one measure of network complexity) have increased from two to six, or 300 percent. A linear increase in the number of trading partners has created an exponential increase in network complexity as measured by the number of message possibilities. This phenomenon can be generalized by the following formula,

$$\text{System Complexity} = \text{N times (N} - 1)$$

where N is equal to the number of parties (nodes) in the system. Try this formula with the Dell examples for both Figure 1-1A and 1-1B to verify our previous intuitive results.

Figure 1-1 Dell Message Paths

A. Old Dell System | **B. New Dell System**

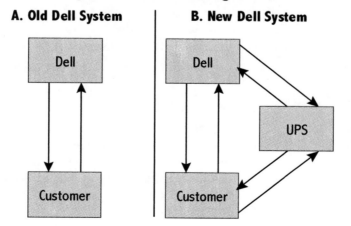

Advances in Internet technology now allow companies such as Dell to greatly expand and expedite their dealings with other supply chain entities such as customers, wholesalers, distributors and third-parties (middlemen). As we increase our number of immediately accessible business partners, the complexity of our information network increases even faster.

<u>Increase in Transaction Complexity</u>: The typical business transaction is becoming more complex. Following is an order request submitted by a technological firm to one of its vendors:

"I want to order 100 units of X to be delivered on 4/15/1999 to my manufacturing plant A. Payment is net 30 days."

Even this simple order results in four separate and ensuing actions:

- the vendor ships the 10 units to the manufacturing plant
- the vendor bills the technology company
- the technology company's receiving section receives, inspects, and warehouses the shipped material
- the technology company sends payment to the vendor within 30 days of receiving the material

This sequence is complex enough. Today, however, technology has enabled that same company to send an order that looks like this:

"I want to order 100 units of X. Split the order between my two manufacturing plants A and B. Deliver to the plant A on 4/12/2004 and the plant B on 4/15/2004. Payment is net 30 days. Apply my volume discount and mark the "Type" box on the Shipping Form with my inventory code."

This new transaction creates the same four actions as described above, but now (a) the vendor must ship twice on different dates, (b) the receiving section performs its functions twice, (c) payment must be delayed until both shipments are received, and (d) the vendor's billing becomes more complex because a quantity discount must be applied and the vendor's Shipping Form must be tailored to this particular customer and this particular order.

In addition, the first order and its ensuing actions were processed on paper via mail or fax. The second order and most of its ensuing actions are conducted electronically between parties with two different computer systems using different electronic transmission languages. The typical business transaction, already complex, has become even more so.

The Bottom Line: So, the number of business relationships is increasing rapidly and the typical transaction (message) between these parties has become more complex. This makes it more difficult for us to fulfill our accounting responsibilities effectively. Complexity is not a friend to accountants. The simpler the business system, the easier it is for accountants to measure, protect and audit it.

THE HETEREOGENEOUS BUSINESS LANDSCAPE

Accountants face another problem in that the companies that they oversee are in different stages of business and technological evolution. There is not a model of a "standard business" to which we can target our accounting and auditing standards. There is an evolution that allows a firm to reach e-business maturity. Yet all firms do not evolve to that state at the same pace or through the same path.

Some firms leap into the latest technology with gusto. Other firms take a "wait and see" approach and adopt only when a technology has proven itself. Other firms have to be dragged into using a technology, sometimes adopting it just when it is facing obsolescence. The result is a mishmash of organization types that accountants must oversee. The evolutionary path that a single firm might follow to reach a mature e-business state includes the following stages.

Islands of Technology: In the traditional, pre-1990s firm, each of the separate business applications (e.g., Accounts Payable) was independent of each other. These separate applications acted as islands of technology that could not communicate with one another. This lack of communication required reentry of the same data many times, harbored files with redundant and inconsistent information, and forced employees to learn many different ways of doing things. Some companies are still at this embryonic stage but their numbers are decreasing rapidly. Yet, many of our current accounting standards were developed with this type of business structure in mind.

Internal Integration: *Integration* is the linking of automated applications in order to reduce the need for human intervention. The first progression from the Islands of Technology embryonic state is for the firm to integrate business applications internally so that, within a single organization, all applications "speak the same language" and can communicate with each other without time-consuming and error-prone human intervention. This can be done by initiating such projects as (a) consolidating all independent data files into one integrated database and (b) deploying a centralized Enterprise Resource Planning (ERP) system.

External Integration: The next stage is for the firm to integrate its external processes. This typically is done in three steps: (a) electronically integrate the purchasing function with key vendors, (b) electronically integrate the firm's supply chain (e.g., distributors), and (c) provide electronic linkages with customers. A particular firm may choose to integrate in a different sequence, but the ultimate destination is a mature e-business firm that is fully integrated, both internally and externally.

Increase in Business Complexity: It is clear that technology and its resulting complexity is pervasive and will continue to penetrate all levels of businesses. This increase in business complexity presents significant challenges to accounting. The accounting profession is attempting to respond to these new challenges.

THE CHANGING ACCOUNTING PROFESSION

There are new challenges and forces reshaping the Accounting profession. These forces may not necessarily change what accountants are, but they likely will change how they do things – or at least the targets for their activities.

Forces Affecting Accounting: Some of the primary forces that are refocusing traditional Accounting are:

Demise of Bookkeeping: The manual calculating and data-gathering tasks once assigned to accounting clerks and bookkeepers are now done almost entirely by computers. Lower-level accounting positions are disappearing. Some educators even are questioning the need to teach debits and credits to introductory accounting students. The traditional accountant is taking a more proactive role as financial consultant and guardian of organizational assets. Business system planning, technology alternative selection, and performance measurement are becoming a larger portion of the accountant's skills portfolio.

Increased Business Access: The physical store has a fixed number of entrances and exits. It is relatively easy to guard against undesirable visitors (e.g. bank robbers) and customers leaving the store with stolen merchandise. Even internal theft (some 75 percent of total business theft) is easier to prevent and detect since employees having access to assets are limited in number and are visible to management.

It is much more difficult to prevent or detect fraud or sabotage in an Internet environment. There are multiple entry portals, particularly in a wireless setting. The visitors are unseen and could be spoofing – posing as a legitimate customer. Accountants are the guardians of organizational assets, but now the intruders that we must guard against have proliferated and seem almost invisible. Even internally generated transactions can be generated anonymously.

Complicating our dilemma is the fact that electronic transactions, including financial transfers, are moving at the speed of one per billionths of a second. The enemy is unseen and moves too quickly for humans to spot. Does this sound like a Science Fiction horror movie? This is intrusion detection in today's world.

Faster Reporting Needs: The business world is evolving rapidly and now has many more permutations than even ten years ago. Top-level executives must make decisions more rapidly using more up-to-date information. Annual or monthly publications of financial information will not suffice in today's business world. Intel, as an example computes weekly and even daily cost-benefit (ROI) statistics by department, by product, and for the company as a whole.

Financial reporting is becoming more frequent. Some predict that, with the advent of innovations such as the Extended Business Reporting Language (XBRL), financial reporting may become continuous rather than periodic. In addition, what we report may change as well as when we report. The information in our financial statements is based upon old business models that are disappearing. Some legislators and business executives are asking whether entries included in current financial statements are the requisite information needed for today's decision makers.

Increase in Business Risk: The old paper audit trails have disappeared. We now rely on electronic records which can be modified or erased more easily. This record alteration can be done through multiple electronic entry points, many now coming from wireless connections. In addition, we now are plagued by "hackers" who may not want to steal from us, but instead seek to create havoc in our workplace. Our increased business risk comes not so much from increased incidents of fraud or disruption as it does from our needing a new technological tool set to monitor and counter the pathways and characteristics of this new breed of incidents. Fraud now occurs in cyberspace, and we need cyberspace skills in order to prevent, detect and correct that fraud.

More Competitive Markets: There are fewer cost or other entry barriers to prevent new companies from engaging in e-business. In addition, easy Internet access is allowing customers to "shop around", thus driving prices down. As a result, one can project an e-business future where there are many more sellers, but each seller's profit margin is comparatively low. These low profit margins will force an even stronger emphasis on reducing the cost of goods sold. Accountants will be asked to make cost-cutting more visible and pronounced. There also will be an increased effort to measure performance in order to determine which products and services must be abandoned and which departments must be outsourced to outside service vendors in order for our companies to survive profitably.

Increased Public Scrutiny: The Enron and other financial scandals have given public visibility to the accounting professional as the recorder, reporter, custodian, and guardian of organizational records. While this arguably has increased the perceived importance of our profession, it also has reduced the margin of error that we will be allowed in performing our functions.

<u>Legislative Pressure</u>: This increased public scrutiny has prompted lawmakers to enact laws creating more oversight of our financial reporting and auditing functions and to impose more drastic penalties for noncompliance with these laws. The most notable of these new laws are the Baines-Oxley and U.S, Patriot acts

<u>Accounting Profession Blurring</u>: The definition of what is an accountant is becoming blurred. Emerging career options such as Forensic Accounting, Financial Services, and Risk Management blend accounting principles with other disciplines. At KPMG, Management Information Systems (MIS) trained security experts precede accountants to auditing engagements to assess the strength (risks) of the client's computer environment. California's Board of Equalization has computer personnel travel with accountants to audit firms with large computer systems. There no longer seems to be a clear distinction between who is an accountant or is an IT professional.

How Accounting Changes: We will use the example of electronic books (e-books) to demonstrate how the new electronic marketplace can change significantly how accountants must fulfill their responsibilities.

E-books are digital texts available for reading on a variety of electronic devices including personal computers, personal data assistants (PDA), and specialized readings devices.

There were fewer than 50,000 specialized reading devices sold so far in United States in 2001, but that number is expected to grow to several million in the next dew years. As Claire Zion, editorial editor for Times Warner, said, *"I can't imagine print books surviving at all. Once people try this (e-books), they won't want to give it up."*

E-books present unique problems to traditional accounting systems. In a traditional setting, the author writes a hard-copy book which is printed in a specified number of copies (Figure 1-2a). Thus, there is a variable cost for each copy printed and stored in a warehouse. The printed book then is distributed directly or indirectly to the reader with revenue recorded when the physical book is transferred to the customer.

On-line books, however, are handled quite differently from an accounting perspective (Figure 1-2b). The author still writes the book (no robot writing yet). But now the book remains in digital, rather than hard-copy medium. Thus, there are negligible variable costs per book distributed; you can distribute 1000 digital books over the Internet at about the same cost as 10 books. In addition, revenue is recorded by known download of the book. Table 1-1 shows accounting differences between off-line and on-line books.

Figure 1-2 Off-line and On-line Book Production

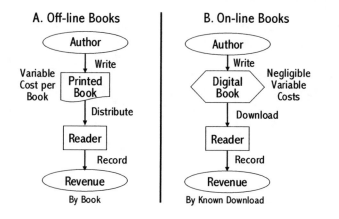

Table 1-1 Accounting Differences between Off-line and On-line Books

CHARACTERISTIC	OFF-LINE BOOKS	ON-LINE BOOKS
Inventory Control	Physical	Digital (???)
Potential Loss	Physical Theft	Web-based Theft
Extent of Loss	Known	Unknown
Type of Loss	Lost Assets	Lost Revenue

These differences fall into the following categories:

Inventory Control: We must store physical books in a warehouse but the one copy of the digital book requires only an infinitesimal amount of computer storage. In addition, physical storage costs increase as the number of stored physical books increases; that is not true for a digital book – there is but one electronic master copy.

Recording of Asset Value: We include on the Balance sheet a physical book value of the number of books stored times the cost per book. What is the value of the one computer-stored, electronic book? How do we record that value on the Balance Sheet?

Potential Loss: Someone can enter our warehouse illicitly and physically remove some books that are stored there. Theft of a digital book, however, is an illegal copying of an electronic master copy – the number of digital books in storage remains the same after the theft.

Extent of Loss: We can discover and compute physical book loss by performing a periodic inventory. If someone illegally downloads a digital book, what is our loss? The original electronic version still exists.

Type of Loss: We record the loss of physical books on the Balance Sheet (number of books missing times cost per book). How do we record the illegal download (copying) of a digital book? We could record it as lost future sales if we were sure that the perpetrator would have purchased the book if he or she was not able to steal it. \We will be discussing these problems in the chapters that follow. It is important to note that accounting responsibilities for e-marketing firms are not reduced; they are changed and may indeed be increased.

ACCOUNTING AND TECHNOLOGY

How then should accountants face this new world of rapidly evolving technology and increasing business technology? There are three different levels of an accountant's increased involvement with technology: the technology savvy accountant, the technology proactive accountant, and the accounting technology professional.

The Technology Savvy Accountant: Today's accountants cannot be concerned only with technology tools that facilitate fulfillment of their everyday tasks (e.g., spreadsheets). Accountants also must be concerned with how current and emerging technologies will affect the very nature of the businesses over which these accountants have oversight responsibilities. How will new technologies affect the accountant's role, in fraud prevention, cost controls, asset protection and auditing? What technologies should command our attention? The American Institute of Certified Public Accountants (AICPA) publishes a Top Ten Technologies list each year. The 2004 list includes:

Business Information Management: capturing, storing, and retrieving, and managing documents electronically

Application Integration: ability of different systems to "talk to each other"

Web Services: using the Internet as an infrastructure and access tool

Disaster Recovery Planning: planning for and managing losses or disruptions in computer processing

Wireless Technologies: transfer of information via airwaves

Intrusion Detection: detecting and managing unwanted electronic messages

Remote Connectivity: allowing users to connect from remote locations

Customer Relationship Management (CRM): managing all customer touch points

Privacy: protection of employee and customer personal information

This annual listing on the AICPA Web site infers that all accountants should know about these technologies as they apply to their jobs and professional responsibilities. We believe, however, that the AICPA list, while important, focuses too much on existing rather than emerging technologies. The technology savvy accountant (particularly the auditor) also should be aware of emerging technologies that will affect the accounting profession in the future. These include grid computing, artificial intelligence, sensory recognition, optical networks, holographic video, and open source software – all of which we will discuss in the next chapter. The technology savvy accountant should be a technology scout looking at the horizon to spot emerging technologies that will require transformation of what accountants do and how they do it.

The Technology Proactive Accountant: Many Accounting Information System (AIS) textbooks and courses stress what technology can do for accountants. While we do not ignore that stress, we are as much concerned with what accountants can do for technology. Accountants can proactively help other business professionals in trying to control technological and business change. Accountants can use their traditional expertise to proactively enhance technology initiatives in the following manners.

Outsource consulting: Most public accounting firms have divested themselves of IT consulting endeavors. There still exists, however, many firms such as IBM or EDS who require accounting expertise in areas such as enterprise-level system development, IT strategic planning, IT feasibility analysis, and auditing of computer operations.

Development of accounting systems: A firm often requires internal accounting expertise in development of enterprise-level IT systems and accounting applications.

Assisting IT personnel in making technology decisions: IT personnel sometimes lack the expertise to make economic decisions such as whether or not to outsource IT functions; whether to build, buy or lease applications software; the estimated profitability (ROI) of making IT investments; and what is the value of IT to the business firm. Accountants can assist and train IT people to make such decisions, or accountants may make these decisions themselves.

Ensuring adequacy of internal controls: IT personnel often consider internal controls as a redundancy which adds time and costs to an IT project. The accountant can be the advocate in justifying the economic value of internal controls in reducing business risk and loss.

Protecting information assets: Information has become one of the firm's most crucial assets. The accountant must guard information assets as carefully as physical assets.

Auditing of IT systems and operations: The accountant is an external or internal watchdog who assures to stakeholders and management that business processes and people are operating in an efficient, effective, and ethical manner.

Alleviating information overload: Businesses used to suffer from a lack of timely information. Now the problem is just the opposite: we suffer from too much information. This often is referred to as *Information Overload*, or *Data Glut*. Accounting expertise must be used to sift, summarize and prioritize information according to its decision enhancing value.

The Accounting Technology Professional: Electronic computing first began to take effect in the business world in the early 1960s. It was the accounting profession which led the way to business automation. Since then, however, accountants have ceded their technology leadership to a new class of business professionals, the Management Information Systems (MIS) specialist. There are signs, however, that the accounting profession is reasserting its technology leadership capabilities. We will focus here on accounting technology certifications and the Accounting Information Systems (AIS) professional.

Certified Information Technology Professional: Probably nothing underscores the challenging relationship between accountants and technology more than the relatively new Certified Information Technology (CITP) issued by the AICPA. One must be a Certified Public accountant (CPA) to be eligible for be awarded the CITP. This certification is intended to serve as a bridge between business knowledge and technology skills. The AICPA's CITP program has several objectives, but the most striking is *"To achieve public recognition of the CPA as the preferred IT professional in the business community"*.

Other Professional Certificates: There are many other professional accounting certifications that do not address technology directly, but imply knowledge of technology going beyond that required of the technology savvy accountant. Some of these are the *Certified Information Systems Auditor*, the *Certified Forensic Auditor*, and the *Certified Fraud Examiner.*

The Accounting Information Systems (AIS) Discipline: Another sign that accounting again is assuming a proactive role in business technology deployment is the increasing number of colleges and universities that are offering degrees or concentrations in Accounting Information Systems (AIS). The job market is beginning to recognize this new career specialty and its differentiation from Management Information Systems (MIS) and Computer Science professionals.

What differentiates the AIS professional from these other two technology professions? There are two dimensions to technology knowledge: domain knowledge and technical knowledge. *Domain Knowledge* is knowledge about the application to which the technology will be applied. This can include deep knowledge of production, marketing, finance or – in the case of the accountant – knowledge of how the business operates as a whole. Accountants are trained in every aspect of a business's operation because accounting records are an umbrella encompassing the entire business organization.

Figure 1-3 AIS Discipline in Context

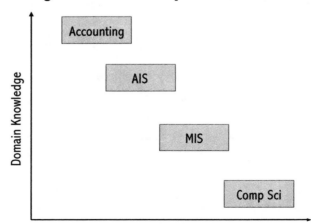

Technical Knowledge is knowledge of how to design, build, and deploy technology to solve a particular business problem. That problem may be how to market a product or how to pay a vendor. There often is a disconnect between domain and technical knowledge in that the jargon used by accounts receivable people, for example, is quite different from the jargon used by network designers. The solution is to place between the domain person and the technical person an interpreter who understands both languages. This is the primary role of the AIS professional. Figure 1-3 shows four professions mapped according to relative domain and technical knowledge.

The accountant has considerable business domain knowledge, but only a minimum of technical knowledge. The Computer Science professional, on the other hand, has very deep technical knowledge but very little business domain knowledge. The MIS profession was designed to be the intermediary between business domain experts such as accountants and technical experts such as computer scientists. The increased complexity of technology, however, has drawn the MIS profession further in the direction of technical knowledge with less emphasis on business domain knowledge. The AIS professional now is inserted as the intermediary between the accountant and the MIS professional.

The Accounting World According to Rob — Profile of an Accounting Executive

Robert (Rob) Taylor is the Accounting Manager for the North America division of Getronics, a financial solutions technology provider for clients such as City Bank and First Services. He is responsible for the day-to-day finance and accounting operations for the North America division's product lines. We interviewed Rob on October, 2002, on a variety of subjects germane to this textbook. We have included the results of this interview throughout the chapters that follow. Here are some of the questions that we asked Rob and his responses.

How did you get into Accounting? "I've been in the accounting/finance field since 1988. I started in public accounting where I did auditing and tax preparation. Then I moved to the private accounting sector where I filed thousands of sales, use, property, and income tax returns, was an accounting supervisor in a manufacturing environment, developed cost accounting systems and performed inventory forecasting."

How has technology helped you? "I started out in electrical engineering and took many computers courses including programming languages. I think that I had an advantage over other finance and accounting people who didn't have some of that computer background." Rob feels that, while technology has increased the complexity of the accountant's role, that same technology has increased accounting capabilities even more. "With four people," Rob says, "we now have four times as much valuable information as what we had with 20 some people."

How has technology changed accounting? "The one thing I see more and more every day is our change in viewpoint. Over the years, accountants have looked at the past. Now, with current accounting systems and tools, we're able to get a better picture of what you're going to do in the future."

Robert (Rob) Taylor will share his viewpoints with us on the various topics discussed in this book. Join us as this accounting executive explains to us "the world according to Rob".

Ideally, AIS professionals are those who have augmented (not replaced) their accounting domain knowledge with sufficient technical knowledge to be able to (a) alert accounting and other business professionals to technological opportunities, (b) apply accounting knowledge and principles (including internal controls) to specific technology deployment tasks including systems development and database design, and (c) use performance measurement and cost-benefit skills to help determine the feasibility of technology initiatives.

It must be noted that not all scholars or practitioners would agree with the position we have described above. The AICPA, for example, has as one of its goals for the Certified Information Technology Professional (CITP), "...to achieve public recognition of the CPA as the preferred IT professional in the business community." This implies that the AIS professional will displace the MIS professional. Nevertheless, it is our contention (and a theme throughout this textbook) that, given the increasing complexity of business and technology, there is room for both the AIS and MIS professional in the new business landscapes.

SUMMARY

Technology is evolving at an ever increasing rate. Business processing is becoming more complex and varied, thus making the business arena more difficult for the accountant to measure, manage, and audit. These and other forces are changing the focus and scope of traditional accounting. Accountants today must be increasingly knowledgeable of and proactive in the use of new technologies and their resulting effects on business practice. Accountants must know not only how to use technology, but also how to target their traditional domain skills (e.g., measurement, risk assessment) to business and technology landscapes that are becoming more complex and thus more difficult to control effectively.

Traditional accountants could disappear gradually in this century as their past roles are automated or are mired in obsolete business models. This fading away is happening to bank tellers today. We believe, however, that new accountants with refocused skills, increased technological knowledge, and a more strategic emphasis will replace their traditional counterparts. This will not happen, however, unless we are willing to change as rapidly as is technology and business practice. It is towards this end that this textbook is directed.

KEY TERMS

Certified Forensic Auditor (CFA)

Certified Fraud Examiner (CFE)

Certified Information Systems Auditor (CISA)

Certified Information Technology Professional (CITP)

Data Glut

Domain Knowledge

Exponential growth

Information Overload

Integration

System complexity

Technical Knowledge

REVIEW EXERCISES

1. What is exponential growth? Draw a graph showing what an exponential growth curve looks like.

2. What is the Network Effect? How does it relate to System Complexity?

3. Dell actually has an additional trading partner. A Texas firm ships a computer monitor to an UPS regional center to meet and be shipped with the Dell computer that UPS is delivering to the customer. (This is referred to as *Merge in Transit*). Show how does the Dell system complexity increases with the addition of this fourth party.

4. What are the forces that promise to reshape the accounting profession?

5. Go to the AICPA website and print out that society's latest list of Top 10 Technologies and its Technology watch List.

7. Give examples of Information Overload or Data Glut in

   a. buying a large appliance (e.g., big screen TV)?

   b. requirements for attaining your college degree?

8. What is the difference between Domain Knowledge and Technical Knowledge?

9. How could inventory and customer order applications be integrated?

CRITICAL THINKING OPPORTUNITIES

1. Visit a medium- to large-sized firm in your area.

   a. Describe in what sequence this firm has progressed or plans to progress from operating independent business applications to becoming a totally integrated firm.

   b. Ask for an example of how their typical business transaction has become more complex over the past 10 years.

2. Interview the chair of your school's Accounting Department. Ask that chair how that department's curricula have been changed to address the forces now affecting the accounting profession. Prepare PowerPoint slides to demonstrate these changes.

3. Research the Internet for the "XBRL" reporting language. Prepare a short memorandum for a Finance professor of why you think that this language should or should not be included in that professor's course(s).

4. Research the CITP on the Internet. Write a short report on (a) what specific body of knowledge is required to attain this certificate, and (b) how you can attain this knowledge.

5. Have a debate in class as to whether or not financial reports should be published continuously (on-line). Also debate which items in the Balance Sheet need continuous reporting and which do not.

REFERENCES

AICPA, "*About the CITP*", http://aicpa.org/about.htm

Downes, L. and C. Mui; **Unleashing the Killer App: Digital Strategies in Market Dominance**; Harvard Business School Press. 2001

Glover, S., S. Liddle, and D. Prawitt; **E-business: Principles and Strategies for Accountants**; Prentice Hall, 2004

Kurzwell, R. **The Age of the Spiritual Machine**; Viking Press, 1999

O'Leary, D.; **Enterprise Resource Planning Systems**; Cambridge Press, 2004

CHAPTER 2 emerging technologies

> "First you figure out what is inevitable.
> Then you find a way to take advantage of it."
>
> *— Russell Ackoff*

Have you ever wondered why it rains when the *expert* meteorologist said it was going to be clear, prompting you to leave your umbrella at home? Have you ever wondered why five different *expert* economists can't agree whether or not the economy will recover or inflation will return? We don't trust *expert* doctors' diagnoses any more – we seek a second *expert* opinion. It's hard to trust the experts these days because we can't tell the difference between who really knows what's going on and who merely is getting paid as if they knew. Witness this story.

A very famous professor was traveling on a lecture tour. He had a very lucrative consulting practice, so he could afford to hire a limousine and chauffeur to drive him across the country rather than travel by commercial airline. One day they were entering Boston where the professor was to speak before the faculty at Boston College on the topic of, "A Few Fundamental Contributions to Generalized Network Flows".

As the limousine approached the campus, the chauffeur said to the professor, "I really admire what you're doing. I'd give my soul if I could get up there in front of an audience and talk on any subject on which I was considered an expert." The professor responded, "Well, thank you, Ralph. But it's not that special. Anyone could give my lecture with a minimum of preparation. When the audience thinks that you're an expert, they will believe everything that you say."

The professor thought for a moment and then he said, "I'll prove it to you. Stop at that service station just ahead and we'll switch clothes and you can be the professor giving the lecture and I'll be your chauffeur." Ralph's eyes widened and he stuttered, "Oh, that won't work. I don't know anything about that stuff." "Nonsense," countered the professor, "I'll coach you on everything you'll need to know in the ten minutes it will take us to get to the lecture hall." So they switched their clothes and the professor drove them into campus while briefing the chauffeur.

Ralph's lecture went exceedingly well, surprising both him and even the professor who was sitting in the front row. But just as Ralph was about to walk off the stage, a young faculty member in the audience stood up and said, "Professor, I've been waiting a long time to ask you a question about your research. How do you compare out-of-kilter with the simplex method in semi-constrained networks?" The professor thought to himself, "Oh, oh! We're in trouble now!"

Ralph thought for a moment, and then, his voice dripping with sarcasm, he answered the young faculty member. "I can't imagine why you'd ask such a simple question here? Why, it's the kind of thing my youngster has already mastered in his fifth-grade mathematics. To prove that, I'm going to ask my chauffeur to give you the answer"

C. West Churchman (1968) told this story to emphasize the basic humor of science – to demonstrate how little even "experts" know. Who is the expert and who is only bluffing? How little do any of us really know? This is particularly true when it comes to the future of technology.

Technological knowledge is changing so rapidly that, if you take a coffee break, you may have to be retrained. It is said that the half-life of the knowledge of a PhD in technology may be as little as six years; in six years, half of technology PhD's knowledge will be obsolete.

So what? Why do we care about a PhD's knowledge? We will stress in this chapter that it is critically important for accountants to proactively look into the future into what business technologies are emerging. We cannot reactively wait for the experts to tell us what is coming and how it will affect our profession. The experts can provide us with some direction and insight, but they really don't know what will be happening in technology 15 or 30 years into the future.

We discuss emerging technologies impact upon accounting in the sequence of (a) Future Trends, (b) Technology Diffusion, (c) Emerging Technologies, and (d) Technology Scouting.

RELEVANCE OF THIS CHAPTER TO ACCOUNTING

The time given to us to react to new technological advances is becoming increasingly short. This is true particularly for the accounting profession. Why is this so? Technology changes the very nature of how we do business. Since accountants are the scorekeepers and overseers of business, any changes will change accounting directly or indirectly. When it comes to technology, we can afford no longer to wait and see what is happening now. We must be proactive and predict what *may* happen several years into the future. Only in this way will we acquire the lead time necessary to make the changes that technology requires and to do so in an orderly manner. Only then will we be able to take advantage of the technological advances that appear to be inevitable.

FUTURE TRENDS

It is not easy to forecast the future. Long-range forecasting is more art than science. It is a form of structured guessing. Technology forecasting has been the focus of many past predictions that seem absurd when viewed in today's context. Here are but a few of them.

Forecasting the Future

– "Computers in the future may weigh no more than 1.5 tons." (Popular Mechanics, 1949)

– *"There is no reason anyone would want a computer in their home."* (Ken Olsen, President, Chairman and Founder of Digital Equipment Corporation (DEC), 1977)

– *"640K (memory) ought to be enough for anybody."* (Bill Gates, 1981)

– *"$100 million dollars is way too much to pay for Microsoft."* (IBM, 1982)

As you can see, it is not easy to forecast the future. Even some of our computer geniuses have issued forecasts that missed the mark considerably. Indeed, Microsoft did not have the Internet in its long term strategic planning documents as late as 1995.

Another of Bill Gate's axioms seems closer to what we will try to do in this chapter. He says, *"We almost always overestimate where technology will be in five years, and underestimate where technology will be in ten years."* We will attempt to estimate future trends gingerly, relying on the works of experts who specialize in such long-range forecasting (references at the end of the chapter).

We will present our selective view of the future using Figure 2-1's structure.

Figure 2-1 Future Trends

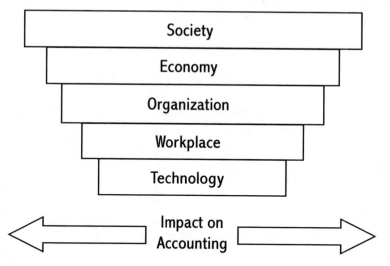

Future Social Changes: As the global cyber-culture grows, local cultures will disappear; they will be subsumed into one global culture. Hundreds of languages will disappear. Family structures will become more diverse as continuing urbanization aggravates most current environmental and social problems.

Time will become the world's most precious commodity as change becomes more rapid and the need for quick decisions becomes more critical. Technology will continue to de-socialize people, making them more prone to antisocial and criminal behavior. Privacy will become harder to maintain. There will a growing division between the *cybersavvy* and the *cyberklutzes* - the computer resource "haves" and "have-nots".

If these social forecasts are beginning to depress you, remember the old Aggie adage that "*When you gain you lose, and when you lose you gain.*" The elderly population will grow dramatically throughout the world as rapid medical advances increase human life spans. Technology will make it almost impossible to hide information or to control events; it will be difficult if not improbable for dictators to maintain a closed society because citizens will be more aware of their government's failures. Some even suggest that unification of global values and the decreasing ability to hide information will lead to fewer human wars.

Future Economic Changes: The global economy will grow more integrated each year. The increased complexity of this global financial system will make it highly vulnerable to disruptions, with financial anomalies in one location quickly affecting all other parts of the globe. Criminals will use cyberspace increasingly to commit thefts. At the same time, burgeoning fields such as Forensic Accounting will use cyber-technologies to more quickly and effectively prevent, detect and prosecute such thefts.

The continuing rapid growth of information industries will create a knowledge-dependent society. The "one size fits all" mind set will disappear as consumers demand customization of products and services, not only in business but in government and education as well. Cash will become unpopular with everyone except thieves, tax dodgers, and the truly paranoid.

Future Organization Changes: Information-based organizations will replace the old command-and-control hierarchy model of management. For example, the limited span of control preached in management books the past 70 years will expand to the point where one person may have direct responsibility for hundreds of others. This will be facilitated by the ability to communicate globally and instantaneously. Indeed, the typical large business of 2010 may have fewer than half the management levels of 1990. This would displace some two-thirds of our middle-managers.

The size of institutions will undergo a transition to a binomial distribution. The big institutions will get bigger, the small companies will survive, and the midsized organizations will be squeezed out. Institutions increasingly will grow more transparent in their operations – more accountable for their misdeeds. This will come about through two factors. Consumers will increasingly demand social responsibility from companies – and from each other. This will lead to an avalanche of federal, state and local .regulations. Indeed, government regulations will take up a growing portion of management's time and efforts.

Services will continue to be the fastest growing sector of the global economy. Distributors will disappear. These and other non-value-added middlemen will be replaced by information brokers (e.g., Price Line) and transaction facilitators (e.g., customer authentication). There will be more competition; more customers will have access to accurate price information. Some market entry barriers will fall. We will experience the demise of fixed prices with all dealings subject to rapid computer price negotiations. As a result, we will have a "profitless prosperity" where it is easier to find buyers, but profit margins become lower (Cairncross, 2001).

Future Workplace Changes: Workers will retire later as life expectancy increases. Specialization will spread throughout industry and the professions. However, the generalist (accountant?) still will be important as the person who can orchestrate specialist efforts into comprehensive and complex missions and projects. Skills and knowledge will become obsolete faster than ever. This will deprive many workers of their jobs as they are left stranded in the cyber-society. As a result, education may become compulsory for adults as well as for children.

Future Technology Changes: The pace of technological change will accelerate with each new generation of discoveries and applications. For example, Internet use and global reach will grow logarithmically. Technology costs will decline rapidly to the point where computers, for example, become common commodities like bread or nails. Older technologies will not necessarily disappear; they will persist despite the constant arrival of newer rivals. This will tax the human mind as new technological knowledge is added to rather than replaces existing knowledge.

Technology will become more portable and miniaturized – even implanted within our bodies. This will enable the blind to see and paraplegics to climb stairs. Computers will take over more and more of our mental tasks, leading some to believe that computers will replace humans. We are reminded of one anonymous Stanford Research Institute researcher who many years ago stated, *"Don't worry about computers taking over the world. Maybe they'll keep us as pets."*

Technology will become more ubiquitous – so prevalent and common that we don't notice their existence. Computers commonly will talk to other computers. Your television will automatically turn down the volume when the phone rings. When you use the last of your milk, you'll pass the empty carton over a refrigerator scanner. The refrigerator computer will send a message to the local grocery store computer to send you immediately more milk. You will electronically attach your automobile's computer to the computer system of an Interstate freeway. The freeway will drive your car accident-free and at great speeds. Your automobile sitting in your garage will be automatically tuned-up from a remote service location.

Key stroking will disappear. Data will be entered to computer systems by such unobtrusive means as voice recognition, touch screens, and other biometric sensing devices. Databases holding all of the world's knowledge will be available to everyone and will fit on the palm of one's hand. These databases will be updated automatically from a remote location.

What _will_ be the Future? Will all of the preceding forecasts come to pass? Who knows if or when? If we did know, we could become famous and quite wealthy. These forecasts merely are an amalgamation of the thoughts of many futurists cited at the end of this chapter. We must be reminded that the future holds not only what can be imagined, but the unimaginable as well. As was stated a few years go, _"Tomorrow's employees and managers will face the opportunities and challenges of advancing technology in ways we cannot possibly envision today" (Scientific American, 1998)._ While somewhat dated, this quote is relevant today. Nevertheless, we will attempt to paint the technology landscape of the future using today's imagination. But first, let's investigate how emerging technologies evolve – how they are "diffused" into society and the workplace.

TECHNOLOGY DIFFUSION

Emerging technologies are deployed throughout a society by a process call Technology Diffusion. **_Technology Diffusion_** is the spread of usage for a new technology throughout a population of interest, such as an industry or a country. There are two types of emerging technologies subject to such diffusion. A **_Disruptive Technology_** is a new technology, often in its infancy, which unexpectedly replaces an existing technology or business practice. The Internet in the 1990s is one example. A **_Sustaining Technology_** is an established technology which is undergoing incremental changes and improvements. For example, the cellular phone is a sustaining technology that is undergoing incremental changes but could eventually be replaced by a disruptive technology such as thought transfer.

As shown in Figure 2-2, sustaining technology costs decrease at a much lower rate than do disruptive technology costs. Information Technology (IT) specialists are very good at improving existing (sustaining) technologies. The best value for any organization, however, is to spot on the horizon a possible disruptive technology that will lead to a substantial competitive advantage.

Any specific technology's diffusion in any particular period of time can be described by Moore's (1995) Technology Adoption Life Cycle model (Figure 2-3).

This model attempts to explain how technology follows a diffusion process for non-mandatory technologies. By **_Non-mandatory Technologies_** (sometimes called **_Discontinuous Technologies_**), we mean those that are not imposed upon prospective users by edicts such as, for example, government laws that require use of touch screens for voting. Moore applied diffusion theory to the adoption rate of discontinuous innovation.

The **_Technology Adoption Life Cycle_** consists of the five specific adopter classes of Technology Enthusiasts, Early Adopters, Early Majority of Pragmatists, Late Majority of Conservatives, and Laggards or Skeptics.

Technology Enthusiasts: This group receives intrinsic enjoyment from experimenting with any new technology whether or not it is practical or cost effective. Every business organization needs at least a few employees in this category to raise the general consciousness as to the potential usefulness of emerging technologies.

Early Adopters: These people look for an immediate high value in the use of a new technology. This early value is specific to this group's needs but not necessarily to the larger

Figure 2-2 Disruptive and Sustaining Technology Cost Patterns

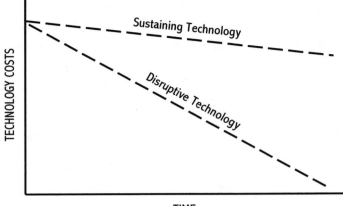

group of potential users. For examples, frequent travelers were the first group to begin using electronic books although those books were not yet culturally and economically viable for most users.

Early Majority of Pragmatists: These potential adopters don't wish to be pioneers. For example, they may be skeptical of the risks of changing their ways of doing business to an e-business setting. They want *complete* technological processes that have *proven* to produce a *high value* relative to price. Members of this group look to the experiences of the two earlier groups in order to judge adoption. This was certainly the case with e-marketing where established firms studied the experiences of dot.com firms before entering the Internet arena.

Late Majority of Conservatives: These risk-averse users wait until a new technology surrounds them before adopting it. Often their adoption is forced by collateral events such as a hardware or software supplier discontinuing support for older technologies.

Laggards or Skeptics: This group goes down fighting; they only adopt the new technology under absolute duress. We know of one business school where five members of the faculty refused to use e-mail. The Dean of that college attempted to force adoption of e-mail by insisting that *all* school communication be transmitted *only* by e-mail. The five faculty members didn't

Figure 2-3 Technology Diffusion in Specific Time Period

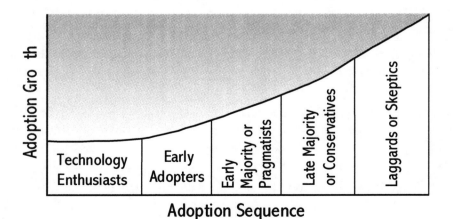

budge; they had their department secretary print out for them in hard copy all school communications. All of the e-mail skeptics eventually retired and the school lived happily ever after.

The "Chasm": Moore places what he calls a "chasm" between the Early Adapters and the Early Majority of Pragmatists (Figure 2-4).

Figure 2-4 Adoption Life Cycle with Chasm

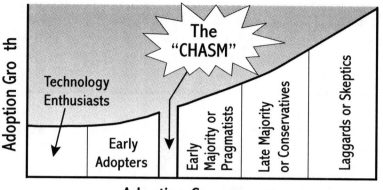

Some technologies are delayed from progressing from the Early Adopter to the Early Pragmatist stage. Some technologies never are able to leap the chasm in order to continue on the adoption growth curve. Other technologies are bypassed by newly deployed technologies diffusing at a faster rate. For example, in the film medium, video cassettes were being replaced by writable CDs, but that changeover now is being interrupted by the development of writable DVDs. The writable CD film revolution seems to have become stuck in the Chasm while writable DVDs move past it to the right of the Technology Adoption Life Cycle curve.

Figure 2-5 shows what can happen inside the chasm. The figure illustrates the dot.com "bust" of 2000 and 2001, but it can be generalized to the adoption of almost any newly developed technology. The entry into the chasm is preceded by discovery of the technological device or approach and high expectations for its use. But then a reality check halts the progress of the innovation. The technology in its current state doesn't function as well as predicted or it costs more than currently is feasible.

This happened in 2001 with new dot.com companies. New companies were started too quickly with insufficient business plans. (See the boxed discussion on Dot.com Companies and the Chasm). Many if not most of these companies failed. Established, more cautious companies (Early Majority of Pragmatists) waited on the sidelines to learn from the mistakes of these failed ventures. Then, beginning in 2002, these established and pragmatic companies and a handful of surviving dot.com companies began to push e-marketing up the other side of the Technology Adoption Life Cycle.

Dot.com Companies and the Chasm

The massive failure rate of dot.com companies in the early 2000s was a shock to many people, particularly to investors. Yet, that failure was not totally unexpected to those who peered deeply into the underlying economic forces in play. These forces included the following:

Dot.com Company Immaturity: A typical, long-term business first automates, then integrates its processes, and then reengineers those processes to make them more competitive. Most dot.com

Figure 2-5 Inside the "Chasm"

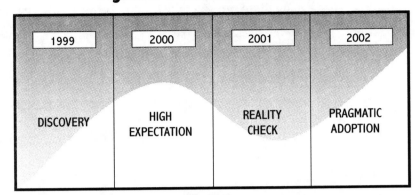

Adapted from Intel (Doug Busch) presentation 4/10/02

companies bypassed these early stages of development. Thus, their products and services often could not be offered at a competitive price or at a high enough quality. This was particularly true for the delivery and customer service processes.

Cultural Barriers: There was and continues to be uneven access to the Internet, particularly in developing countries. In the United States, for example, it is estimated that some 75 percent of Internet sales are made to persons in the top 15 percent of income distributions. Also, many people consider physical shopping to be a social experience and do not want to sacrifice a "try-on" environment. It takes time to gnaw away at such cultural barriers.

E-business Marketing Cycle: There is a lengthy path from initiation to profit realization for a service or product. You have to (a) let consumers know that you are on the Internet and where to find you, (b) encourage these consumers to buy something (70 percent of initiated Internet sales are aborted before completion, (c) satisfy customers so that they will revisit the site, and (d) increase volume of sales to the point where you are making a profit. Amazon.com still was not making a profit after three years.

Investment Pressures: Many dot.com companies were startups that relied on entrepreneurial funding. Their entrepreneurs expected to see a return on their investments within a certain time frame often called the *Investment Cycle*. During this period of dot.com high expectations, entrepreneurs became concerned that companies such as Amazon.com and Netscape, while hugely successful, still were not making a profit. Their concerns caused them to decrease the Investment Cycle from about three years to as little as 18 months.

Thus, the first three economic forces described above required more time for dot.com companies to develop. Yet investment pressures reduced the time necessary for these companies to demonstrate profitability (Figure 2-6). This can be viewed as what was happening in the "chasm" of the Technology Adoption Life Cycle for many dot.com companies.

EMERGING TECHNOLOGIES

Let us now embark upon the hazardous journey of predicting specific technology developments in the next 20 years and how these developments may affect business in general and accounting in particular. We must remember, however, that such predictions are only possibilities, and that other technological alternatives may emerge very quickly. As Downes and Mui pointed out, *"The future arrives so quickly that the designers of Disney World's Tomorrowland have given up. They can't build an environment that doesn't look stale before it's opened"*

Figure 2-6 E-marketing Forces

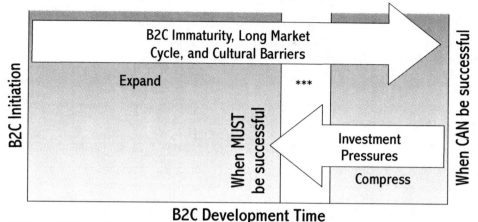

*** Moore's "Chasm"

We will start with a model used by the Gartner GP Group (2003) which looks surprisingly similar to Intel's prior description of what happens within the Chasm of Moore's Technology Adoption Life Cycle.

Gartner's Emerging Technologies Hype Cycle: The Gartner Group's model (Figure 2-7) carries the provocative title of the Emerging Technologies Hype Cycle. This cycle consists of the five phases of (a) Technology Trigger, (b) Peak of Inflated Expectations, (c) Trough of Disillusionment, (d) Slope of Enlightenment, and (e) Plateau of Productivity.

Technology Trigger: A scientific breakthrough, public announcement, product launch or other event generates significant press and industry interest. According to Gartner, business technologies now falling into this phase include:

Grid Computing: Connecting user workstations together without messages having to go through a central routing point (server)

Mobile Retail Applications: Conducting retail transactions such as a sale using a mobile device such as a cell phone

Instant Corporate Messaging: Exchanging corporate-level messages through a continuous stream much like an Internet "chat" site

Figure 2-7 Emerging Technologies Hype Cycle

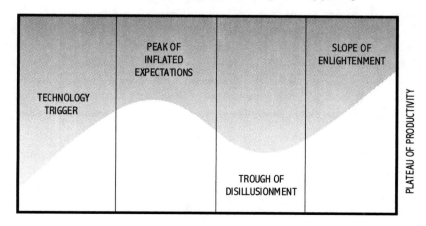

Peak of Inflated Expectations: Over-enthusiasm and unrealistic projections characterize this phase. There are some successes but even more failures as the technology is pushed to the limit. Technologies falling into this phase now include:

Instant Retail Messaging: Exchanging messages between a buyer and a retailer through a continuous stream much like an Internet "chat" site

Web Services: All business applications and messages flowing through a Web browser.

Mobile Corporate Applications: Conducting corporate-level transactions (e.g., budgeting) using a mobile device such as a cell phone

Mobile Payments: Making point-of-sale (POS) payments using a mobile device

Trough of Disillusionment: The technology becomes unfashionable as it fails to meet its inflated expectations. Business technologies now falling into this phase include:

Artificial Intelligence: Use of computer reasoning/physical skills in lieu of a human

Biometrics: The use of physical characteristics such as iris- or face-scanning to serve as the identification of a valid party attempting to enter a system

E-signatures: A unique electronic sequence or symbol representing a human signature and used to sign a document

Speech and Voice Technologies: Use of a human sensory attributes in lieu of key-stroking to enter data to a computer system

Slope of Enlightenment: Focused experimentation leads to a better understanding of the technology's applicability, risks, and benefits. According to Gartner, business technologies that fall into this phase include:

Intelligent Agents: The use of computer programs to perform human decision making tasks such as evaluating on-line loan applications

Document Imaging: The accurate conversion of paper documents into an electronic format

Business Rules Engines: Centralized computer storage of formulas and other decision logic criteria used in business applications (e.g., "Give 5% discount to vendors submitting payment within 10 days of billing.").

Plateau of Productivity: The practical benefits of the technology are demonstrated and it gains world-wide acceptance. The only technology that the Gartner report includes in this phase is Data Mining – the sorting through a database to identify patterns and establish relationships.

The Gartner study deals primarily with technologies that are focused on financial services. While this focus certainly is important, the accountant's reach is much broader including such non-financial aspects as protection of information assets, detection of destructive programming code, and intrusion detection. Therefore, we have chosen to discuss in more detail some emerging technologies that we believe can have the most dramatic effect on hoe accountants in general, and auditors in particular, effectively perform their professional responsibilities. We have ordered our discussion by the estimated time in the future (a consensus of forecasters) when the technology will mature,

Sensory Recognition: This technology converts human sensory stimuli into electronic patterns that a computer can recognize. All human senses including smell and touch accept or emit some form of energy. Ideally, then, all of the human senses could be converted to electronic patterns (the "0's" and "1's" binary language of the computer).

The most imminent of these senses that are being digitized is the human voice. It is estimated that, by 2009, key-stroking will disappear as a means of entering data to a computer system. Voice will be the predominant entry medium. Even today, voice recognition software can produce the accuracy of an experienced typist, computers can identify voices of humans that are angry, and a Russian telephone speaker can have her message translated automatically to English or Spanish.

Conversion of human handwriting is becoming more accurate each year. This might become a viable alternative for the voice-impaired or when voice recognition devices are not available. The electronic conversion of other senses such as smell or touch is a distinct possibility in the not so distant future. Many experts believe that thought patterns are a form of energy – that when we think we generate distinguishable energy emissions. Will our future thoughts be subject to computer sensing, translation, and dissemination? This is a troubling conjecture.

Effect on Accounting: We can establish an electronic voice audit trail as easily as a keystroke audit trail. Authentication of the message-entering party will not become more difficult since specific voice identification will be at least if not more accurate than keystroke pattern identification. So our internal control, auditing and asset protection responsibilities may experience only a minor impact.

However, our responsibilities for reducing costs and increasing process efficiency will be enhanced by sensory recognition in general and voice recognition in particular. Whenever a person enters a keystroke, three bad things happen. The human is slower than a computer, the human makes more errors than do computers, and the human may be motivated to deliberately enter the data erroneously (we call this "data diddling"). Thus, by bypassing human keystroke entry, we gain time, reduce errors, and reduce the risk of fraud – all of these are costly events.

Optical Networks: Current communication networks including the Internet are based upon electronic pulses ("0's" and "1's"). It is estimated that, by 2012, optical networks will be replacing electronic networks. Optical networks are comprised of 160 channels (or colors of light) transmitted in single fiber no thicker than a human hair. Messages can be transmitted over 1000 concurrent wavelengths. This non-electronic medium will increase exponentially the amount of data that can be transmitted via telecommunications networks. This means that data can be sent at much faster speeds than now. It is estimated that optical networks initially will be focused on long-distance, Wide-area Network (WAN) capabilities, thus making communications between different parts of the globe almost instantaneous.

Effect on Accounting: The switch to optical networks probably will be transparent to and thus have little impact on our day-to-day functions. However, the conversion from an electronic to an optical network infrastructure may require a considerable investment of organizational resources. We then may be called upon to use our cost-benefit skills in evaluating the feasibility of the timing for such a conversion. In addition, technology department training costs will likely increase with this shift in technology infrastructure.

Extreme Software: It is estimated that, by 2012, we will see the introduction of software programs that utilize artificial intelligence constructs to operate independently of the human programmer. This intelligent software fixes its own errors, adapts to specific user patterns and needs, and never fails (crashes). It can correct human program design errors. Indeed, after a period of time the original programmer probably won't be able to tell how extreme software program works.

Impact on Accounting: One of the most difficult accounting responsibilities is the overseeing and auditing of computer software programs. We have a difficult time today detecting errors or malicious code that has been imbedded into software applications such as Inventory or Accounts Payable. With Extreme Software, the software is constantly changing under machine control to the point where the original human programmer doesn't know what the program is doing and why. Our current software auditing problems may become a nightmare! At the same time, a world without human programming errors and software "crashes" would seem to be a blessing from the perspective of efficiency and consistency. When you gain, you lose, and when you lose, you gain.

Grid Computing: The emerging technology that may have the greatest impact upon accounting is *Grid Computing*: connecting directly together user workstations without having to go through a central routing point (server). It is estimated that this advanced form of peer-to-peer (P2P) networking will be commonplace by 2015. After the 9/11 terrorist attacks, many companies found that their central computer and message routing systems were inoperable. As a result, customers and vendors could not communicate with these companies; employees could not communicate with each other. There was an upsurge of interest in using P2P networks which bypassed vulnerable, centralized message routing servers.

Grid Computing is a complete P2P system with no reliance on centralized routing points. It also has the capability to harness the capacity of underutilized machines. Suppose that we could tap into all of our organizational computers that are shut down from 5 p.m. to 7 a.m. We would have harnessed an aggregate computer power that would exceed that of the world's largest supercomputers. We could, for example, perform large complex economic and market simulations and forecasts that exceed our central computer capabilities today.

We also could break our sensitive data files (e.g., customer, inventory) into small segments and distribute these segments to be stored in the multitude of workstations within our organization. Whenever we needed a complete record or file, we could retrieve the requisite fragments and reassemble them into the whole. Some futures experts even predict the extension of Grid Computing into a World-wide computer that taps the unused capacity of millions of computer workstations around the world.

Impact on Accounting: The ability to fragment data files into a multitude of varied locations would reduce the risks of complete or substantial file destruction through natural disasters or sabotage. However, it could be a nightmare trying to audit such dispersed files and their constant dispersal, update, and reassembly.

Other Emerging Technologies: These are only a few of the emerging technologies that may impact the accounting profession in the near-future. A few other emerging technologies that may impact us are the following:

Holographic Video: This is the electronic presentation of 3-dimensional, life-size images in spaces apart from computer monitor screens. Potential customers could inspect products and instructors could present live training from distant locations.

Adaptive Antenna Wireless Communication: This technology allows mobile communication devices to adapt to different weather or other conditions that deter effective usage today.

Streaming Media: Now pictures and sound can be transmitted (streamed) live over the Internet. In the future, all human senses (e.g., smell) may be transmitted by this medium as well.

Accounting Questions: Table 2-1 summarizes the possible impacts that emerging technologies discussed may have upon accountants.

Yet, there are several generic questions which we should use to gauge how any emerging technology may impact what we accountants do and how we do it.

How will new technologies affect the way we do business? Will the technology be disruptive and change our basic business models as did the Internet? If so, our accounting models also will have to change.

How much will we have to know about these new technologies to be effective? Will we need detailed or only conceptual knowledge? Will our education system be able to incorporate this knowledge quickly or will we need to develop organizational or professional association alternatives?

Will these new technologies make it easier for to commit fraud/sabotage? Unfortunately, utilization of new technologies is much like using a wrench. I can use the wrench constructively to fix a child's bicycle or destructively to hit someone over the head. How can we protect our organization from the worst-case uses of new technologies?

Can accounting / auditing standards keep up with technology? Electronic Data Interchange (EDI) was implemented in business in the early 1980's. Our accounting standards for dealing with EDI were promulgated in 1998 – some 15 years later. How can we speed up our standards revision process to accommodate the ever increasing pace of business technology development?

Of course, you cannot begin to answer such questions without first discovering what technologies are emerging. That discovery process is called *Technology Scouting* and is the subject of the next section.

TECHNOLOGY SCOUTING

Adapting to new technologies often is a troublesome process. The technology must be learned, tried, deployed and adapted to in terms of procedures and internal controls. Just when the new technology has become a comfortable part of our workplace, a newer technology arrives to take the old technology's place. It is a constant cycle of upheaval that some clever person once described as "Gate's way to Heaven". The rapidity of this cycle is becoming increasingly fast. Our only defense against this technology change chaos is to place ourselves in the position where we know as far ahead of time as feasible what technologies may affect us in the future. In this way we can give ourselves the lead time necessary to assure an orderly rather than a panic transition between technologies. This process is called Technology Transfer.

Table 2-1 Emerging Technologies Impact on Accounting

Emerging Technology	Estimated Emergence	Accounting Impact	Auditing impact
Sensory Recognition	2009	- Faster processing - Fewer errors - Reduced fraud risk	- Change in nature of audit trail
Optical Networks	2012	- Increased technology investment analysis - Increased IT training costs - Faster data transfer	- Change in nature of file transfer
Extreme Software	2012	- Fewer programmer errors - Less frequent software "crashes"	- Increased difficulty of software auditing
Grid Computing	2015	- Reduced risk of file destruction	- Increased difficulty of file auditing

The British Postal Service

Downs and Mui (1999) use the example of the British Postal Service (BPS) to demonstrate how an organization can be proactive about tracking and using emerging technologies. While this example is somewhat dated, it still stands as a model for today's organizations. In 1997, BPS created an innovation fund as a means of giving managers a way to experiment with technology without preparing extensive cost-benefit analyses.

Submitted proposals had to meet two of the three criteria of (a) dealing with technology new to BPS, (b) preparing a creative new application, and (c) including substantial risk. $4.5 million was made available annually for this project. BPS management received over 30 proposals during the first six months.

The first project to be approved was a prototype for an improved vehicle navigation system for postal vehicles. This project included (a) experiments with global positioning satellite (GPS), (b) collision avoidance technology, and (c) real-time congestion reports. All three of these technologies were in their infancy stages in 1997.

Perhaps the most important benefit of the BPS experiment was that it created an organizational mind of Technology Transfer — searching for emerging technologies that could enhance the organization.

Technology Transfer: *Technology Transfer* is the process for ensuring an orderly transition between a current and an emerging technology or technology application. This process is comprised of the following stages:

- Scout emerging technologies by, for example, reading technology magazines and searching the Internet.

- Map prospective use of a particular technology onto your company by asking how you or your competitors could use or be affected by it.

- Convene a "Think Group" to play with the future – to ideate how, when, and why the technology could be used. The sessions should be vigorous marketplace of ideas that are floated, argued, selected or rejected. Use brainstorming and technology fairs. Play the roles of your competitors and try to see how they could use the technology to destroy your company. Some companies have even developed video tapes containing alternate versions of the future.

- Hold demonstrations such as workable prototypes or vendor demonstrations of the technology. Let people "play with" the technology in order to generate ideas on how it will effect the organization in general and accounting in particular.

- Secure organizational commitment to experiment with the technology; this may involve developing a cost-benefit analysis to justify experimentation costs.

- Pilot test the technology at one location or one non-critical application. Build a full cost-benefit analysis based upon the results of the pilot test.

- Deploy (implement) the technology throughout your organization.

Technology Scouting: Technology scouting is the most critical stage of technology transfer. It also may be the hardest to justify from a cost-benefit perspective since it is almost impossible to demonstrate tangible benefits this early in the process. You will need a fast and sensitive pipeline of information on what technologies are beginning to emerge 10, 15, or even 20 years from now. Technology magazines, technology Web sites, technology conferences, or any other technology information source can be the flow for this pipeline.

You also will need a radar screen that is sensitive to what is a real emerging technology versus what merely is science fiction hopes or "hypes". Finally, you will the triage skills of an emergency room doctor to determine which of this myriad of new ideas really will be relevant to your organization.

The Technology Advocacy Group: Many companies establish technology advocacy groups which track and demonstrate future technology developments. Daimler-Bentz, for example, has established a Circle Member Group which includes 150 renowned researchers; the group meets regularly. The goal of this group is to anticipate long-range changes in tomorrow's technology landscape. The group has developed and updates regularly a Technology Scouting database.

Savants and Gurus: Technology scouting often can be initiated using existing personnel and personal interests. Any organization of even moderate size has several individuals who might be labeled technology "savants and gurus". These people are fearless about technology and optimistic about the possibilities. They often are self-appointed and not formally supported through organizational resources. An organization can find these individuals and form them into the nucleus of a formal, resource-supported technology advocacy group. These individuals tend to be deeply but narrowly focused on technology and they are not always cognizant of the firm's strategic goals or processes. However, they make excellent technology scouts as long as they are surrounded by mission-oriented persons who can filter savant/guru ideas to keep the ones that have practical use.

SUMMARY

Forecasting the future of technology is not easy. Yet we must make the attempt to do so proactively in order to give us the lead time necessary to adapt in an orderly rather than in a reactive manner. Technology is diffused in a relatively predictable manner as portrayed by the Technology Adoption Life Cycle. We presented in this chapter several emerging technologies which may have important impacts upon the accounting profession. Finally, we stressed the importance of the Technology Transfer process in general, and the Technology Scouting process in particular.

KEY TERMS

Chasm	Grid Computing	Sustaining Technology
Discontinuous Technology	Investment Cycle	Technology Adoption Life Cycle
Disruptive Technology	Non-mandatory Technology	
Empty Shopping Cart Syndrome	Optical Network	Technology Diffusion
	Sensory Recognition	Technology Scouting
Extreme Software		Technology Transfer

REVIEW QUESTIONS

1. Why is it important for accountants to track emerging technologies?
2. What is Technology Diffusion?
3. What are the differences between sustaining and disruptive technologies?
4. What are Non-mandatory or Discontinuous Technologies? Give an example of a mandatory technology.
5. Describe the Technology Adoption Life Cycle.
6. What is the Chasm? Why is it important?
7. What transpires within the Chasm?
8. What will be the importance of Optical Networks to accountants?
9. What will be the advantages and disadvantages to accountants of Grid Computing?
10. What steps comprise Technology Transfer?
11. What does a firm need to do effective technology scouting?
12. Why is a Technology Advocacy Group important?

CRITICAL THINKING EXERCISES

1. Consider the adoption of DVD technology. Describe the Technology Adoption Life Cycle for this technology.

    a. Which types of people belong to each adoption class?

    b. What is the Chasm in this situation?

2. Survey senior accounting officers in five to 10 companies in your geographic area. Ask them the following questions:

    a. Are you aware of what Optical Networks and Extreme Programming entail?

    b. If so, what do you think will be the impact upon accounting of these two emerging technologies?

    c. Does your firm have a Technology Advocacy Group? If so, are you a member?

3. Interview the Dean or an Associate Dean of your Business School. Ask him or her how that school keeps abreast of emerging technologies that may impact business education.

REFERENCES

Cairncross, F.; **The Death of Distance**; Harvard Business School Press; 2001

Churchman, C.; **Challenge to Reason;** McGraw-Hill, 1968

Cornish, E.; **The Cyber Future: 93 Ways Our Lives Will Change by the Year 2025**; World Future Society, 1999.

Downes, L. and C. Mui; **Unleashing the Killer App**; Harvard Business School Press 1999

Gartner G2, **2003 Emerging Technology Hype Cycle for Financial Services**; Gartner G2 RPT-0603-0053, 2003

Gates, B.; **The Road Ahead**; Viking Press, 1995

Halal, W.; **The Top Ten Emerging Technologies**; Futurist, June 2000

Khan, M. and M. Martin; *Technological Barriers to E-Business*; Proceedings of the **International Applied Business Research Conference**; Acapulco Mexico, March 2003

Kurzwell, R.; **The Age of the Spiritual Machine**; Viking Press 1999

Moore, G.; **Crossing the Chasm**; Harper Business Press 1995

Zuckerman, A.; **Tech Trending**; Capstone, 2001

CHAPTER 3 integrated e-business systems

> "Isolated applications and data, no matter how impressive, can produce idiot savants, but not a highly functional corporate behavior."
>
> — *Steve Haeckel*

Have you ever wondered why your new address shows up on your semester registration billing but not on your end-of-semester grade report? Have you ever wondered why, when you ordered a fruitcake, the company ships you gourmet coffee? We are in the age of marvelous technological advances, but sometimes things seem to be more messed up than they were without these new toys. Sometimes this type of problem can be quite serious. Consider this story.

Assistant District Attorney Peter Gonzalez walked into his colleague's office shaking his head. "What's wrong?" asked Tracy Waller. Peter Replied, "I've got an arraignment hearing an hour from now and I'm not sure if I've got the right defendant." Tracy looked puzzled and said, "What do you mean? How could that happen?"

Peter explained, "I have the defendant's hearing notice from the Court System. I also have the police report, but it has a different address and only a middle initial – no middle name. Finally, I printed out this guy's criminal history record and it has a different birth date than the other two records. Are all of these different records for the same person?"

Tracy said, "Probably so. The courts, police and prosecutor's office all have different computer systems that don't talk to one another. The birth date, for example – it had to be entered by three different people and one of them might have entered it wrong. Or there could have been an address change that was corrected in one system but not the others." "Are you serious?" Peter asked. "These computers had better start talking to each other before we throw the wrong person in jail!"

This situation was not uncommon in the early 1990s, both for business and government information systems. Still today the biggest IT challenge, barring security, is integration of disparate systems – whether these systems lie within one organization or are shared by many organizations in an e-business setting. Without such integration, each separate department or business partner *owns* its own data file; no other entity is allowed to change or even access the data in that file. These islands present problems for accountants and others who then must gather data from multiple, often conflicting data sources. Information output from one application must be reentered manually to other applications. This slows down the business process and increases the risks of errors and fraud. This setting also makes it difficult for managers to extract information quickly since it must be gathered from many sources and may not have a consistent format.

In this chapter we discuss integrated e-business systems – the various ways of conducting business on a global scale. We will focus primarily on Business-to-business (B2B) models. We also will discuss the underlying B2B need for third-party interpretation and translation between business parties who conduct their events in different ways. We will stress how this new e-business world is changing the targets of traditional accounting activities. This will be done in the sequence of (a) Business-to-business (B2B) Models, (b) Enterprise Resource Planning (ERP) Models, (c) Business-to-business Integration, and (d) the XML Standard in B2B Integration

RELEVANCE TO ACCOUNTANCY

As Professor Dan O'Leary, University of Southern California, says, "Accounting is process, process, process!" We agree, and the nettlesome fact is that those business processes for which we have been trained and with which we have worked are changing – both internally and externally. We must redirect our traditional accounting focus on a new set of business models, conditions and processes. Yet, before we can do so, we first must learn just what the integrated B2B world is all about.

BUSINESS-TO-BUSINESS (B2B) MODELS

Business-to-business (B2B) is comprised of several different approaches or models which include:

- electronic data interchange using protocols such as Electronic Data Interchange (EDI) or the extensible Markup Language (XML)
- internal sharing of the same data and processes using Enterprise Resource Planning (ERP) systems
- controlling the flow of vendor information and goods through Supply Chain Management (SCM) systems
- controlling flows of product information across product life cycles using Product Life-cycle Management (PLM) systems
- controlling flows of information and products sold to customers using Customer Relationship Management (CRM) systems
- procuring goods by leveraging technology (E-procurement).

We will be describing these B2B models and protocols throughout the remainder of this chapter. Figure 3-1 is derived from Professor O'Leary's work and shows how these B2B models relate to one another.

Supply Chain Management: *Supply Chain Management (SCM)* models connect enterprises electronically with their suppliers (vendors) and facilitate partnering with suppliers. SCM removes inefficiencies in the supply chain by providing real-time information visibility across all supply chain players.

How SCM Models Function: Figure 3-2 demonstrates how an "ideal" SCM model would work for paper towels. A consumer buys a roll of paper towels from a retail supermarket. This sales event is transmitted immediately to a Foresting company which decides that it needs to cut another tree to meet future demands for paper towels. The felled tree is shipped to a Pulp Maker who has been alerted to the tree's imminent arrival. The resulting paper pulp is shipped to Proctor and Gamble who uses that pulp to make another roll of paper towels to ship to the retailer (supermarket) to replace the roll that the consumer purchased.

Figure 3-1 B2B Flow

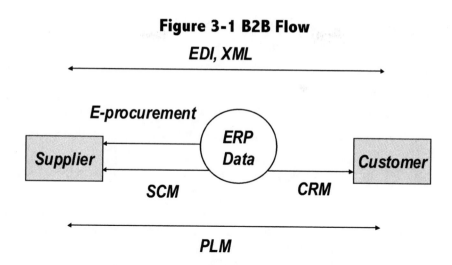

Adapted from D. O'Leary presentation at 2002 American Accounting Association

In reality, this type of immediate reaction to a *single* consumer purchase does not happen. Indeed, such overly quick response could result in inefficiencies and incorrect anticipations throughout the supply chain. Yet, the salient point is that SCM models *can* move such consumer demand information rapidly to all supply chain players, even if these players choose not to immediately act on this information.

Supply Chain Elements: SCM models transmit information which leads to the following supply chain decisions.

Location: Along which paths will goods flow?

Production:

Figure 3-2 SCM Towel Example

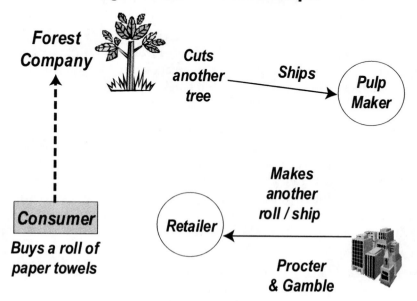

Adapted from D. O'Leary presentation at 2002 American Accounting Association

- What products do we create at which plants?
- Which suppliers will service these plants?
- Which plants will supply which distribution centers?

Inventory:

- What should we stock?
- For each item that we stock, what should be the order quantities, reorder points, and safety stock levels?

Transportation: What's the best way to transport goods while balancing shipping costs and shipping time?

These questions are not new. What Supply Chain Management adds is that these questions are asked across the entire supply chain rather individually within each firm. In addition, the answers to these questions are rapidly communicated throughout the supply chain. This allows immediate response to changing customer demand patterns and thus a reduced need to carry expensive safety stock as a "buffer" to such changing patterns.

Effect on Accounting: The effect of SCM models on accounting parallels that of other B2B models. A firm's internal information is shared with external partners through multiple electronic portals. It then becomes more difficult for accountant's to prevent and detect fraud, to protect the firm's strategic information, and to audit a system which now surges beyond brick boundaries.

Thus, the accountant's traditional responsibilities for establishing and evaluating internal controls do not change, but the focus is shifted to a new arena with new threats and risks.

CRM: *Customer Relationship Management (CRM)* is an approach that treats customers as organizational assets that must be managed. This includes giving customers the information they want when they need it. CRM starts with *Customer Targeting*: finding out which customers you really want, then deciding how you want them to relate to you. CRM uses database search techniques in an attempt to treat each desired customer uniquely through means of on-line ordering and customization. It is important to note that both of these functions can be used by a firm without a CRM model. CRM, however, adds value to these functions by integrating them in a seamless manner.

On-line Ordering: On-line ordering enables the organization to shift order entry work to customers. This also allows the organization to learn more about these customers at the same time. On-line ordering will allow a firm to bypass traditional distribution networks to reach customers directly. This can lead to lower marketing and product distribution costs.

Customization: The "one size fits all" mentality of the 20th century will not work any more. Most customers now expect products that have been tailored to their unique needs, whether the products are automobiles, laptop computers, or greeting cards. E-business requires and facilitates cheap customization of consumer goods. For example, Proctor and Gamble created a company called Reflect which allows Internet sales of beauty care products. This online ordering site bypasses distributors and retailers on Proctor and Gamble's traditional supply chain. Customers fill in Web forms with such details as skin color or hair quality. They then receive shampoos and cosmetics made to their specifications.

Interestingly, this on-line ordering system has allowed Proctor and Gamble to deal with the "Abandoned Shopping Cart" problem. Two-thirds of customers shopping over the Internet abandon the purchasing process after partially completing it. The Reflect system makes custom lipstick to match the type that the customer seemed about to order. Then Proctor and Gamble mails the lipstick free to the customer with an invitation to revisit the on-line ordering Web site.

Effect on Accounting: Customer Relationship Models (CRM) can reduce costs significantly by outsourcing expensive order entry processes to customers. However, this again increases the number of electronic "doors" into a company, thus increasing the difficulties of fraud prevention, asset protection, and auditing. In addition, on-line customer ordering may eliminate the need for an internal customer order taking function, thus reducing the number of accounting clerks required in a firm.

Product Life Cycle Management: *Product Life Cycle Management (PLM)* is a term used to group all software tools required by an organization for the management of a firm's product through its life. PLM covers all stages of the product's life cycle from design to manufacture to disposal. This methodology may cross organizational boundaries when product life cycle stages are performed by different companies.

PLM Functions: The PLM collection of software packages tracks products by gathering information over time and across partners including customers. The time dimension includes the *Product Life Cycle*: the life of a product from design to obsolescence. PLM models integrate product information from disparate sources including (a) sales histories, (b) product diagnostics, (c) usage and repair histories, and (d) maintenance and service records. Performance alerts are sent when product performance is out of line with expectations. For example, the number of customer return sales of defective units may exceed what would be expected for a product of that type. In such a case, alert messages might be sent to manufacturing and quality assurance.

PLM Software: PLM primarily is a collection of often non-integrated software applications which perform specific product life cycle functions. Some of these functions include:

Specification: definition of a product's requirements and major parameters.

Concept Design: product aesthetics and main functional aspects

Detailed Design and Development: automated design tools (e.g., Computer Assisted Design (CAD)).

Simulation: pre-manufacturing prototyping of how product might work.

Visualization: three-dimensional rendering of what the product would look like.

Manufacturing: Automated manufacturing scheduling and tracking tools including Computer Aided Engineering (CAE)

Quality: Computer aided product inspection.

Enterprise Management and Communication: including Enterprise Data Management (EDM) software which includes (a) linking to SCM, CRM and ERP models, (b) project planning, and (c) documentation (e.g., digital publishing).

Effect on Accounting: Product Life-cycle Management (PLM) models have minimal effect upon traditional accounting functions with the exception that the software can be expensive and difficult to justify using Return-on-investment (ROI) analyses.

E-Procurement: *E-procurement* is the electronic ordering of supplies and material over the Internet. The traditional Purchasing department is bypassed partially or entirely. This may cause that department to be reduced in size or eliminated. These cost savings, however, may be offset by an increased security threat posed by multiple electronic portals leading into the company. An increase in people with technology skills may be needed to counter the increased security risks endemic with software that interfaces with outside parties. E-procurement often is the first step for a company entering the e-business world. Most large vendors provide the means for their customers to quickly and easily order through the Internet. Thus, there is a low entry cost for small-to medium-sized firms to begin e-purchasing.

Effect on Accounting: E-procurement can reduce procurement costs significantly by reducing the number of orders and removing the purchasing department as an intermediary between departments and vendors. However, the purchasing department acts as an internal control that screens for invalid and unnecessary purchases. E-procurement savings could be offset by increases in fraud and superfluous purchasing. A firm still needs someone to ensure that correct business rules are being enforced so that, for instance, we order the correct printer cartridge from the correct vendor.

ENTERPRISE RESOURCE PLANNING (ERP) MODELS

An *Enterprise Resource Planning (ERP)* model is a software package that integrates the processing of an organization's transactions in order to facilitate operations and planning. These integrative software suites sometimes are called simply *Enterprise Resource Models (ERM)*. An ERP ties together into one entity the different business functions that have hitherto been separate software packages that did not communicate with one another (Figure 3-3).

ERP Features: An ERP has certain features that distinguish it from other types of automated business systems.

Centralized Database: ERP software interacts with a centralized database which is updated on a real-time basis. Transaction data need only be entered once because there are no duplicate and autonomous data files. This single update feature reduces organizational resources expended for data re-keying and maintenance of duplicate files. It also prevents inconsistencies when redundant data fields are updated with different values. More importantly, ERP creates a single version of organizational "truth" that cannot be challenged because it is the only information that exists within the organization.

Flexibility: An ERP can be suitable to a wide range of industries and organizations, but have available specific industry templates.

Geographically Broad: An ERP can support organizations with multiple companies or sites in multiple locations. From an international perspective, an ERP can support multiple languages and any number of currencies.

Planning Facilitated: An ERP allows integration of transaction processing with a firm's strategic and tactical planning activities. Typically, planning is performed based on batched activity data in the form of reports which can be one to six months old. An ERP allows real-time planning which is based on information that is current as of the last transaction processed.

ERP Applications: We will use SAP's R/3 software as an example of specific application features that can be found in an ERP package. This software comprises several modules:

Financial Module: This includes Asset Management (AM), Controlling (CO), Financial Accounting (FI), Work Flow (WF) and Industry Solutions (IS). The Financial Accounting portion includes posting of transactions to the General Ledger while the Controlling portion includes cost accounting. Other accounting applications include credit management, product profitability analysis, Activity-based Costing (ABC), and built-in management reporting and analysis tools.

Figure 3-3 ERP Application Integration

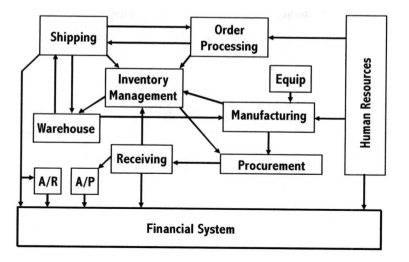

Manufacturing Module: This includes Plant Management (PM), Production Planning (PP), Quality Management (QM), and Materials Management (MM).

Other Modules: Other R/3 modules include Human Resources (HR), a Project Management System (PS), and Sales and Distribution (SD).

ERP Market Trends: The ERP market is in a state of flux. In discussing where this market may be going, it is helpful to define two terms which relate to the extent of business application coverage that a particular package may provide. *Functionality Breadth* refers to what percentage of total business applications a software product contains. For example, if an ERP product includes in some manner all or most of the applications shown in Figure 3-3, then that package is said to have functionality breadth.

Functionality Depth refers to what percentage of any one application's requirements is fulfilled by a particular package. For example ERP product A may not include as many applications as does ERP product B. Product A, however, includes every possible requirement that a manufacturing application could use, while product B only includes only limited manufacturing features. ERP product A would have less functionality breadth than ERP product B but, for the manufacturing application, product A would have more functionality depth than product B. From a marketing and service perspective, it is difficult for ERP software to have both functionality breadth and functionality depth for all applications covered. The resulting model would be too complex, too costly, and take too long to implement. ERP vendors generally have chosen to emphasize either functionality breadth *or* depth.

Top-tier ERP vendors are those which emphasize functionality breadth and appeal to a large-sized company market. Large-sized companies generally have the resources and the needs to add programming code in order to give any specific application (e.g., manufacturing) requisite depth. *Middle-tier ERP vendors*, on the other hand, emphasize less functionality breadth, but have more depth in particular industry segments or business applications. BAAN, as an example, has designed ERP packages that are functionally deep for specific vertical markets such as Chemicals or Primary Metals. Figure 3-4 demonstrates the differences between top- and middle-tier approaches. Table 3-1 shows differing characteristics for the two tiers.

Figure 3-4 Top- and Middle-tier ERP Approaches

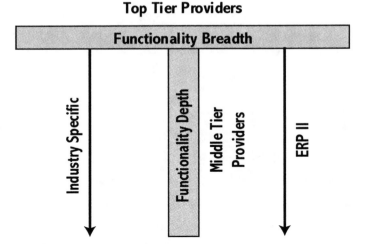

Modified from a figure originally presented by Julie Adam Smith, Arizona State University

Yet who is a top-tier and who is a middle-tier vendor is not always clear. JD Edwards, a middle-tier vendor, attempted to enter the top-tier market, but then they retreated from that endeavor. The firm now advertises itself as a middle-tier vendor although it now has been acquired by PeopleSoft. At least part of the reason behind JD Edward's retreat is that the top-tier market has become saturated; most of the large-sized firms already have implemented ERP models.

Much of this implementation took place in the late 1990s when these firms were faced with massive overhauls of all existing applications in order to make dates compatible with the new millennium (the "Y2K problem"). These firms felt that, instead of expending resources on revamping software, it would be better to devote these resources instead on implementing an integrated, enterprise-wide ERP solution

Table 3-1 Top- and Middle-tier ERP Characteristics

CHARACTERISTIC	TOP-TIER	MIDDLE-TIER
Number of Industries	Many	Few
Number of Countries	Many	Few
Number of Languages	Many	Few
Type of Architecture	Closed	Open
Ability to Integrate with Partners	Limited	More Capability
Complexity	High	Low
Agility (Ease of Change)	Difficult	Easier
Transaction Volume Range (Scalability)	Medium to High	Low
Cost	High	Low
Is Source Code Available?	No	More Often

Modified from a table originally presented by Julie Adam smith, Arizona State University

B2B INTEGRATION

One of the cornerstones of B2B models is their ability to integrate a firm's processes with those of vendors, customers, and other trading partners. *E-business Integration* is the tying together of two or more computer systems in order to enable the seamless, electronic movement of transactions between all supply chain parties through use of a common language (protocol).

Why Integrate Business Systems? There are many reasons why a firm may choose to integrate its processes with firms outside its boundaries. First of all, that integration can save transaction time, thus reducing order and payment cycles and their costs significantly. Second, an outside partner may provide cost savings or preferred treatment to firms which have integrated with that partner's systems. Thirdly, integration may allow a firm to leverage some of its technological assets. For example, General Motors (GM) allows Conrail to access its production scheduling files so that a railcar is ready to load new vehicles as they are exiting the production line. This file sharing would not be possible unless there was data integration between GM and Conrail.

The final reason for integration is that the current e-business landscape is a virtual Tower of Babel; there are a multitude of languages (protocols) being used within industries and among industry partners. This chaotic communication structure is illustrated in Figure 3-5. This would be equivalent to a United Nations where each of its members spoke only his or her native languages. The United Nations would need to (and does) hire a host of interpreters to establish communication between members. This is what B2B integration does – provide translation between the varying ways two partners do business. As in the United Nations example, this translation, or integration, often is done by third parties.

Levels of Integration: There are several levels of integration required to translate business transactions from one firm to another. These include:

Platform Level: This is the computer hardware addressing such concerns as" Can GM's Production Scheduling files be read accurately by Conrail's mainframe computer?"

Application (software) Level: The two firms attempting to communicate may be, for example, use two different types of Enterprise Resource Planning (ERP) software which are closed systems – they aren't allowed to talk to other ERPs from different software vendors.

Network Level: As shown in Figure 3-5, there are a variety of network protocols with intriguing acronyms such as FTP, SMTP, EDI or X12.

3rd Party Middleware) Level: A typical business firm must interact with many external partners who may be using many different ways of conducting and communicating business. It would be difficult for such firms to have to translate its communications to multiple languages. Often these firms opt to use a third-party vendor to act as an integrator between itself and its external trading partners. Such outsourcing firms now have to learn the language of the 3rd party vendor. *Middleware* is computer software that allows transaction processing interpretation and communication with external trading partners. Middleware also can also take on an internal company role of integration platforms which connect disparate hardware and software. Systems such as MS BizTalk or WebLogic translate and dispatch messages sent by one internal application to another.

Modes of Information Exchange: Paper had been the primary mode of information exchange for hundreds of years. It has been displaced slowly by first the telephone, then by such message media as (a) faxes, (b) Electronic Data Exchange (EDI), and (c) Web data transfer technologies. However, according to Blaab's Law, "Old technologies persist n the face of new technologies." Thus all of these successive developments in information exchange coexist today.

Figure 3-5 B2B Tower of Babel

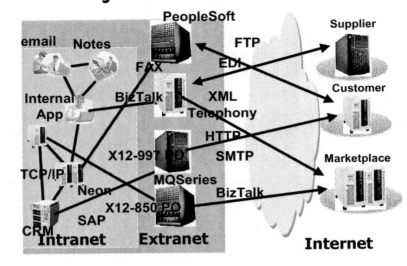

Fax: The Fax technology has serious limitations. These messages are hard to read and easily lost. More critically, information from the Fax document must be reentered to computer systems, thus slowing processing and introducing opportunities for entry errors. Fax processing also is people intensive. Yet, Dr. Pepper/Seven-up still processes up to 70,000 faxes per year.

EDI: *Electronic Data Interchange (EDI)* is a means of communicating business transactions electronically using a standard set of transmission rules (protocol). This technology has been in existence for 20 years. Transaction exchange between trading partners is done through a third party's Value Added Network (VAN) (Figure 3-6).

EDI is a mature technology now being moved to the Internet. Yet it is still being used in its original mode by many companies. Sears, for example, has over 30 mainframe computers that use data in EDI format. Eastman Kodak processes over 65,000 transactions from over 400 partners *each month*. Yet, EDI has limitations which render it increasingly impractical in an e-business world.

EDI is a serial system processing standard chunks of information in a standard form. Needed changes in business processing are limited by this rigid structure. EDI's lease of Value Added Networks (VAN) through a third party is quite a bit more expensive than using the Internet. EDI works best between pairs of companies but not with multiple partners as is often required by today's e-business environment. Finally, there are high entry costs for EDI which makes it difficult for smaller firms to participate. Still, many firms have made a sizable investment in EDI and it still works quite well in many business situations. So, instead of EDI being phased out, it often is translated by firms such as Cisco to a Web setting.

Web Data Transfer: *Web Data Transfer* allows information such as orders to appear and be filled in at Internet sites. Typically these forms are found at the seller's Web sites. Some large buyers, however, implement them at their Web sites and require sellers to do the data entry. Lowes, for example, provides Web forms for small vendors to complete. This has saved them 30,000 faxes per year and $3 million in VAN charges. Unlike EDI, Web data transfer does not require expensive 3rd party leasing of VAN lines. The firm needs only a standard Web browser. Some EDI systems are being translated to a Web-based medium to take advantage of Internet global coverage and decreased costs. It seems likely that Web-based interaction eventually will displace both the Fax and EDI technologies for transaction transmission.

Integration Standards: Certain communication standards (a protocol) must be established between trading partners in order to allow transactions to be transmitted back and forth with accurate and complete information. A ***Communication Standard (Protocol)*** is an agreed upon method for transmitting and interpreting business transactions. Integration standards reduce the complexity of processing business transactions. However, at the present time, no one standard has emerged as a common, universal means of inter-business communication. Therefore, the promised simplification of standards is instead a mishmash that complicates business processing.

Vertical Integration: Some industries are not waiting for the promulgation of global B2B standards. These industries are developing their own standards which are unique to those industries. For example, the computer industry has developed a transaction communication standard called RosettaNet. This standard is being used by all computer industry manufacturers, vendors and customers to transmit B2B transactions.

EAI: In the past, computer workstations did not have individual processing capabilities. They were unintelligent slaves to large mainframe computers. Today, computer workstations are powerful and capable of performing the most sophisticated processing without the assistance of large centralized computers. Indeed, the centralized computer serves the computer workstation, providing it with data or message capabilities only at the workstation's request.

Yet, we have gained but we have lost. Before, we could change the central mainframe computer and all the slave workstations would not be affected because they were merely powerless communication nodes. Now, consider a bank with hundreds of computer workstations linked throughout multiple branches. Whenever bank IT personnel wish to make a common application change or upgrade, they must do so individually for each of the several hundred computer workstations.

Enterprise Application Integration (EAI) integrates a firm's internal and external communications processes including e-mail, document transmission, database sharing, use of Web pages, and all business applications through a central routing point. It translates communicated data and automatically routes them according to automated business processing rules. Common changes need only be made once through this central routing point.

Figure 3-6 EDI Transaction

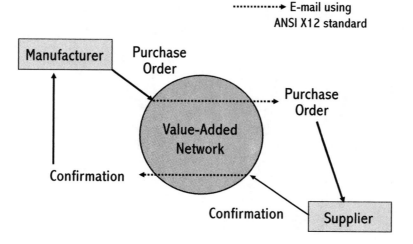

Southern Company and EAI

Southern Company of Atlanta is a $10.6 billion utility and energy firm. It is in the early stages of an EAI effort aimed at bolstering revenue and lowering costs throughout its extensive supply chain. It hopes that the EAI project will provide Southern's executives with greater visibility into its supply chain operations.

Southern currently has a complex materials procurement system which is linked to 75 different work-order and accounting applications throughout the company. Many of these applications are tied to business partners. When a change is made to one work-order system, changes must be made to all 75 systems throughout the company. The company hopes that use of centralized BusinessWare EAI will minimize changes and reduce system support costs. If this EAI project proves to be successful, Southern plans next to develop interfaces to the systems operated by its energy trading partners

EAI embodies the concept of middleware. It allows a Web-enabling server to be placed between internal, non-Internet systems and the Internet. In this way, non-Internet applications can be converted to Web versions in many cases in a matter of days or weeks. The EAI structure is shown in Figure 3-7.

EAI's biggest benefits are speed, cost savings and flexibility. Large companies can save as much as 80 percent of the cost of doing a custom integration project. The simplicity of having a single connector to each business application rather than many is particularly appealing. Required system changes need be made only once at the central connection point (server) rather than having to be implemented many times at many different connection points. However, for large companies, EAI can entail initial investment costs of as much as $500 thousand.

XML Web Services: The next evolutionary step for the Internet is **Web Services** which links external Web portals to a firm's back-office application data and business services. This extends the Internet from a network that provides services to humans to one that also provides services to software attempting to connect with other software. Instead of applications being linked to an internal EAI server, Web servers (e.g., AOL) can become the delivery vehicle for enterprise inte-

Figure 3-7 EAI Structure

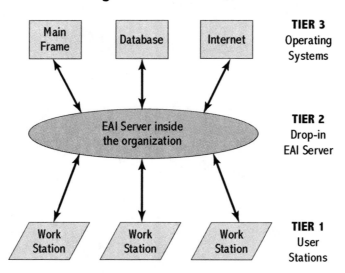

gration (Figure 3-8). Web services can range from a movie review service to a real-time weather advisory to an airline/hotel booking service (Coyle, 2003).

SOAP: The **Simple Object Access Protocol (SOAP)** holds the Web Services approach together. It lets customers, suppliers, and other trading partners to talk to each other and exchange XML data. It translates one firm's way of doing business to that of another firm. Many firms have selected this integration methodology, but there currently are concerns about the lack of a solid security model for XML Web Services.

Microsoft, IBM, and VeriSign formed an alliance in 2002 to craft new standards to address concerns about the security of Web services. They call this standard WS-Security. It is hoped that this new approach will serve as a starting point for solving the security problem. Many believe that the Web Service approach eventually will achieve a high level of security and operational integrity and will replace EAI tools.

XML Web Services Functions: Web Services operates in the following sequence:

Describing: The Web Services application describes its functionality and attributes so that other applications will know how to use it.

Exposing: The application registers this description with a repository that has (a) "white pages" that hold service provider information, (b) "yellow pages" listing services by category, and (c) "green pages" describing how to connect and use the services.

Being Invoked: A remote application locates and invokes the Web service.

Returning a Response: Results requested are returned to the invoking application.

Web Service Promises: Implementation of Web Services promises several financial advantages including (a) new revenue opportunities through creation of private trading networks, (b) increased revenue through expanded distribution networks, and (c) reduced inventory and transaction costs. It also provides the opportunity to improve supply chain effectiveness, thus reducing the customer order cycle.

Figure 3-8 Web Services Structure

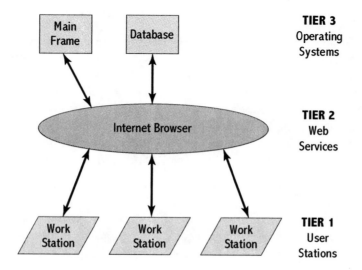

Integration Downsides: The quest for integration within a firm and between firms has taken on almost a religious zeal. Yet, true B2B integration does not come without a price. Following are some warnings about B2B integration.

Integration increases complexity: Integration adds an interpretive party to the process, whether that party is a service provider or 3rd party intermediary software (middleware). The more parties there are, the more complex is the system. For example, the United Nations could reduce its staff considerably if it didn't need all those interpreters. Standards reduce complexity because they reduce the number of variable ways of doing business. Yet, this is true only when there is a single standard in use rather than the myriad existing today. B2B integration will continue to increase business complexity until we can agree on a single or a reduced number of transaction processing standards.

Integration may not be incompatible with change: Change now is a way of life. However, when you make a small change in one part of an integrated system, that change ripples to require multiple changes in other parts of the system. One party in an integrated system may choose to sub-optimize and make changes that are locally beneficial without doing a cost-benefit analysis of the impact to the total system. That small local change can multiply into integrative changes needed for multiple parties throughout the supply chain.

Integration benefits cannot always be measured in dollars: Complex integration projects may take years and this extended period may be beyond organizational time limits for expected project payback (ROI). In addition, the benefits of integration are future-oriented and may be difficult to state in terms of today's dollars.

Integration may be culturally uncomfortable: Integration requires cooperation between competitive firms. This need for cooperation may clash with a firm's cultural values and may even be antithetical to the precepts of a free-market society. On the other hand, standards can establish a fair playing field where firms can more easily enter the marketplace and all competing parties must play by the same rules.

The Bottom Line: B2B integration promises enormous benefits in terms of future sales, market reach, and flexibility to adapt to marketplace changes. For the accountant, however, B2B integration provides a more complex environment of increased portals to firm assets and more parties involved in the transaction mix. This increases the difficulty of ensuring transaction integrity, safeguarding organizational assets, and auditing.

THE XML STANDARD

B2B integration using Web Services requires the establishment of a common method for designing, searching and extracting information from Web pages. The accepted Web page standard today is XML. The *extensible Markup Language (XML)* provides a global data interchange format between organizations and individuals. It is defined by the World Wide Web Consortium (W3C), allows the interchange of data in non-proprietary fashion including over the Internet, and is a common set of rules describing structured data in plain text rather than in proprietary binary representations. No one organization or group owns XML or dictates how it can be used.

XML is a "markup language" which uses tags to describe the meaning of the data within an e-document. These tags differentiate between data, structure (e.g., data sequence), and format (e.g., data is numeric). Suppose, for example, that we wish to purchase an automobile. We could search all the automobile retailers' Web sites to compare automobile prices. This search would

Figure 3-9 XML Hierarchy

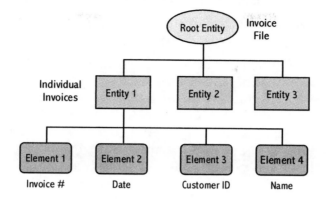

proceed rapidly because the automobile Web sites would have similar XML tags to identify the price fields and extract the price data. In short, XML allows Web sites to be designed with the same structure so that search engines know where to go to find requested data.

XML has had a significant impact on business integration because (a) XML files are human readable unlike binary data formats, (b) widespread industry support exists for XML, (c) numerous tools and utilities are being provided with Web browsers making it easier for smaller companies to import and export data using XML, and (d) major database products now have the capability to read and produce XML data.

XML Structure: XML uses a hierarchical structure of entities and elements (Figure 3-9).

The ***XML Root Entity*** is the equivalent to a file name (e.g., Invoice file). An ***XML Individual Entity*** is equivalent to a single record within the file (root Entity). For example, Entity 1 might be the first record (specific invoice) within that Invoice file. ***XML Elements*** are equivalent to fields within each record (Individual entity). For example, Element 1 is the Invoice #.

Data in an XML document is marked using nested tags. An ***XML Tag*** is a string of characters enclosed within the symbols "<" and ">" (e.g., <invoice>) (Figure 3-10).

XML Advantages and Disadvantages: XML allows Web site access to multiple parties; thus it facilitates B2B integration. One company can easily extract information from another firm's Web site. This facilitates the use of Web Services for B2B integration. XML is not constrained to fixed length fields as is EDI because XML's tags can define variable length fields.

Figure 3-10 XML Tags

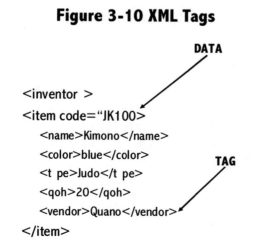

Most importantly, a firm or individual now can use a simple Internet browser to display and extract information. Unlike the much more expensive EDI, the XML protocol makes B2B interfacing available to the smallest firm. Yet, there are disadvantages as well.

It is costly for a business to switch from EDI to the Web-based XML standard. Many firms instead choose to operate through a 3rd party intermediary that translates EDI transactions to XML and vice versa. XML files require up to 10 times more increased processing power and message bandwidth, thus often requiring additional hardware and software investment.

Another downside to XML is that there are many versions of this markup language (Figure 3-11). This complicates the process of ensuring frictionless communication between B2B firms.

EbXML: One of the more promising of these XML derivative standards is the **_extended business XML (ebXML)_**: a set of specifications that facilitate a globular electronic marketplace where enterprises of any size and in any location can conduct business through the exchange of XML-based messages. The direct sponsors of ebXML are OASIS (Organization for the Advancement of Structured Information Standards) and UN/CEFACT (United Nations Centre for Trade Facilitation and Electronic Business). The participants represent hundreds of big businesses from the technology, industrial, shipping, banking and other world-wide industries.

EbXML uses standard message structures within standard business process sequences as mutually agreed upon by trading partners (Figure 3-12). When a business wants to start an ebXML relationship with another company, that business queries the Registry in order to (a) locate a suitable partner, and (b) find information about how to deal with that partner. The Registry contains three elements:

Business Process Catalog: This describes in detail activities in which a business can engage and for which it would want one or more partners (e.g., purchasing). Variations from or enhancements to the standard flows are described in the Collaboration Protocol Profile.

Business Object Type Library: A set of standard process objects (parts) that may be used to assemble larger ebXML elements. An example of a business object is a Purchase Order which is but one element we find in the Purchasing process.

Collaboration Protocol Profile (CPP): Profile of how any particular firm (e.g., Intel) conducts business. This is used as a means of translating between differing business partner rules.

This intermediary "language" is viewed as the global successor to EDI. It first must compete, however, with prior established industry standards such as RosettaNet.

Figure 3-11 XML Taxonomies

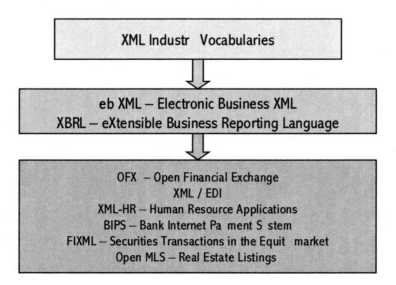

Figure 3-12 ebXML Structure

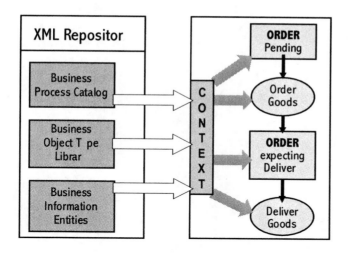

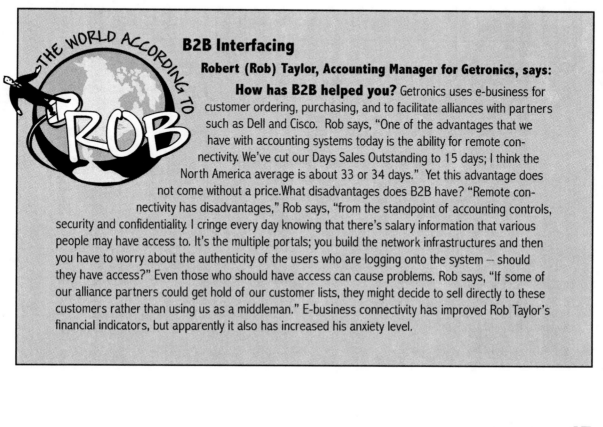

XBRL: The *eXtensible Business Reporting Language (XBRL)* is an XML-based open specification for e-business reporting including financial statements. The "open" designation refers to the use of a common standard that will accommodate all technology platforms.

Although it encompasses all business reporting, XBRL answers the need for a common vocabulary for e-financial reporting. A company can use HBRL to post all of its financial statements on the internet so that all interested parties (e.g., potential investors) can retrieve that information and rapidly compare the financial postures of many firms. XBRL is hastening the movement towards continuous financial reporting.

HBRL is implemented by another XML-based language called the *eXtensible Stylesheet Language Transformations (XSLT):* the formatting (e.g., sequence) of information for the report to be published on the firm's Web site. Figure 3-13 shows the language relationships.

The Bottom Line: Integration between trading partners increases the complexity of the business world by introducing more parties to the mix and the need to translate between these parties.

B2B Interfacing

Robert (Rob) Taylor, Accounting Manager for Getronics, says:

How has B2B helped you? Getronics uses e-business for customer ordering, purchasing, and to facilitate alliances with partners such as Dell and Cisco. Rob says, "One of the advantages that we have with accounting systems today is the ability for remote connectivity. We've cut our Days Sales Outstanding to 15 days; I think the North America average is about 33 or 34 days." Yet this advantage does not come without a price. What disadvantages does B2B have? "Remote connectivity has disadvantages," Rob says, "from the standpoint of accounting controls, security and confidentiality. I cringe every day knowing that there's salary information that various people may have access to. It's the multiple portals; you build the network infrastructures and then you have to worry about the authenticity of the users who are logging onto the system – should they have access?" Even those who should have access can cause problems. Rob says, "If some of our alliance partners could get hold of our customer lists, they might decide to sell directly to these customers rather than using us as a middleman." E-business connectivity has improved Rob Taylor's financial indicators, but apparently it also has increased his anxiety level.

This complicates the asset protection, fraud prevention, and auditing responsibilities of the accountant. Standards simplify business processing because all parties are now speaking the same language – that is, if there only is one standard rather than many. EbXML promises to subsume all existing e-business standards into one global means for businesses to communicate and trade with one another. XBRL also is promising since it will standardize and increase rapid dissemination of financial reports. This may lead to the emerging process of continuous financial reporting.

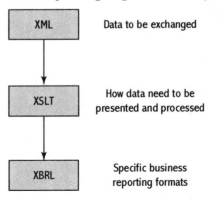

Figure 3-13
Markup Language Hierarchy

XML — Data to be exchanged

XSLT — How data need to be presented and processed

XBRL — Specific business reporting formats

SUMMARY

As Professor O'Leary of the University of Southern California has said, *"Accounting is process, process. process."* Yet, our business processes are changing into an alphabet soup of systems such as B2B in general, and ERP, CRM, and PLM in particular. We need not change our basic skill set of analytical thinking, a global perspective, and a watchdog vigilance. Nor do we need to change the way we apply these skills through auditing, cost-benefit analysis, performance measurement, or implementation of processing controls. We need to change the targets of our professional attention to new alternative ways of doing business rapidly and dynamically.

KEY TERMS

Communication Standard

Customer Relationship Management (CRM)

Customer Targeting

E-business Integration

e-business XML (ebXML)

Electronic Data Interchange (EDI)

Enterprise Application Integration (EAI)

Enterprise Resource Planning (ERP) Models

E-procurement

eXtensible Business Reporting Language (XBRL)

eXtensible Markup Language (XML)

eXtensible Stylesheet Layout Transformation (XSLT)

Functionality Breadth

Functionality Depth

Middle-tier ERP

Middleware

Product Life Cycle

Product Life Cycle Management

Protocol

Simple Object Access Protocol (SOAP)

Supply Chain Management (SCM)

Top-tier ERP

Web Data Transfer

XML Elements

XML Individual Entries

XML Root Entries

XML Tag

XML Web Services

REVIEW EXERCISES

1. Compare and contrast:
   a. ERP and CRM
   b. SCM and PLM
   c. PLM and E-procurement

2. What is "customer targeting"?

3. What is the Product Life Cycle?

4. What are the distinguishing features of an ERP model?

5. What does SAP R/3's Financial module include/

6. What is an "extended" ERP?

7. Compare and contrast functionality depth with functionality breadth.

8. Compare top-tier to middle-tier ERP vendors. Which tier's products;
   a. use a more open architecture?
   b. are easier to make changes?
   c. include more languages

13. Describe what is meant by the term "e-business integration"?

14. Compare and contrast EDI with Web Forms and XML Web Services.

15. Why does integration increase business complexity? accounting complexity?

16. How may integration be incompatible with system change?

17. Describe the XML hierarchy.

18. What does an XML tag do?

19. Why is ebXML important?

20. Describe the ebXML Registry.

21. How are XML, XBRL and XSLT related?

CRITICAL THINKING EXERCISES

1. Survey several companies in your geographical area to determine which B2B models (e.g., SCM) are being used.

2. Write a practice memorandum to an executive in the computer industry explaining why RosettaNet should be subsumed within the ebXML standard.

5. Reference Figure 3-2. Redraw this figure to show how SCM would work for a Business school.

6. Survey several companies in your geographic area to determine which of them accept customer orders by:
   a. Fax
   b. EDI
   c. Web Forms

7. Write a practice memorandum from a Chief Accountant to a Chief Executive Officer explaining the problems posed in assuring transaction integrity for:
   a. 3rd party intermediaries and middleware
   b. transactions involving on-line trading partners

REFERENCES

Brady et al; **Concepts in Enterprise Resource Planning**; Course Technology, 2001

Coyle, F. *"Web Services, Simply Put"*; **Computerworld**; May, 2003

Executive Summaries; *"Enterprise Application Architecture"*; **Search CIO.com**; http://64.28.70.70/summaries/enterprise/integration/

Glover, S., S. Liddle and D. Prawitt; **E-business: Principles and Strategies for Accountants**; Prentice Hall, 2002

Mertz, D.; *"Understanding ebXML"*; **IBM developerWorks**; June 2001http://www-106.ibm.com/developerworks/library/x-ebxml/

Norris et al; **E-Business and ERP**; PricewaterhouseCoopers; 2000

O'Leary, D.; **Enterprise Resource Planning Models**;

data warehousing & mining

> "Knowledge is power."
>
> – *Francis Bacon*

Have you ever wondered why everyone has to put a number on everything? Our television preferences, the state of our health, the state of our economy and of Wall Street – all these are converted into an overwhelming mishmash of numbers that flood our television screens. We humans (particularly human accountants) love numbers; they are not ambiguous and so can be communicated with a minimum of misunderstanding. But sometimes this penchant for quantifying everything can be counter-productive.

In the early 20th century, a visitor named Peter Atchison visited the Ford Motor Company. He happened to meet Henry Ford himself. Pointing to a finished car, Ford proudly declared, "There are exactly 4,719 parts in that model." Peter was impressed that the president of a company would have such details at his fingertips. The visitor later asked a company engineer if Ford's statement had been true. The engineer shrugged his shoulders and answered, "I'm sure I don't know. I can't think of a more useless piece of information.

Perhaps Peter had met an engineer who didn't know what information he needed. On the other hand, Peter may have met an executive who was too immersed in trivial data. We are in an age of data explosion and rapid information availability. However, we also are in an age of data glut, information overload, and knowledge abundance. Knowledge *is* power, but only when you can obtain what is really needed and can ignore the rest. Today's information technology allows us to capture mountains of data in a variety of formats, store them in different data storage facilities, and retrieve them rapidly. Perhaps as with Henry Ford, we still have a problem in separating useless data from critical information. Most of our collected data end up in data tombs which never will be transformed into useful knowledge for decision-making purposes.

There is, however, hope that we may learn to separate cluttering data from useful information. This hope is in the form of advanced database organization and rapid retrieval capabilities. We will discuss these advances in this chapter in the sequence of (a) the Data-Information-Knowledge Hierarchy, (b) Data Warehousing, (c) On-line Analytical Processing, (d) Data Mining, and (e) Business Analytics.

RELEVANCE TO ACCOUNTING

Accountants have three major roles in the capture and use in information systems. First, accountants can be *designers* of data storage structures. An accountant may serve as a participant in a team designing data storage and data warehousing systems. We can take advantage of such an opportunity by designing essential audit features into those structures. We have seen many auditing difficulties arise because data structures could not be retrofitted to implement data tracking without extensive reprogramming of existing applications.

Second, accountants can be *auditors* of data storage structures. In order to fulfill auditing responsibilities, an accountant has to have comprehensive knowledge about different data storage structures, their applicability, strengths, weaknesses, and audit risks. Third, accountants are end-users of data storage structures. Accounting is basically a data-intensive profession that keeps track of different accounting sub-systems and transaction cycles. The in-coming and out-going data stream in an organization is subject to internal and external control practices as coordinated and managed by accountants.

THE DATA-INFORMATION-KNOWLEDGE HIERARCHY

Numeric data has been virtually the only medium that accountants needed in order to understand and describe business processes in organizations. Mandated reporting requirements largely have ruled out any information that cannot be quantified and captured in numbers. However, the hierarchy of data-information-knowledge shows us that vital information can be represented in formats other than numeric quantities.

Traditional Knowledge Hierarchy: Traditionally, we have been taught the knowledge hierarchy shown in Figure 4-1. The lowest level of the hierarchy is *Data* which are discrete, objective facts about reality. For example, in a census, we record different households' number of persons, their ages, genders, occupations, education, and income - all of which are raw facts about household characteristics. The middle level of the hierarchy is *Information*, which are data transformed to fulfill reporting, decision making and coordination purposes. Information is data that makes a difference – that changes a person's outlook or insight. If we try to present the relationship between a household's income level and its total number of persons, we can present the data in a two-dimensional table with the columns listing different categories of total number of persons, and the rows listing different categories of income level. Each cell in the table has the number of households for a certain category of income level and total number of persons. Notice that the process of compiling household data into the two-dimensional table is *Quantitative Compression*, the condensing of data into another precise format for a specific purpose.

Figure 4-1 Data-Information-Knowledge Hierarchy

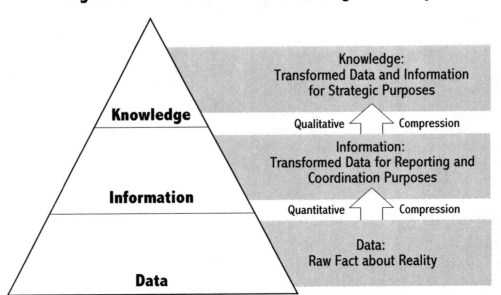

The highest level of the hierarchy is **Knowledge**, which is a fluid mix of framed experience, contextual information, and expert insight. Knowledge provides us with an historical perspective in which to view and understand new situations and events. If we want to predict the income level of households for city planning purposes, we need to look at more variables than just the total number of persons in households. We can build a predictive model using age, education, gender, and number of persons to predict household income.

This process of converting data and information into knowledge involves **Qualitative Compression**, the changing of both the quantity and quality of the data and information. Compared with data and information, knowledge is multi-dimensional and future-oriented.

Davenport and Prusak (1998) have extended this traditional structure by adding the characteristic of **Experience**, which is what we have done and what has happened to us in the past. Experience provides us with an historical perspective in which to view and understand new situations and events.

Data Collection Process: Data must be collected and processed before it becomes useful information. Data collection follows a certain processing path (Figure 4-2).

Datum: This is a raw stimulus – a characteristic or event capable of being moved or stored. An example might be a customer's age.

Database: This is data organized into fields, records and files or, in relational database terms, rows, columns and tables. We could have a customer file comprised of individual customer records. Each record would be comprised of fields such as Customer Name or Customer Address.

Database Management System: This is software that stores multiple incidents of collected data, handles security, and ensures access only to authorized parties.

Data Warehouse: This is a collection of completed and integrated data organized to support the strategic decision-making processes for the entire organization.

Data Mart: This is a smaller-scale and functional-area-oriented data receptacle that is usually dedicated to a specialized portion of an organization's mission. For example, there may be separate data marts for customer and product information, or for different sales regions.

Data Cube: This is a relatively small segment of a data mart set aside to allow intensive processing such as regression analysis or other mathematical routines.

Figure 4-2 Data Collection Process

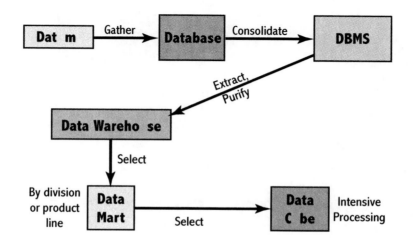

DATA WAREHOUSING

Data Warehousing supports the total physical separation between data storage for transaction processing (e.g., inventory processing) and decision support. While data for transaction processing are kept in databases, data for decision support are kept in a data warehouse. The comprehensiveness of a data warehouse renders it a difficult, enterprise-wide project to implement. Therefore, organizations often concentrate on first developing functional area data marts rather than an integrated data warehouse.

Data Warehousing Benefits: The primary benefits reported from data warehouse usage include:

Higher data accuracy, since database elements are screened and purified before entering a data warehouse

Ease of use, since the data warehouse has as its primary purpose the rapid presentation of information suitable for management decision making.

Faster response time, because the data warehouse is focused on rapid retrieval. This leads, of course, to a shortened time span for making decisions.

Data Warehouse Characteristics: A data warehouse has certain characteristics which differentiate it from a database management system. These characteristics include:

Organized by detailed subject such as vendor or product

Consistent, by standardizing usage for data gathered from multiple sources into a data dictionary

Time Variant, by including 5 to 10 years of data for trends and forecasts

Non-volatile, in that data is not updated once it enters the warehouse

Data Warehouse Functions: Building and maintaining a data warehouse requires exercising the functions of extraction, consolidation, filtering, cleansing, conversion and aggregation.

Extraction: This is the taking of data from the original database and transferring it to a data warehouse infrastructure. Often there are restrictions on what can be extracted. For example, changes to database data that are older than 24 hours may be ignored.

Consolidation: This is combining data from several sources. For example, a complete view of each customer may be compiled by combining data from the separate sources of the order entry system, a sales contact database, and a technical support database.

Filtering: Not every piece of data that is extracted may be needed (e.g., order confirmation number). This function will pick out the relevant data and eliminate unnecessary data.

Cleansing: This function uses an intelligent agent to identify and correct incorrect data. For example, suppose that we have extracted customer data from three different sources. We then find three customer records with the different names of (a) John Jones, (b) Jack Jones, and (c) J. Jones. Are these the same person? The intelligent agent would compare other record characteristics such as date-of-birth or social-security-number to ascertain if these records are for the same person and thus should be consolidated into one record.

Conversion: This function also is called **Translation**. It is the mapping of raw, imported data onto new data fields within the warehouse data model. Imported data are translated into required warehouse formats. For example, this function may change unit of measurement of an imported unit-of-issue from "gross" to "each".

Aggregation: This function summarizes individual data in target groups (e.g., orders by product group). Metrics are computed for management analysis (e.g., warehouse turnover rate by product).

Data Warehouse Examples: This section presents some data warehouse showcases in different industries.

Financial Applications: MasterCard International's data warehouse has increased client size from 22,000 in 1997 to 25,000 in 2003. The credit card giant's data warehouse processes millions of credit card transactions in one day. As soon as a credit card is swiped, the transaction data is transferred to the data engine for data analyses such as identifying purchase habits, buying trends, detecting usage anomalies, verifying fund eligibility, flagging fraud alarms, and reporting portfolio information to business partners. One major emphasis of MasterCard's data warehouse is on "squeaky clean" data. It is very important to have accurate, consistent, validated, and audit-trail-enabled data in financial applications to ensure the trust of customers and business partners. Another significant issue is how to keep up with business partners' ever-increasing demand for more information.

Manufacturing Applications: 3M embarked on a data warehouse effort to consolidate company information for improving the company's business relationship with its partners and customers. 3M has more than 500,000 varieties of products considering different packaging, shapes and sizes. The goal of the data warehouse project is to standardize and digitize product data from all divisions to support supplier, distributor, retailer, and inventory decision making. The data warehouse in 3M supports 5,000 active users with the goal of rolling it out to a minimum of 76,000 users. The data warehouse has the primary data marts of goods and services, trading partners, and global sales.

Transportation Industry: United Airline has an enterprise-wide data warehouse which includes a customer relationship management system (CRM) that manages customer and flight information across 27 countries. Data from reservation centers and United.com are analyzed to reveal customers' most frequently traveled routes, types of travel, travel periods, seat selections, and promotion usage. Analysis results have indicated that personalized offers and promotions identify cross selling opportunities and strengthen customer loyalty. In the future, data from call centers, airport ticketing counters, flight kiosks and other operational and planning centers will be added as data sources into the data warehouse. United Airline projects full payback from its data warehouse investment occurred in one to two years.

Telecommunication Industry: MCI built its data warehouse mainly to perform profitability analysis. The data warehouse was a top-down initiative by senior executives at MCI. Top management realized the necessity of examining business operations in greater detail in order to survive and succeed in the highly competitive telecommunication market. This data warehouse enables MCI's employee to investigate and analyze information in the company's data warehouse via the Internet. Decision makers can access highly detailed customer and product information in order to understand profit margins and key performance metrics. The final goal is to deliver efficient and targeted service to customers.

Health Industry: Kaiser Permanente, the largest health maintenance organization (HMO) implemented an enterprise-wide data warehouse that includes 400 workstations, 25 hospitals, 200 clinics, 250 pharmacies, and 800 users in various sites. Kaiser's warehouse collects data from disparate sources including current and historic, clinical and research, and medical and non-medical data. The goal is to analyze certain practices and to find out which procedures will produce the most efficient and effective results for health-related treatments. Kaiser has encountered several challenges during the data warehouse project effort. First, in order to get management buy-in, the project team selected a pilot area that provided fast and accurate delivery of concrete results. This proof of concept effort demonstrated to top management and physicians what the data warehouse could provide to them. The data warehouse can answer questions posted by physicians using what-if scenarios in just minutes as compared to hours in the past.

The second challenge was to provide training to technical staff and end users. Kaiser solved this problem by implementing an internal education program that trained over 20 employees per month. The third challenge was to evaluate hardware and software products. The last and continuous challenge was to recruit and retain qualified and experienced data warehouse practitioners to manage and maintain the data warehouse. Kaiser's data warehouse has resulted in millions of dollar in savings.

Retailing Industry: Wal-Mart's data warehouse is the largest of those found in Fortune 500 companies. Wal-Mart is planning to increase its data warehouse size to capture and analyze four million retail transactions every minute nationwide. The data warehouse supports analyses on merchandise demand in terms of quantity, seasonal fluctuation, regional differences, and sudden shifts due to social incidents.

Public Sphere: The US Postal Service (USPS) uses data warehousing to track down money launderers. USPS management discovered that postal money orders are a favorite instrument for drug traffickers to do money laundering. Criminals engage in the practice of "layering" - breaking up large amount of cash and converting that cash into money orders for easy deposit into bank accounts. The data warehouse "Focus" in USPS keeps track of 4,700 money order transactions each month nationwide to detect suspicious patterns and large transactions. Data are analyzed together with bank account information compiled by the Federal Reserve Bank to confirm the existence of money laundering activities.

ONLINE ANALYTICAL PROCESSING (OLAP)

Getting data into a warehouse is not an easy or inexpensive endeavor. Yet, it would be fruitless if we then could not retrieve information from that warehouse in an efficient, timely, and customized manner. That retrieval is the role of *Online Analytical Processing (OLAP)*: the immediate processing of management requests for information in specific formats from a data warehouse.

Suppose that we wish to ask the question, *"What would be the effect on soft drink costs to distributors if syrup prices went up by $.05/gallon and transportation costs went down by $.05/ mile?"* We would use an OLAP query on our data warehouse. Decision makers would not need to submit a request to the information system department and wait for several weeks or months for the reports to arrive. Instead, they can use their own computers, do some simple point and click operations, and immediately see the results on their computer screens.

A typical OLAP query might be *"Display the profit of my highest and lowest products last quarter in my domestic sales region."* The key words by which the data warehouse is categorized and indexed would be "profit", "highest / lowest", "last quarter", and "domestic sales region".

OLAP Uses: OLAP often is used in the following areas:

Finance and Accounting: Budgeting, Activity-based-costing (ABC), financial performance analysis, and financial modeling

Marketing: Sales forecasting, promotion analysis, customer analysis, and market segment analysis

Manufacturing: Production planning and defect analysis

Southwest Airlines OLAP Project

Southwest Airlines implemented an OLAP project in two phases in 1995. First; the Hyperion Solution Corporation's Essbase software was installed at a cost of one million dollars. Southwest almost immediately realized Return-on-investment (ROI) savings, which is unusual for such business analytics implementations. Prior to Essbase, people had to (a) write queries by hand, (b) spend 30 minutes running the queries, and (c) enter the results into spreadsheets which would be used for further analysis. The entire process consumed up to four hours of an employee's time. Essbase reduced this process to as little as two minutes.

In the second phase of the project, Southwest linked the OLAP software to their ERP application. After the 9/11 terrorist attack on New York City, management found that they needed this integrated system to help prepare for a severe market downturn. Southwest was one of those rare firms that exploited its intelligence applications successfully during this chaotic period. Management used its OLAP system to run best- and worst-case scenarios of future market conditions. Forecasts were created and plans were devised to stabilize Southwest's finances. The essential question that was asked was, *"How fast would we burn through our cash?"* Southwest's forecasts using OLAP proved to be within two percent of what was actually realized.

OLAP Characteristics: An effective OLAP system will have the following characteristics:

Multidimensional: Different data views (e.g., by product or market) offered to different users.

Transparent: The architecture, system, and software supporting OLAP is transparent to end users who can work using familiar interfaces such as spreadsheets.

Accessibility: The OLAP systems allows access to data from different sources in different formats.

Consistent reporting performance: A consistent response time which is not significantly affected by the number of dimensions and amount of data in the system.

Shared: with multi-users supported concurrently and containing all security requirements for confidentiality and concurrent update locking

Simple: Users carry out data manipulation by point and click or drag and drop without extensive programming effort.

Flexible reporting: Users are allowed to change presentation formats easily such as swapping columns and rows, summarizing cells, and using graphs and charts.

Support for unlimited number of dimensions and aggregation levels: There are no artificial limitations on the number of dimensions and aggregation levels.

Fast: delivering responses to users within 5 seconds

Analytical: coping with any relevant business logic and statistical analysis

Sufficient Capacity: to handle requisite amounts of input data

Cost Effective: where benefits exceed costs, although benefits may be hard to quantify

OLAP Operations: Figure 4-3 shows a data cube storing sales data by the dimensions of product, region, and time. Following are some common OLAP operations.

Figure 4-3 Sales Data Cube

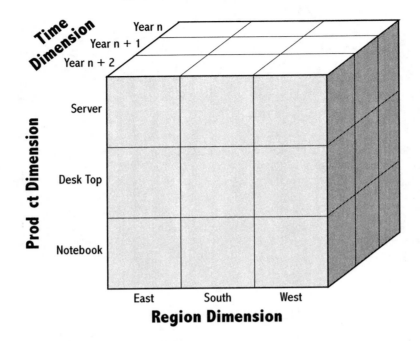

Slice is the cutting off of one dimension from a data cube. For the data cube in Figure 4-3, we can slice the product dimension out and just look at an aggregate sales figure for all products as classified by region and time.

Dice is similar to the "pivot" concept in spreadsheet software, which means rotating the data cube to create a different view based on a set of different dimension values. Suppose the existing table view of the data cube in Figure 4-3 is the product in columns, region in rows, and time as a drop-down menu for time selection. When we rotate the data cube, we can have region in columns, time in rows, and product as the drop-down menu for product selection.

Nesting is to embed one dimension inside another dimension to create a multi-level presentation.

Drill Down for a hierarchical dimension means to move down to a lower level, away from the root of the hierarchical tree. Drill down presents more detailed data to users.

Roll Up is the reverse of drill down to move closer to the root of the hierarchical tree and show aggregated data

OLAP Examples: Following are a few examples of OLAP use.

Office Depot: The Essbase OLAP tool allows Office Depot's 100 merchandisers to review the gross margin return on investments by store and by product. Data analyses showed that there was too much fringe stock in the wrong stores. This result helped the company adjust its inventory levels; its return on computer business has improved substantially. A single data cube can store up to 30,000 products for 53 weeks and 600 stores.

GHS Data Management is a company that provides pharmacy benefit management service. It collects pharmaceutical data for Medicaid programs and private sector companies. One task of the GHS data analysts is to identify problematic spending patterns and ways to reduce spending. Before GHS adopted MS Analysis Server and Databeacon to implement its OLAP operation, the staff had to run a query and generate a new report every time they received a phone call from customers requesting some information. The high number of phone calls from customers prevented data analysts from carrying out the high-impacted task of fraud identification. The OLAP tool allows users to access data, carry out analyses, and generate reports via an intuitive Web interface. Now, instead of calling the GHS staff, GHS customers use the Web to perform their own queries. OLAP not only releases GHS staff to perform high-level data analyses, but also cuts cost and reduces reporting errors.

Lockheed Martin: The motivation of Lockheed Martin Aeronautics Company to use Essbase as an OLAP tool was to collect all data from engineering, purchasing, and manufacturing to support aircraft design and manufacturing. The OLAP tool has helped reduce the analysis cost up to 20 percent. It also provides ways to evaluate project costs; analyze manufacturing time, cost, and other variables; and provide staffing forecasts to determine future needs.

Prudential Insurance uses Cognos' PowerPlayWeb OLAP tool to deliver customer information to marketing users. Prudential's first data mart has life policy information. The second contains information for property and casualty business. The third focuses on life attrition, and the last one is for Prudential's financial products. The common data in all data marts include number of policies held, the types of products purchased, customer status, their tenure, and segmentation. Marketing users now can identify customer trends at a high level including understanding attrition rates by product, tenure, and status. The OLAP tool has made technical queries possible in just seconds using non-technical language.

DATA MINING

Data Mining is a software system for accessing data warehouse information by means of statistical and artificial intelligence algorithms. Traditional OLAP tools focus on presentational techniques (such as slice, dice, drill down) which perform quantitative changes on data. Data mining relies on modeling and other mathematical processes to perform qualitative changes on data and information. The output we receive from data mining is knowledge which has a different structure and format from the input data.

OLAP and Data Mining: OLAP is reactive, seeking out known relationships – a process called verification. Data mining is proactive, sifting through unknown relationships – a process called discovery. The difference between these two analytical paradigms can be seen by the following queries:

OLAP Query: *"How many widgets did we sell in the spring of 2000 in sales region A versus sales region B?"*

Data Mining Query: *"What are the drivers that cause people to buy these widgets from my catalog?"*

Note that the OLAP query looks for the results of *what has already happened*. The data mining query, on the other hand, searches for the causes of *why these results have occurred*. Thus we can be more *predictive* of what will happen. In addition, we may be able to deal directly with the causes in order to *change* rather than predict the future

Data Mining Characteristics: Data mining has the characteristics of being novel, non-trivial, valid, understandable, action-propelling, and valuable knowledge to support organizations' tactical and strategic decision making.

Novel requires that the knowledge be new and interesting rather than some known or common-sense information.

Non-trivial refers to not using a common computational process such as calculating means, standard deviations, or using a statistical procedure such as ANOVA.

Valid points to the required process of verifying the accuracy of discovered knowledge.

Understandable is an important characteristic of the output from data mining because users are reluctant to apply mining results they don't comprehend.

Action-propelling means that decision makers can act upon the knowledge to solve their problems.

Valuable refers to knowledge that has significant impact on the bottom line performance measures of an organization.

Data Mining Classifications: There are five major data mining classifications:

Supervised Classification is a model that can predict the classification of a new case such as whether a company will file for bankruptcy, a stock will go up, and a loan will become defaulted. An example of supervised classification is: *"Classify characteristics of GOOD, MEDIUM, and POOR credit risks where the GOOD characteristic are income over $25K, age between 45 and 55, and lives in XYZ neighborhood."*

Unsupervised Classification entails output of a predictive model to categorize new cases into different groupings, which is a perfect tool for performing customer segmentation – putting customers into different demand classes so that each class (e.g., teenagers) can be dealt with differently.

Cluster Analysis takes unclassified data and places them into similar clusters. It is used for such business purposes as market segmentation, determining affinity groups (people with similar tastes), and defect analysis. The input to sequence analysis is transaction log data that show the movement of subjects from one state to another state. The output is a set of frequent and valid paths for the data set.

Sequence Analysis identifies sequential path patterns. An example of a discovered sequential pattern is: *"68% of the time when stock X increased its value by at most 10% over a 5-day trading period AND stock Y increased its value between 10% and 20% for this period THEN stock Z's value also increased in a subsequent week."*

Association Analysis takes transaction data with the quantities and types of transaction items as input, and generates a set of association rules with different degree of confidence and support for the transaction data. Association analysis is frequently used for market basket analysis that identifies shoppers' purchase patterns. An example of a detected data association is: *"72% of all records that contain items A, B and C also contains items D and E."* Another example, taken from IBM's Market Basket Analysis is: *"20% of the time a specific brand of toaster is sold; customers also buy a set of kitchen gloves and matching cover sets."*

Data Visualization that can take very large scale data sets as input and generate 3D data representation in different formats for users to visually inspect, analyze, and evaluate the data. For example, by revealing population density and transportation flow in cities, data visualization is useful in determining whether a certain location is suitable for important public facilities such as schools and hospitals.

Data Mining Examples: Following are some examples of data mining use:

Wal-Mart: This data mining application manages Wal-Mart's inventories one store at a time by identifying patterns, relationship, and moment-to-moment sales variation. NeoVista Software can process a year's point-of-sale data from Wal-Mart's data warehouse and generate buying patterns and other inventory relationship for 700 million merchandises for more than 2,000 stores in only two days. The results are used to adjust Wal-Mart's inventory replenishment system so that customers can get what they want when they step into a store, and there are no more inventories on store shelves than what will be demanded by customers

IBM and Farmers Insurance Group has co-developed a data mining insurance policy application called Underwriting Profitability Analysis (UPA). Using claims data for policy holders, UPA discovered 40 characteristics (rules), some of which were previously unknown, for predicting automobile insurance claims. Using these rules can yield a net profit of several million dollars in only one year. For example, insurers have known that high-performance-sport-car drivers have more accidents than others. However, UPA discovered that if the sport car is not the only vehicle in the household, the accident rate is about the same as for other drivers. Because of that finding, additional policies from re-classifying Corvettes and Porches into the preferred premium policy could bring in more than four million in premium revenue without a significant rise in claims.

Emerging Issues in Data Mining: The next generation of data mining tools has to face several challenges. First, data mining tools have to accommodate very large scale databases with many dimensions from distributed data sources. Second, other than data mining, we will hear more about text mining, Web mining, voice mining, motion mining, and graphic mining. There is the need to develop mining algorithms to accommodate different data types and their combinations.

Third, as data mining technology becomes mature and gains acceptance from decision makers, data mining may become an end-user productivity tool in the near future, just like a worksheet program or word processor. In order to be widely available to and used by end users, data mining tools need a more user-friendly interface that makes mining processes transparent to users. Fourth, in order to enable data interchangeability for data mining, there is the advocacy for data mining standards. The Predictive Model Markup Language (PMML), as a branch of XML standard, is being developed by the Data Mining Group (www.dmg.org).

On the other hand, data mining has encountered some social and legal issues. Casinos are utilizing data mining tools to identify association rules to predict gamblers' behavior; this may be considered socially unethical. There have been lawsuits involving companies' data mining activities intruding on individual privacy. Two measures were introduced in Congress on January 16, 2003 to halt the Total Information Awareness Project (TIA), which is a research program targeting at analyzing individuals' financial transactions, travel records, medical records, and other activities using data mining tools. TIA is operated under the Department of Defense as part of counter-terrorism response.

DATA MINING FOR FRAUD DETECTION

"Finding fraud in masses of (transactions) is more difficult than finding a needle in a haystack. In the haystack problem, there is only one needle that does not look like hay, the pieces of hay all look similar, and neither the needle nor the haystack changes much over time." (Cahill, 2000). There are goals to be pursued when attempting to discover fraud. The first is to minimize the incidents of undetected fraud. Failure to accomplish this goal is referred to as a ***Type I Fraud Detection Error*** (Table 4-1). The second goal is to minimize "false alarms" – detecting what appears to be fraud when it really isn't. Failure to accomplish this goal is referred to as a ***Type II Fraud Detection Error***.

Both types of fraud detection errors can result in financial losses to the firm. Failure to detect fraud (Type I) results in the loss of organizational assets. Detecting fraud when it isn't there (Type II) increases processing costs and leads to loss of revenue from angry customers.

Yet, we cannot merely reduce both types of errors simultaneously. For when we strive to reduce undetected fraud (Type I), we will increase the incidence of false alarms (Type II). The opposite also is true. Thus, we determine the relative costs associated with each type of error and try

Finger Hut Data Mining

Finger Hut uses data mining for catalog mailing, credit granting decisions, and inventory stocking decisions. Its data mining software sifts through databases containing the records of 12 million customers. The software discovers which customers are more likely to buy products from one of Finger Hut's many catalogues. In one example, Finger Hut studied the past purchases of customers who had changed residence. The Data mining software discovered that these customers were three times as likely to buy items such as tables, fax machines, and decorative products. At the same time, these customers were less likely to purchase high-end consumer electronics. Based on these data mining results, Finger Hut created a special catalogue that was mailed only to customers who had moved recently.

to strike a balanced approach. One method of striking this balance is to establish fraud thresholds or *account specific thresholds*. Data mining software then alerts a human operator when a threshold is exceeded so that the operator can investigate the case more closely.

Fraud Thresholds: To establish thresholds, we first must reduce transactions to statistics such as average dollar value, typical transaction times of day, or the number of times a customer accesses sensitive files. Then we compare account summaries to these threshold values. Accounts exceeding a threshold value are placed in a special file for human analysis.

Account Specific Thresholds: In this method, the latest customer transaction is compared to past customer transaction history. Unusual activity is flagged. For example, a Nebraska customer shows higher than normal purchasing activity in Mexico, a place that customer has not shown prior purchases. The fraud detection is heuristic – it changes its thresholds if customer patterns change. American Express uses this technique and that is why the company does not impose credit dollar limits on its credit cards.

Detection Requirements: In order for thresholds to work, the data mining software must be (a) tailored to each account's uniqueness, (b) event driven, detecting fraud *WHILE* it is happening rather than after the fact, (c) memory driven, weighing recent events more than past events, and (d) adaptive to legitimate changes in behavior.

Blue Cross Case: Empire Blue Cross/Blue Shield is New York State's largest Health Management Operation (HMO). Its data mining software profiles each of its client physicians on patient claim records included in its database. It compares the results to a peer physician group. Any deviations are reported to investigators as a "suspicion index". An example would be a physician who performs a high number of procedures per visit, charges 40 percent more per patient, or sees many patients on weekend. By the third year of operation, Empire's data mining fraud detection savings had reached $39 million annually.

Table 4-1 Fraud Detection Risks

Actual Condition	Fraud Detection Result	
	Detect Fraud	Don't Detect fraud
There is Fraud	DESIRED CONDITION	UNDETECTED FRAUD (Type I)
There isn't Fraud	FALSE ALARM (Type 2)	DESIRED CONDITION

BUSINESS ANALYTICS

Business Analytics is a special branch of data mining targeted to business. It is software driven including industry specific programs for business performance data, financial analysis, and CRM-related analysis. The market for business analytics software is projected to over $12 billion in the next few years. One of the fastest selling software products is Microsoft .NET architecture. We will use this package as an example of the many new products now available. Microsoft.NET performs Customer Resource Management (CRM) and data analytics.

CRM Analytics: Microsoft.NET analyzes a company's relationship with its customers and attempts to reduce shopping cart abandonment (currently is estimated to be as much as 70 percent of a typical company's Web site accesses). This software also can (a) improve post-sales service, (b) build customer loyalty, and (c) find new clients by *Cross-prospecting*: searching sales files for one product in order to find potential clients for other products.

Microsoft.NET also performs Web traffic analysis in order to assess the marketing effectiveness of the company's Web site. For example, we might ask the question, "How did our customers find our Web site? Was it through portal site advertising (e.g., AOL), a search engine, or directly? Are we getting our money's worth for the fees we are paying to a referral Web site?"

Data Analysis: Microsoft. NET and other business analytics software allow users to find business anomalies by visualizing multiple sets of data through a single interface. For example, one could view a complete customer history by consolidating information from payment, sales, warranty, and service files. Microsoft.NET allows managers to identify areas for further exploration through a series of standardized business questions. The software also identifies key performance indicators such as Customer Return-Sales Rate.

Business Simulation: One specific area of business analytics that is receiving increased attention is *Business Simulation*: computer software that models the company's business environment in order to allow managers to improve their decision-making skills by repetitively practicing in a zero-risk exercise. Smithkine Beecham, for example, used simulation tool to plan a strategy for a new competitive product launch. After running a series of simulation trials, management decided to run an advertising campaign that neutralized competitive offerings. That decision alternative was not considered seriously before.

THE WORLD ACCORDING TO ROB

Robert (Rob) Taylor, Accounting Manager for Getronics, says:

How has database technology affected your company? It has improved our operations immeasurably. It's allowed us to be more efficient — to better manipulate and review the large amount of details we have.

How has it improved your efficiency? We have specific data entry points and business rules on how the data should be put into our relational database. That data is stored in tables which makes it easier to manipulate and transfer electronically — all quicker than we used to be able to do it.

But aren't these database technologies expensive? Well, somebody has to pay for them and they're not cheap. But how do you say, "Here's what I've spent and here's what I've gained. How do we do a cost-benefit spreadsheet?" Now we spend less time on getting the information and more time on analyzing it. We used to have two full-time people who did nothing but gather information to prepare commission statements for our sales force. Now, I do that myself in two hours each month.

Complex Adaptive System Theory (CAS): The increasing speed and decreasing costs of computer technology have allowed companies to use more powerful and interactive forms of simulation software. One such powerful version uses an operations research methodology called *Complex Adaptive System Theory (CAS)*. Traditional simulation models start with assumptions from historical data. CAS models start with world as it is and tracks the results of a possible event's effects and impacts in future. Currently, CAS uses supercomputers and high-end PCs and so is still relatively expensive. But the costs of operation are decreasing steadily and may be practical for small- to medium-sized companies to use in the near future,

Possible CAS uses include (a) Financial (simulate capital markets), (b) Pharmaceutical (model effects of different chemicals on organisms), (c) Aerospace (create materials that perform under stress), (d) Airlines (optimally balance cargo for smoother rides), and (e) Manufacturers (supply-chain modeling). It remains to be seen how business analytics in general and business simulation in particular can or will be used by future accountants. However, this is an emerging area of business potential and demands our continuing attention.

SUMMARY

The fundamentals of data storage structures are required knowledge for accountants in their roles as designers, auditors and users. Data warehouses are important because they separate storage of decision support information from transaction processing data. This makes the data warehouse more amenable to rapid, accurate and customized retrieval of management information through such processes as Online Analytical Processing (OLAP) and Data Mining. A rapidly emerging field called Business Analytics focuses data mining techniques on business problems.

KEY TERMS

Account Specific Threshold	Database Management System (DBMS)	Nesting
Aggregation		Online Analytical Processing (OLAP)
Association Analysis	Data Cube	
Business Analytics	Data Mart	Qualitative Compression
Business Simulation	Data Mining	Quantitative Compression
Cleansing	Data Visualization	Roll Up
Cluster Analysis	Data Warehouse	Sequence Analysis
Complex Adaptive System Theory (CAS)	Dice	Slice
	Drill Down	Supervised Classification
Consolidation	Experience	Translation
Conversion	Extraction	Type I Fraud Detection Error
Cross Prospecting	Filtering	Type II Fraud Detection Error
Data	Information	Unsupervised Classification
Database	Knowledge	

REVIEW EXERCISES

1. What are the differences between:

   a. data and information?

   b. knowledge and experience?

2. Compare and contrast Quantitative with Qualitative Compression.

3. Describe three (3) characteristics of a Data warehouse.

4. What are the differences between:

   a. a Data Warehouse and a Database?

   b. A Data Mart and a Data Cube

5. What are the differences between:

   a. Consolidation and Aggregation?

   b. Cleansing and Filtering?

6. What is OLAP? What does it do?

7. What are the differences between:

   a. Slice and Dice?

   b. Nesting and Drill Down?

8. Compare and contrast OLAP with Data Mining.

9. Describe three (3) Data Mining characteristics.

10. Compare and contrast Supervised with Unsupervised Classification.

11. Describe Association Analysis.

12. What are the differences between Cluster and Sequence Analysis?

13. What is the relationship between the Type I and Type II Fraud Detection errors?

14. What is an Account Specific Threshold?

15. How does CAS differ from traditional business simulation models?

CRITICAL THINKING OPPORTUNITIES

1. Modify Figure 4-1 to include the Experience characteristic.

2. Annotate your modified Figure 4-1 to give an example of how it would appear for a CPA. (e.g., what data does a CPA deal with?)

3. Survey five to 10 companies in your geographic area and compile the answers to the following questions in a formal Word report.

   a, Do you have a Data Warehouse? If no, why not?

   b. Do you use Data Marts? If so, for what functional areas?

4. You wish to query a Data Warehouse to determine which of your company's products have shown the largest profit margin over the last six months.

   a, Construct an OLAP query.

   b. Construct a Data Mining query.

5. Search the Web for five (5) Business Analytics software products. Record and compare their characteristics (including price) in a PowerPoint presentation.

REFERENCES

Cahill et al, *"Detecting Fraud in the Real World*,*" **Bell Labs**, 2000

Cannataro, M., and D. Talia; *"The Knowledge Grid"*; **Communications of the ACM** 46:1, 1/2003, 89-93.

Davenport, T., and L. Prusak; ***Working Knowledge***; Harvard Business School, 1999

Fayyad, U., and R. Uthurusamy; *"Evolving data mining into solutions for insights"* **Communications of the ACM** 45: 8, 8/2002, 25-31.

Grossman, R., M. Hornick, and G. Meyer; *"Data mining standards initiatives"*; **Communications of the ACM;** 45:8, 8/2002, 59-61.

Han, J., R. Altman, V. Kumar, H. Mannila, H., and D. Pergibo; *"Emerging scientific applications in data mining".* **Communications of the ACM**; 45:8, 8/2002, 54-58.

Higgins, K. J. *"MasterCard International – Warehouse Data Earns its Keep"*; **Network Computing**, 5/1/2003, 111-113.

Hollis, J. *"Deploying an HMO's Data Warehouse"*; **Health Management Technology**, 19:8, 7/1998, 46-49.

Lam, M.; *"Neural network techniques for financial performance prediction: integrating fundamental and technical analysis"*; **Decision Support Systems**, in publication.

Lin, F. Y., and S. McClean; *"A data mining approach to the prediction of corporate failure"*; **Knowledge-Based Systems**, 14, 2001, 189-195.

Lin, Q. Y. Chen, J. Chen, and Y. Chen; *"Mining inter-organizational retailing knowledge for an alliance formed by competitive firms"*; Information **& Management;** 40, 2003, 431-442.

Little, R. G., and M.Gibson; *"Perceived Influences on Implementing Data Warehousing"*; **IEEE Transactions on Software Engineering** 29:4, 2002

Moad, J. *"Stamping Out the Bad Guys – U.S. Postal Service Uses Data Warehouse and Analysis System to Help Track Down Money Launderers"*; **eWeek**, 6/18/2001, 47.

Sammone, D., and P. Finnegan; *"The Ten Commandments of Data Warehousing"*; **Database for Advances in Information Systems;** 31:4, 2002.

Shaw, M, C. Subramaniam, G. Tan, and M. Welge; *"Knowledge management and data mining for marketing".* **Decision Support Systems** 31, 2001, 127-137.

Songini, M.; *"Home Depot's next IT project: Data Warehouse"*; **ComputerWorld;** *36:41*, 10/6/2002, 15-16.

Stedman, C.; *"Wal-Mart mines for forecasts"*; ComputerWorld; 31:21, 5/26/1997, 63-65.

Watson, H., D.Goodhue, and B. Wixom; *"The Benefits of Data Warehousing: Why Some Organizations Realize Exceptional Payoffs?"*; **Information & Management;** 30, 2001.

Wixom, B. and H. Watson; *"An Empirical Investigation of the Factors Affecting Data"*; **Warehousing Success**; 25:1, 2001, 14-41.

CHAPTER 5 **new business models**

"He who mounts a wild elephant goes where the wild elephant goes."

— *Randolf Bourne*

Have you ever watched an old-fashioned 1950's or 1960's western movie with Jimmy Stewart or Gary Cooper or even John Wayne? If you haven't, you should; they're pretty exciting. You can tell the good guys from the bad guys, justice always prevails in the end, and there are a lot of horse chases and shootouts. Well, some would say that this Wild West has returned in the form of e-business. Exploration of this e-business world has been compared to exploration and settling of the American West in the 19th century – as sort of a new gold rush.

"*There are rogues, heroes, philanthropists. There are big winners and big losers, fortunes made and lost, and (new technologies) providing the equivalent randomness of a giant gold strike or a railroad's routing around a booming city and reducing it, overnight, to a ghost town.*" (Downes and Mui, 1999) The rogues might include the management of Enron, or even Arthur Anderson. One of the heroes might be Bill Gates, although some of his competitors might regard him as a rogue as well. Today's ghost towns are the host of dot.com companies that raised investor expectations and then went bust. Yet, there still are a multitude of firms panning for the gold which may come from e-business success.

We discuss in this chapter how traditional business models – the ones that accountants have been operating with – are changing. We emphasize that these changes are rapid and unpredictable but that, nevertheless, our accounting profession must keep pace with this new "Wild E-West." Otherwise, our form of accounting justice may not prevail. Our discussion is organized into the sections of (a) E-business Technological Forces, (b) the Coasian Rules of Organizational Survival, (b) E-business Models, and (c) Reinventing the Business.

RELEVANCE TO THE ACCOUNTING PROFESSION

Our entire accounting profession has been developed around rules and standards pertaining to business models that have been working effectively for many years. Now these traditional models are changing rapidly. Our profession must change just as rapidly if we are to remain a viable professional force in the years to come. We must learn, adapt to, and master the new business paradigms emerging so rapidly.

E-BUSINESS TECHNOLOGICAL FORCES

We described a **Disruptive Technology** in Chapter 2 as "one that can displace an entrenched technology, not because it performs better, but rather because it provides an overall better (business) value" (Glover et al, 2002). This definition is similar to what Downes and Mui refer to as a "**Killer App**". These significant technologies change the way we think about and do business.

Technologies that have revolutionized the ways we do e-business include wireless telecommunications, e-payment systems, security policing, and biometrics (e.g., speech recognition). There are other emerging technologies such as optical networks that will influence our business models in the future. However, this chapter is not about technologies as much as it is about the economic forces that drive technology development and use and the impacts of that use on our ways of doing business.

These principles include Moore's Law, Metcalf's Law, and the Coasian Rules of Survival. Figure 5-1 shows the interaction of these forces.

Moore's Law accelerates geometrically the introduction of new technologies. Metcalf's Law spreads the usage of these new technologies, again geometrically. The Coasian Rules of Survival suggest that this proliferation of new technologies drastically reduces business transaction costs on the open market (e.g., Internet). In order for established business firms to be able to compete with plunging open market costs, these firms must reduce their size (overhead). This latter phenomenon is called Coase's Law of Diminishing Firms.

This reduction in business firm size can be realized only by destroying traditional business models and creating new models that are more adaptive and competitive. Yet, since our accounting models and standards are based primarily upon these traditional models, we are faced with the pressing question, *"What will these E-business forces do to the accounting profession as we now know it."*

Moore's Law: This law attempts to explain the exponential growth of technological capabilities that we have witnessed in the past century. Simply stated, ***Moore's Law*** holds that *"every 18 months, processing power doubles while cost holds constant"* (Kurzwell, 1999).

Causative Factors: The Moore's Law phenomenon results from several factors including;

Faster Speeds: New algorithms allow data to be compressed into smaller and smaller space; thus more data can be sent for period of time or, conversely, the time it takes to send a specific amount of data decreases.

Miniaturization (density): A given amount of physical storage (e.g., chip) constantly is being reduced in size. Thus a given amount of physical storage space can hold more data.

New Technological Media: New technological media are being designed that are more efficient than current media. For example, optical networks promise a multiple factor increase in data transmission speeds at the same or less cost over than that of the current Internet

Figure 5-1 E-Business Forces

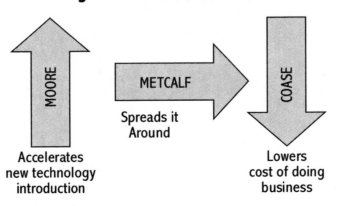

Moore's Law at Work: Table 5-1 shows Moore's Law at work in Intel's manufacturing of computer chips. Note that the number of transistors in Intel chips has increased at an exponential rate. Some question whether such a growth can continue indefinitely without some intervening force (e.g., a new ice age?) causing that growth to slow into what economists refer to as an "S-shaped curve

In human history, we rarely have experienced such an unabatedly increasing phenomenon as we see today in emerging technologies. What typically happens is that some external forces(s) conspire to suppress the exponential growth (Figure 5-2). For example a shortage of fossil fuels could hamper the discovery and implementation of new technologies. Interestingly, some suggest that one suppressing force may well be that we develop technologies beyond our needs – at least the needs of the consuming business public.

Table 5-1 Moore's Law and Intel's Computer Chip

Year	Number of Transistors in Intel's Latest Microchip
1972	3,500
1978	29,000
1985	275,000
1993	3,100,000
1997	7,500,000
2000	20,000,000

Another suggested phenomenon that may create the S-shaped curve effect is the physical limits of a type of technology. For example, some have suggested that we are reaching the physical limits of designing silicon chips that are smaller and faster. Yet history has shown that such physical constraints often are bridged by the invention and development of a new physical medium. This was exemplified 50 years ago by the development of plastic as a new fabrication medium So there is a high likelihood that, when the silicon chip or its technology counterparts reach their intrinsic capacities, someone will already have been working on their successors (Figure 5-3).

Moore's Law and Software: This law was formulated with computer hardware in mind. Some would argue that the law is not applicable to computer software. There have been studies showing that programming applications have not become more efficient during the last 20 years. Indeed, today's software may be less efficient. What these critics miss is the fact that today's soft-

Figure 5-2 Exponential Growth of Computing

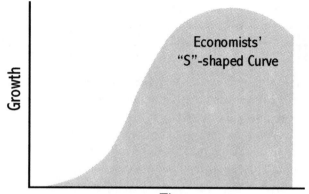

Figure 5-3 Successor Technologies

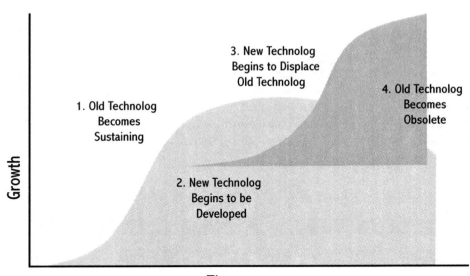

1. Old Technolog
Becomes
Sustaining

2. New Technolog
Begins to be
Developed

3. New Technolog
Begins to Displace
Old Technolog

4. Old Technolog
Becomes
Obsolete

Growth

Time

ware applications are much larger, more functional, and more integrated than their predecessors. For example, a typical business software application today has been expanded to include functionality for everyone from novice to experienced users.

The typical person using MS Access, for example, only employs about 20 percent of that package's functionality. On the other hand, a master user may use 95 percent of Access's functionality including the ability to modify databases in its Visual Basic source language. The Access source programmer must design his or her program to accommodate both user extremes.

Yet, it is the integration aspect of today's software applications that most resembles the effect that Moore's Law has on hardware. Today's software applications must mesh and communicate with a multitude of other software programs performing functions such as telecommunications messaging, security handling, client authentication, system administration, and audit facilitation. In addition, as explained in Chapter 1, use of the Internet multiplies the number of message paths in an e-business setting; it also multiplies the number of different parties and systems with which today's software applications must integrate.

Metcalf's Law: *Metcalf's Law* can be stated as, "*The usefulness (utility) of a network equals the square of the number of users*" (Downes and Mui, 1999). Some call this the ***Network Effect*** (Glover et al, 2002). Metcalf's Law operates much as a disease which, if not isolated and contained, spreads throughout a population (number of users?) at a rapidly increasing rate. Of course, we hope that Metcalf's Law spreads more positive effects than does a disease...

This law often is referred to as the ***Gate's Accelerator***. As more people buy a particular type or brand of computer hardware, more software designers gain an incentive to write software applications for that hardware. This increased availability of application software makes the hardware more appealing to more purchasers. This expanded volume of sales encourages more software development, and so on. Some pundits have referred to Gate's Accelerator as Gate's Way to Heaven. They contend that increased software development requires increased hardware requirements which, when built into newer versions of the hardware, encourages development of even larger versions of application software, and so on. This phenomenon renders technologically obsolete previous versions of hardware because new software releases exceed the processing capacity of older hardware versions.

The Need for Standards: The full explosive effect of Metcalf's Law can occur only when there are open standards. **Open Standards** is defined as the access of all potential users to all hardware, software, and network protocols, regardless of the specific technology package that users possess. Open standards become a common language (**Protocol**) with which all potential users can communicate. We discussed open standards in Chapter 3. Open (shared) standards have many economic advantages for business communities, including:

- Selection of computer infrastructures is made easier since all brands or types interact with each other. These infrastructures become easier and cheaper to modify.
- Exponential linkages are enabled with a firm's buyers and suppliers.
- Creative use of standards drives innovation; the best innovation becomes the standard.
- Metcalf's Law operates in an unimpeded manner, thus allowing new technologies to spread at an exponential rate.

Where We Are: Moore's Law describes why technology increases exponentially. Metcalf's Law acts as a multiplier of Moore's Law. In an open standards environment, Metcalf's Law acts to spread any given period's technology to potential users, also at an exponential rate.

COASIAN RULES OF SURVIVAL

Ronald Coase (1995) developed the concept of a **Transaction Cost**, which he defines as the cost of completing a business transaction between a buyer and seller. **Search Costs** are costs of the buyer and seller finding each other. **Information Costs** are costs of the buyer learning about the product. **Bargaining Costs** are the setting of transaction terms. **Decision Costs** are the costs of the buyer choosing from alternative products or services.

Policing Costs are associated with ensuring that terms of the sale are fulfilled. Finally,

Enforcement Costs are the costs for remediation of unsatisfactory dealings. For an e-business or other technology driven environment, the Coasian cost structure seems to lack one vital category which we will call an Establishment Cost. An **Establishment Cost** is an expense incurred from building the structure necessary to conduct business in the first place. Table 5-2 equates these Coasian costs to General Ledger accounts.

Table 5-2 Coasian Transaction Cost Types and General Ledger Accounts

COASIAN COST TYPE	TYPICAL GENERAL LEDGER ACCOUNT
Search	Advertising Expense
Information	Salaries Expense
Bargaining	Salaries Expense
Decision	Salaries Expense
Policing	Warranty Expense/Liability
Enforcement	Legal Costs/Loss
Establishment	Indirect Cost Pool

Table 5-3 E-business Accounting Costs and Coasian Cost Categories

E-BUSINESS ACCOUNTING COSTS	COASIAN COST CATEGORY
Network Infrastructure	Establishment
Customer Authentication	Search (allowing only valid traffic)
Intrusion Detection	Search (detecting invalid traffic)
3rd Party Payment Systems	Decision (after buyer makes choice)
Fraud Prevention and Detection	Policing
Alliance Partner Integration	Establishment
Audit Functions (e.g., Integrated Test Facilities)	Policing

Table 5-3 shows typical e-business accounting costs and where they fall within the Coasian structure. We now can see that the Coasian economic cost structure, with one addition, fits reasonably well with our accounting perspective of transaction costs.

Coasian Theory of Firms: Firms exist to develop transaction costs that are lower than that of individuals dealing with one another. Firms can do this through such practices as specialization of labor (e.g., purchasing clerks) or economies of scale (e.g., purchasing volume discounts). Ideally, a firm includes only those activities that cannot be done more cheaply in the market by another firm or by individuals dealing with one another.

Coase postulates that firms will expand *exactly* to that point where the costs of organizing one more transactions equal the costs of carrying out that same transaction on the open market (Figure 5-4). If open market costs increase, then the firm can expand profitably. If open market costs decrease, then the firm must contract its size to maintain its profitability. Of course, this Coasian theory assumes that the firm (a) has full and immediate knowledge of open market conditions, and (b) acts immediately and logically on that knowledge.

Technology and Transaction Costs: Technology wisely used drives down the costs of both firms and the open market. However, it drives down open market costs at a much greater rate than it drives down firm costs. This phenomenon is explained by the application of Metcalf's Law.

Technology can reduce a firm's operating costs, but only incrementally. This is because a traditional "brick" firm is a relatively closed system – it mostly operates within fixed physical boundaries. Metcalf's Law can operate at best only in its low numbers range. This is equivalent to spreading rumors in a small office. Only a few people can share that rumor. There is a restricted multiplier effect. Technology reduces open market costs (Internet) much more rapidly. There are no brick impediments to the spread of new technology. Metcalf's Law acts as a full multiplier of Moore's Law. This is analogous to spreading a rumor on the streets of San Francisco. Who knows how far that rumor will spread? This difference in technology diffusion within the firm and in the open market place leads to the next postulate.

Diminishing Firms: There is another phenomenon which Downes and Mui call the ***Law of***

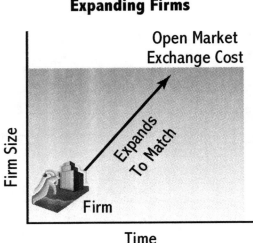

Figure 5-4 Coasian Theory of Expanding Firms

Figure 5-5 Law of Diminishing Firms

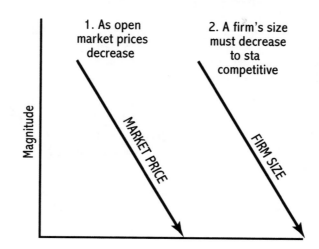

1. As open market prices decrease

2. A firm's size must decrease to sta competitive

Magnitude

MARKET PRICE

FIRM SIZE

Diminishing Firms which is: "*As transaction costs in the open market approach zero, so will the size of the firm*". Figure 5-5 illustrates this law. An E-business society in which there are no barriers to communications between buyer and seller is called a ***Frictionless Economy***. As Downes and Mui suggest, "*A truly frictionless society needs no permanent firms*".

According to this theory, firms will shrink in size as e-business (the Internet) becomes the predominant business model. Firms will outsource non-critical processes, split them into specialized business units, reengineer their processes to achieve more competitive costs, or go out of business. A new type of organization will appear called the ***Virtual Organization***, which:

- achieves *low overhead costs* by using part-time or contractual employees,
- *shares assets* (e.g., buildings and distribution systems) with other firms,
- is *boundless* with a hazy separation between what is inside and outside the firm, and
- is *temporal*, perhaps existing for only one or two interim transactions (projects).

Thus, Moore's Law and Metcalf's Law operate as multipliers to exponentially increase the use of technology and to drive open market (individual to individual) costs down. Coasian theory then suggests that decreasing open market costs will force firms to become smaller and smaller (Law of Diminishing Firms). Ultimately, all firms may become virtual organizations.

Of course, events rarely proceed along the neat lines of economic theory. There are differing rates of change among and within countries, and among and within any one country's industry segments and regions. Still, the possible interaction between the three models we have discussed presents an interesting picture of what may be the future of business practice.

E-BUSINESS MODELS

There is a shifting definition of what is within or outside the firm. Processes are shared, customers are unseen, and brick walls with assigned parking spaces are disappearing rapidly. Many more business transactions are being handled more efficiently on the Web, forcing off-line firms to decrease operating costs in order to compete. There also is pressure to transform internal functions to the Web or to outsource them entirely. Operating cost pressures are creating new opportunities for companies to forge supplier and customer alliances.

The underlying supposition guiding past business practices is that a firm must guard its processes jealously and consider all other entities, including customers, as threats. That supposition now is being seriously questioned given the new forces associated with e-business. Current accounting models are based largely on traditional business models. Therefore, our accounting models must be questioned as well.

New Business Forces: What are these new forces that are changing the order of things in our business world? The four most dominant forces are digitalization, globalization, deregulation, and cooperation. None of these forces really are new; they just have reached critical mass at about the same time.

Digitalization: More and more entities are being converted to a digital format. In addition, digital messages are being squeezed into smaller and smaller packages using more powerful data compression algorithms. The result is more information available to facilitate more rapid change.

Globalization: More and more players are able to share the information marketplace without regard to physical location. This creates more competitors and smaller profit margins.

Deregulation: Many legal and political marketplace entry barriers are being discarded, thus opening the field to more competitors.

Cooperation: Suppliers, customers, middle-men, and even competitors are being forced to work together on industry models in order to reduce costs and cycle times for all parties.

These new forces are changing the way we view and use traditional business models. First of all, there now are more alternative modes and channels and thus ways of doing business. Secondly, these new forces allow or even dictate customer access to parallel, coordinated processes rather than serial, proprietary processes. This speeds up cycle times and makes information available more rapidly and across a greater range of participants. These forces do not necessarily invalidate current business models. They do, however, make these traditional models more unstable, dynamic and complex.

Now let's look at how these forces are affecting different elements of the traditional supply chain.

New Organization Structures: Traditional internal, hierarchical organizations are being transformed into more flexible and therefore faster-acting, more flexible structures organized about new business models that consider the Web as the primary marketing channel. Among these new models are the following:

E-Value Chain: A business model organized on a business process perspective. An example would be a manufacturing company.

E-Value Network: A business model organized on connectivity and partner relationships, rather than on specific processes. An example would be a telephone company.

E-Value Shop: A business model organized on a customized problem solving perspective, rather than a continuous operation. An example would be a consulting company that operates on a project by project basis. Now let's see how these new forces and organizational structures are affecting traditional marketplace participants.

New Market Entrants: There are two phenomena that are allowing new entrants ready access to the e-marketplace. First, cost entry barriers are being destroyed. New companies can enter an e-marketplace with no inventory, no buildings, or no production facilities. New entrants also can share with other companies such assets as technology, thus reducing individual company overhead costs.

Secondly, costs for consumers to switch to new entrants often are quite low. Hardware switching costs (e.g., shaving razor) are the highest. You have to purchase the new hardware. Software switching costs are the next highest. For example, if you switch from an accounting program such as Intuit, you may be forced to reenter your data to the new accounting package. Information switching costs (e.g., books) are the cheapest. The courts have held consistently that there are no patent violations in using published Internet information.

The lack of new entrant cost barriers coupled with low consumer switching costs poses a dilemma for many traditional, or "legacy" businesses. These businesses are saddled with overhead costs associated with a large sales forces, main-frame computer systems and applications, and physical buildings and production plants. These "assets" were designed to sell a product or service in a certain way. Unfortunately, that certain way is changing. Burdened with these obsolete (often called "stranded") fixed assets, legacy companies find it difficult to compete with the newer, slimmer versions of e-business competitors.

The Customer: Customer expectations have changed dramatically in the e-business world. Consumers are now getting used to mass customization at a nominal initial price. No longer can companies force customers into a "one size fits all" mode of thinking. Even the smallest customer has bargaining power to force product or service customization. Dell Computers is an example where you can order a computer specifically tailored to your specific needs. The customer has become a product designer. Customers now will willingly part with personal information at a marketing site if a firm gives them value in return. This personal information can be used by the firm for marketing purposes. For example, if you give to Hallmark your important dates, Hallmark will e-mail you when it's time to send a card (hopefully, a Hallmark card).

It now is easier for a firm to outsource its order processing function to the customer. When you let customers enter their own orders, they use their own resources. Customers also can perform their own order follow-up without the firm expending funds on expensive inquiry centers. In addition, there are less order errors because the data only is entered once. When an error does occur, the customer cannot blame the seller. However, while this new customer behavior can reap benefits to a company, there are additional threats and costs involved. For one thing, a company now must give customers access to some of its internal system files. This increases the risk of fraud, data theft, and mischievous behavior. Therefore, the company must expend more resources on preventive, detective, and corrective Internet controls

The Death of Middlemen: There is continuing emphasis to reduce time for the customer order cycle – to deliver products and services faster to customers with ever increasing expectations. One way to do this is to shorten that supply chain by-passing middlemen such as distributors. Many middlemen's values were based on transaction costs of a non-Web environment. However, those transaction costs are decreasing in an e-business setting. Therefore, unless a middleman adds clear value to e-business transactions, that middleman will be bypassed as shown in Figure 5-6. Some have forecast that, for example, wholesalers will disappear within the next ten years.

There now is a transformation of the middleman as an intermediary function rather than as a handler of goods and services. For example, Expedia.com allows customers to acquire lower cost

The Travel Agent

The traditional travel agent is a middleman positioned between the traveling customer and the travel vendors such as airlines, rental car agencies, and hotels. The travel agent does not work without income; where does that income come from? Either one of the travel vendors allocates a share of its profits to the agents or there is a processing cost tacked onto the customer's total travel bill.

Incidents of travel providers sharing profits with travel agents have been declining. For example, airlines discontinued this practice several years ago. This effectively leaves only the second option of adding costs to the traveler's total travel bill. The questions then become, "Why should travelers be willing to pay more by using a travel agent? Why won't travelers make the arrangements themselves and save money? What value does the travel agent add to this transaction to justify his or her additional costs?

The answers to these questions were clear before the Internet meddled with the travel agent's business. Most travel consumers didn't have the time to contact each travel vendor separately and arrange trips. The travel agent could put the entire trip together with just one phone call from the traveler. In addition, the travel agent could provide information brochures and such personal experience tips on what were the best restaurants or what sights to see. Therefore, many consumers were willing to pay higher prices in order to receive the increased value provided by the travel agent.

Then along came the Internet. It became much more convenient for travel consumers to make the arrangements themselves. Their task was made even easier by travel vendor alliances. For example, when you make an airline reservation on-line, you may also be able to schedule a hotel and a rental car on the airline's Web page. But what about the brochures and personal tips provided by travel agents? You can search the Internet for Chamber of Commerce or other agency information on the location to which you are traveling. In addition, you can get personal travel tips by searching for Web pages established by individuals who have traveled to the location in which you are interested.

What then is the value of using a travel agent? This is a question now being tackled by travel agents as well as other business middlemen.

hotel rooms while allowing hotels to sell unsold rooms. Expedia.com adds value to both the customer and the hotel.

Yet, many industries have had a long-term symbiotic relationship between manufacturers and distributors. It often becomes difficult for manufacturers to jettison loyalty to its distributors. For example, Levi's experimented with selling its jeans on-line to its customers. It abandoned this strategy after a flood of complaints from retail outlets. Coca Cola's culture encompasses distributor loyalty so much that this company paid to implement its ERP system at its bottlers' locations.

Figure 5-6 Bypassing the Supply Chain

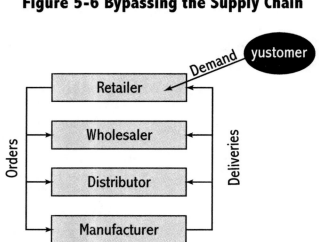

Substitute Products and Services: The Web has become a customer buying channel alternative to the physical ("brick and mortar") store. As explained before, it is cheaper for new entrants and substitute products to initiate sales on the Web. Brand loyalties are not disappearing, but these loyalties must be quite strong in order to deter consumers from switching to substitute products or services. Internet switching costs are very low. As a result, many Internet firms are substituting service for lower product cost in order to compete with lower price substitutes. Indeed, the terms "product" and "service" are starting to be melded into the concept of an "offer".

An *Offer* is a combination of product and service. For example, a training course (service) could try to compete more effectively by offering a free software package (product) to enrollees. Alternately, a computer company could offer a year's free Internet service when you purchase a computer. Amazon.com offers a Web chat-room at its book marketing Web site.

Brand names such as Coca Cola or Cadillac will continue to command loyalty. Weaker brand names will blend with substitutes into product or service commodities for which value rather than name will be the key to consumer sales. *Value* is defined as quality divided by price.

Suppliers: Firms are finding that it is advantageous to share information with suppliers in order to make them a dependent part of the firms' systems. The Just-in-time (JIT) inventory model is an example of melding supplier and company transaction systems. In another example, Dell outsourced its computer delivery function to UPS, thus requiring Dell to share its production scheduling data with UPS.

Industry Competition: Traditional business thinking has been that a successful company (a) were stand-alone and vertically integrated within an industry or industry sector, (b) ran the full gamut of activities within that vertical umbrella, (c) dominated the competitive landscape, (c) did not share resources but hoarded them internally, and (d) considered all of its business processes to be proprietary and therefore secret.

Firms now are acknowledging reluctantly that not all of their business processes are proprietary – that some 80 percent of their processes are common to their competitors. Therefore, there is a growing inclination to share, jointly reengineer, and thus standardize common processes industry-wide or through other alliances. Indeed, there is a proliferation of e-business alliances which allow common companies to share skills and assets. New business thinking suggests that:

- Firms can profit from using resources they don't own such as another company's customer database.

- A firm does not need to own all of its business processes, but can outsource to vendors those processes that are not critical and proprietary.

- Partnering with other firms (even competitors) can be profitable and may allow a firm to gain entry into new markets.

<u>Why E-Business Alliances?</u> There are many benefits that a company can realize through an e-business alliance with suppliers, customers or other firms with common interests. These include:

New Skills: A firm can acquire new skills or strengths quickly without major investment outlays. For example, a textbook publishing company may not possess the technical skills necessary to develop Web courses to support its textbooks. That company may form a temporary alliance with a Web-site development company to develop such courses.

Exit Ease: A firm who wants to expand its market sphere doesn't have to merge with or acquire other firms. An alliance allows partners to remain as separate entities with pre-defined exit strategies.

Sharing Resources: Alliance partners can share resources. This includes customer data, technology, and even common processes such as procurement.

Alliance Examples: This new way of thinking has led to a proliferation of e-business alliances. Many of these alliances are not long-term, but instead are short-lived ventures to complete just one business activity (e.g., design of a university's Web curriculum). These short-term organizations may replace traditional partnerships that require long-term contracts or strategic alliances. Thus, e-business alliances are proliferating rapidly; Microsoft itself has entered into over 100 such alliances. Some examples of e-business alliances are:

- AOL with eBay and Nintendo for mutual e-advertising benefits

- Microsoft with the NBC network to produce the MSNBC cable news network

- Intel with Dell, Cisco and Microsoft for mutual development and use of technology products and e-advertising

- Prentice Hall with Microsoft to produce e-education curricula

- RosettaNet is an example of an industry-wide alliance among customers, suppliers, and other technology players. The alliance was formed to standardize how business transactions are transmitted processed within the vertical computer industry.

Strategic Planning Revisited: Microsoft didn't even have e-business in their 1996 strategic plans. Why? Strategic planning addresses such fundamental organizational questions as "Why are we in business?", "What products or services shall we provide?", or "What will be our basic cultural values?" It is a lengthy, time-consuming process that may produce significant changes that reverberate throughout the organization.

It used to be the tradition to build a 5-year strategic plan once a year. If you were really forward thinking, you might update that plan every six months. That strategy doesn't work in today's cyber-speed world. Now changes to technology and business models are becoming so rapid that such long-term strategic plans become hopelessly dated and non-competitive. The question has become, "Should we abandon all efforts at long-range strategic planning, or should we embrace new planning models?" Continuous long-range planning, sometimes called push-pull planning, is the model more amenable to today's business environment (Figure 5-7).

Figure 5-7 Push-pull Planning

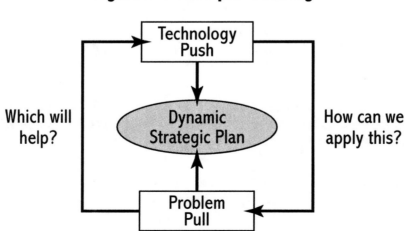

Push-pull Planning is a virtuous cycle between finding technology to solve problems and surmising how we can use emerging technologies. We are still reactive in that, when we face an unanticipated problem, we may search our technology options to see if we can apply a technology to solve that problem. However, we couple this reactive thinking with a proactive approach that searches for technology use *before* the problem occurs. This proactive approach is called technology transfer. **Technology Transfer**, as described in Chapter 2, is the proactive search for emerging technologies that may be of strategic and operational use to the organization.

REINVENTING THE BUSINESS

U.S. Computer Services (USCS) used to hold regular strategic planning sessions for their executives. The goal of these sessions was to invent ways in which its competitors could destroy USCS. Executives would play roles different from their day-to-day responsibilities. For example, the Finance person might assume the role of the Marketing person in a rival firm. Roles might be switched many times during the futures exercise. Ken Taylor, formerly USCS's Vice President for Information Technology, said, *"We thought that we had better figure out ways to destroy ourselves before our competitors did. Then we could reinvent our company before it could be destroyed."* Often it is faster and cheaper to tear down an old house and build a new one than it is to remodel the existing house.

There are great needs and many opportunities for a company to reinvent itself in the e-business world. These opportunities might include such tactics as wholesalers bypassing distributors on the supply chain or even a company competing with itself by opening Web-marketing channels competitive to existing channels. The key is to "Think big." A company can no longer tinker with its transaction processing system. This is similar to repairing the plumbing on a house that is starting to topple over a cliff. A company must find a way to either alter its processing system dramatically or to destroy it and replace it with a faster, more economical and higher value version.

Marshall Industries, a large distributor of electronic components and systems, appeared to be committing corporate suicide when it opened up a Web site that (a) let customers view its price list, (b) provided direct links so that customers could order directly from manufacturers rather than through Marshall, and (c) made their Web site easier to use than their traditional sales

---

The Death of Print

In December 1999, Dan Okrent, Editor-at-large for Time Magazine, gave a lecture at Columbia University entitled "The Death of Print". This lecture occurred just after several e-business events which seemed to have future implications for the paper publishing industry. These events includes (a) the merger of America Online (AOL) with Time Warner, (b) increased use of the Cable medium for internet transmission, (c) and dramatic increases in Internet bandwith which made the Internet more attractive for on-line print distribution. The question that Mr. Okrent was addressing in his Columbia lecture was, "Do such new events mark the end of the newsprint medium as we know it?" Following is an excerpt of his remarks on this subject.

"My colleagues and I did not grow up wanting to be in the ink and paper and staples business. We wanted to be in — we are in — the business of words and pictures and ideas. Don't worry about the future of newspapers or magazines or books any more than you would worry about corrugated boxes or shrink-wrap. They are containers; the substance resides elsewhere."

Mr. Okrents message could provide a wake-up call to the accounting profession. Look carefully at some typical financial statement. You will note that these statements largely reflect production and distribution of products or services. Our financial statements deal more with the container (e.g., fixed assets, conversion processes) than with the substance of the company (e.g., culture, morale, education).

channel. But Marshall's executives felt that if they didn't provide these capabilities to customers, someone else would. For example, the manufacturers might decide to bypass Marshall on the supply chain and sell directly to customers. Marshall realized unanticipated gains from this tactic because it moved from a national to a global distributor at very little cost. Their losses in one marketing channel have been offset by their gains in a new marketing channel. Marshall has successfully cannibalized its own business.

Cannibalizing a Business: Airplane mechanics often borrow parts from an aircraft under repair in order to quickly fix another aircraft that is more ready to fly; they call this cannibalization. In a more formal sense, **_Cannibalization_** is implementing a new business opportunity (e.g., marketing channel) at the expense of an existing part of the business. Figure 5-8 illustrates this strategy.

The Wall Street Journal publishes an on-line (Web) version of its paper in direct competition with its tradition paper version. The on-line version has caused its paper market marketing channel to lose sales and thus become less profitable. Yet, the combined distribution for both old and new channels has increased. Losses in the old channel have been offset by gains in the new channel. This cannibalization example emphasizes an important feature of e-business directly affecting accounting – product/service content is more important than distribution.

Many former "Brick and Mortar" firms such as Barnes and Noble have opened up Web outlets competing with their physical stores. After the dot.com fiasco of the early 2000s, most companies have come to recognize that becoming a "Brick and Click" operation is optimal, even if one channel cannibalizes from another.

Serendipity: an Innovative Strategy: _Serendipity_ is defined as "taking advantage of an unexpected and unplanned business event or condition. Some would say that serendipity is blind luck – that, by some quirk of fate, we benefited by an event we did not anticipate. However, this is not always the case. Serendipity can be the result of lucky foresight – a positioning of our firm so that it has an optimal probability of taking advantage of whatever happens in the future. This is similar to placing a fishing pole in a mountain trout stream. No trout may come along to nibble

Figure 5-8 Cannibalizing a Business

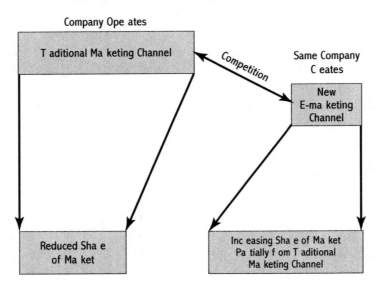

on your line, but you're ready if one does. Of course, if an unexpected whale comes along, you're sort of ready for that also.

A firm must create an environment where lucky foresight (serendipity) is more likely to make an unexpected appearance. The firm can do so by:

- designing modular, expandable Web pages so that you can employ Web marketing if the right set of future circumstances occur.

- investing in infrastructure technology (e.g., extranet capability) so that you quickly can take advantage of e-business alliance opportunities.

- employing group thinking to arrive at most likely future scenarios. Intel holds such planning sessions with its executives to (a) narrow future scenarios down to a most likely set, and (b) determine how the company currently is positioned to take advantage of these most likely future scenarios.

From an accounting perspective, serendipity is a difficult proposition since (a) the value of a current investment equals the possible benefits multiplied by the probability of success, and (b) neither the benefits nor the probability of success are easily anticipated.

Reversing Course: Reinventing the firm is a dangerous undertaking because such redesign is based on what we expect the future to be. Sometimes a new business model doesn't work the way it was perceived. The future is a very unpredictable, volatile partner. Therefore, the firm must be nimble; it must be prepared to change quickly when circumstances dictate. This change ability can be facilitated by planning and technology, but it is mostly a matter of modifying a firm's culture to embrace change.

Amazon.com presents one example of having to quickly react to he sudden, unanticipated conditions. Amazon.com began business as a Web-book clearing house with no book inventories. Ordered books were transshipped to customers from outsourced delivery and warehousing

THE WORLD ACCORDING TO ROB

Robert (Rob) Taylor, Senior Financial Officer for Getronics North America says:

How do you gain from e-business alliances? "We have business alliances with Cisco and Dell. This allows us to bring their products to our clients. Cisco and Dell give us discounts on their products, so we're able to pass these products on to our customers and make some profit on it."

What do you add as a middleman in this process? "We're adding some additional components and we're staging and configuring the complete units. This is value added. Otherwise these clients might have to buy printers and cables and load all different kinds of software. We also have somebody there to install it on a certain day so we can minimize down time on the equipment being installed."

What's the downside of these alliances? "One of the downsides is the pressures on pricing. Dell and Cisco continue to drive down their profit margins because of competition. They put pressure on us to absorb some of that reduced margin by accepting smaller discounts on their products. Another problem is that, particularly with Dell, we have to show our clients the value of using Dell rather than some other vendor. We also have to show them the value Getronics adds by procuring, staging, and configuring the equipment. Otherwise, the clients could buy directly from Dell and Cisco."

vendors. In this way, Amazon could be a virtuously fixed-asset-free entity. This approach was so successful that it forced competitors such as Barnes and Noble to establish their own Web sites. However, Amazon's outsourcers produced a poor product delivery history, and this affected Amazon's sales negatively. Complaints increased and the Percent of Repeat Customers decreased. Yet Amazon had little control over its outsiders except to terminate contracts and look for new partners with no greater likelihood of improved service.

Amazon's solution to this problem was to establish its own warehousing and delivery system. This change was contrary to its original e-business model. This was a costly change that had to be done rather rapidly. Yet this reversal of course proved to be successful although cost recovery for this change may be many years away. The lesson here is that an e-business company cannot become complacent, but must be aware of the need to change and be nimble enough to make that change rapidly and relatively efficiently.

SUMMARY

Rapid technology diffusion is forcing companies to change their old ways of doing business and to adopt new, e-business models. Yet our traditional accounting standards are based upon the old business models. These standards are changing, but not nearly as rapidly as the business world that the standards try to address. The very nature of accounting is in a state of transition.

Accountants must change with the changing. They must enhance their knowledge and skill capabilities in such areas as technological capabilities and application integration. Accountants also must redirect traditional accounting skills such as performance measurement, cost monitoring and reporting, and auditing to a new set of process circumstances. That is the basic premise of this book.

Scary? Maybe. Exciting? Very much so. The future accountant will be in an environment that rarely will be dull or stagnant. More importantly, that future accountant will possess the requisite skills and global mindset to help prevent our Cyber-world from dissolving into chaos.

KEY TERMS

Bargaining Costs	Gate's Accelerator	Policing Costs
Cannibalizing	Information Costs	Protocol
Decision Costs	Killer Apps	Push-pull Planning
Enforcement Costs	Law of Diminishing Firms	Search Costs
Establishment Costs	Metcalf's Law	Serendipity
E-Value Chain	Moore's Law	Technology Transfer
E-Value Network	Network Effect	Transaction Costs
E-Value Shop	Offer	Value
Frictionless Economy	Open Standards	Virtual Organization

REVIEW EXERCISES

1. What is Moore's Law? Why it is important?

2. What is Metcalf's Law? How does this law interact with Moore's Law?

3. Why does Metcalf's Law require Open Standards?

4. What are the differences between the following Coasian transaction costs?

    a. policing and enforcement

    b. search and information

    c. bargaining and decision

5. Explain the Law of Diminishing Firms. What effects would this law have on:

    a. traditional business firms?

    b. an Accounting department

6. What are the new forces that are influencing e-business?

7. Describe the three organizing e-business models?

8. What are switching costs? What type of product has the lowest switching cost? Why?

9. Why are middlemen "disappearing"? Give an example of a middleman that is prospering in today's e-business environment? Why do you think that firm is successful?

10. What is an Offer? Give two examples of offers not described in this chapter.

11. What motivates firms to create e-business alliances?

12. Describe Push-pull planning and why it is necessary today.

13. What is Technology Transfer?

14. What is Cannibalization? Why is it important in e-business?

15. What is Serendipity? List three ways to enable serendipity in a business.

CRITICAL THINKING OPPORTUNITIES

1. Make an inquiry to the manager of the IT Department for a business firm in your area as to what (s)he thinks will be the future effects of Moore's Law.

2. Prepare a memorandum to Susan Smythe, the Chief Accounting Officer of Somewhere Incorporated, as why the economics of e-business are important to that company.

4. Consider how you enroll in classes and pay fees to your university. Identify for this process at least one cost for each of the Coasian Transaction Cost categories.

5. Search the Internet to find five examples of E-business alliances other than the ones discussed in this chapter. Prepare presentation slides to briefly describe these alliances.

6. Describe five different types of Offers.

7. Interview the owner of a local travel agency. Describe that owner's opinions of how the travel agency business has changed with the advent of e-business.

8. Find and describe three cases of businesses cannibalizing traditional marketing channels by establishing e-marketing Web sites.

REFERENCES

Accounting Media Group; *"Firm of the Future"*; **Accounting Today**, June 2003

Baldock, R.; **Destination Z: the History of the Future**; Wiley, 1999

Davis, S. and C. Meyer; **BLUR: the Speed of Change in the Connected Economy**; Warner Books, 1998

Coase, Ronald; **Essays on Economics and Economists**; University of Chicago Press 1994

Downes, L. and C. Mui; **Unleashing the Killer App**; Harvard Business School Press 1999

Gates, B.; **The Road Ahead**; Viking Press, 1995

Glover, S., S. Liddle, and D. Prawitt; **E-business: Principles and Strategies for Accountants**; Prentice Hall, 2001

modified accounting models

> "An organization's ability to learn, and translate that learning into action rapidly, is the ultimate competitive advantage"
> — *Jack Welch*

Have you ever stopped suddenly in the middle of the morning and wondered if you had brushed your teeth because you can't remember having done so? Have you ever known somebody who wakes up at the same time each morning, even on weekends or holidays? Humans get comfortable with a fixed way of doing things; we then can turn repetitive routines over the automata function of our mind which then can perform the routine (e.g., brushing our teeth) without us having to consciously think about it. Here is an example.

There was a party at the house of the renowned mathematician, David Hilbert. His wife noticed that her husband had neglected to put on a clean shirt. She ordered him to do so. He went upstairs. Twenty minutes passed, but the mathematician did not return, His wife went up to the bedroom to find her husband lying peacefully asleep in bed. She later explained to her guests, *"You see, it was the natural sequence of things. He took off the coat, then his tie, then his shirt, and so on, and went to sleep"*.

We described in the previous chapter how our models or ways of doing business are changing rapidly. Accounting is the language of business and accountants are the watchdogs of organizational assets. Therefore, accountants and accounting practice must change to keep up with business changes. Accountants, as with other humans, tend to be slaves to habits. Still, we cannot afford to continue our current routines and then, as the renowned mathematician, fall asleep to our new obligations. We must heed Jack Welch's advice and translate what we are learning about e-business into timely action.

We discuss in this chapter several examples of how the current technological and business revolutions have changed or must change the way we do accounting. The traditional models which have sufficed in the past must be modified to fit the future. We do not attempt to cover all topics of possible accounting change, but concentrate on some of the more significant ones. Our sequence of discussion will be (a) Information Technology (IT) Asset Valuation, (b) the Changing Role of the Auditor, (c) the Changing Nature of Internal Controls, (d) Revenue Recognition, and (e) Taxing the Internet.

RELEVANCE TO ACCOUNTING

It is important that the material discussed in this chapter merely be used as a bridge to discussing changes that will be required in the near and far future to accounting professional standards, certifications and differentiation of skills. This chapter only dusts off the surface of the possibilities ahead. There was a quote from a past issue of Scientific American which said,

"Tomorrow's employees and managers will face the opportunities and challenges of advancing technology in ways we cannot possibly envision today." This quote is as relevant to the accountant as it is to the computer scientist.

INFORMATION TECHNOLOGY (IT) ASSET VALUATION

Asset valuation is not a new topic for accountants. Technology valuation, however, presents some unique problems in light of current accounting practice. A colleague of ours recently was consulting with a firm which was trying to acquire a software development company. Our colleague had to help this firm decide the appropriate acquisition price for the software company. This entailed in part determining the value of the acquired company's software in the market, in production, and on the drawing board. The acquiring firm had a difficult time determining that value, even with our knowledgeable colleague's assistance.

A New Value System: Technology valuation problems are aggravated by the fact that e-business models are creating a new value system which our current financial statements have not yet been conditioned to reflect appropriately. Today's e-business world is more concerned with the means of production, rather than the production assets themselves. This is because technology is changing so rapidly that physical production assets quickly become obsolete or, become, as some call, them, "stranded assets". As we shall see in what follows, the Financial Accounting Standards Board (FASB) is attempting to solve this problem but only has reached a tentative solution to date. Here are a few problems that technology growth lends to traditional asset value calculation.

Virtual Inventories: How do we place value on on-line books or music products which only exist electronically and can be reproduced at almost no variable cost?

Stranded Assets: How do we value and write-off production assets such as newspaper presses or dated hardware and software that have become largely obsolete and are "stranded" in our balance sheets?

Information as Wealth: Information is now a commodity that is bought and sought. What is the asset value, for instance, of a customer database that can be shared or used to leverage business alliances?

Stress on Adaptability to Seize Future Opportunities: How do we value investments in technology infrastructure that may not have much current organizational value, but that allow us to seize future value opportunities should they arise?

Are these addressed in today's balance sheets? The answer is, "maybe", or "somewhat", or "with a great deal of difficulty".

Why Value IT Assets: There are a number of practical reasons why an organization should develop a structured and perhaps novel approach to evaluating IT assets:

Justifying Technology Upgrades: Needs for technology upgrades often are based upon specific operational needs and goals. Sometimes, however, an organization has a policy to replace a certain portion of their technology every year or two. Intel, for example, has a goal to replace a third of employee computer workstations each year. In such cases, the value of the assets being replaced is needed for budget and depreciation calculation purposes.

Determining Merger Values: As was the situation with our colleague, mergers and acquisitions require that the value of a merged company be computed. Information Technology accounts for as much as 40 to 60 percent of many firms' total assets.

Preparing financial Statements: The public view of a firm's worth emerges from financial statements. The value of IT assets can be a critical component of those statements.

Computing Return on Assets (ROA): ROA is an important financial analytic used by analysts to assess a firm's financial health. IT value is an important element in this computation.

Benchmarking: A firm can compare its IT posture with that of other firms of similar size or mission. For example, the amount of IT dollar investment divided by total employees often is used as a gauge to whether or not a firm is investing appropriately in the technology area. One California County Court recently reduced its IT expenditures because they were far above the national average for county courts."

Outsourcing IT Functions: A common company tactic is to outsource its entire IT operations to a vendor. This type of agreement often requires transfer of all IT hardware, facilities, software and personnel to the outsourcing vendor. Obviously, the value of IT assets will be a major determinant of the financial terms reached in such an agreement.

It is important to stress that the IT value computed for financial statements may not be the same value computed for benchmarking, outsourcing agreements, or other purposes. Computation of IT asset value must be tailored to the specific decision setting.

Deriving IT Asset Value: The methods used for computing IT asset value include

Acquisition (Historical) Costs: what you originally paid for the IT asset

Market (Current) Value: what you would receive for the IT asset on the open market

Book Value: acquisition cost minus depreciation

Replacement Cost: what it would cost today in order to provide the same functionality; for example, (a) a firm purchases new PCs for $2000 each, (b) it sells the old PCs for $500 each, then (c) the net Replacement Cost is $1500 per PC.

Value in Use: the productive value that the firm receives from the IT asset (e.g., how that asset alters cash flow)

Current Value: This value includes a deduction for depreciation, but formal accounting depreciation values may be deceiving. If the IT department has taken especially good care of its hardware, software and facilities, then the Market Value will be greater than the Book Value. If, on the other hand, the IT assets have been abused, then the firm may not be able to receive full Book Value on the open market. The above point is critical in determining an organization's technology budget tactics. During lean financial times, future-oriented budget lines such as computer maintenance tend to be eliminated or decreased. That short-sighted tactic may result in serious IT value loss in the future. Paraphrasing an AMCO television advertisement, *"Pay me (a little) now or pay me (a lot) later."*

Value in Use: This emerging metric is somewhat subjective and is difficult to calculate; therefore, it is not proscribed in current accounting standards. It is important, however, because it forces an organization's management to couple IT value with strategic goals such as increased profit or share of the market. Value in Use considers intangible factors such as future benefits or customer satisfaction. These are difficult to quantify and so they rarely enter a firm's formal financial statements. Value in Use can include other positive considerations such as faster processes, greater productivity, and generation of better organizational insight (e.g., Data Mining). Yet there are negative aspects as well. These can include equipment breaking down frequently (through lack of maintenance?) and IT hardware and software being difficult for users to learn and use.

The primary point we wish to make here is that the Value in Use measure of IT value may be more important to an organization's attitude about technology than any of the other easier-to-calculate metrics. We cannot ignore this difficult and new way of thinking merely because it is difficult to measure and therefore not amenable to our financial statements.

Balance Sheet Recognition of Intangible Assets: Paragraph 39 of Financial Accounting Standard (FAS) number 141 (June, 2001) states that an acquired intangible asset shall be recognized as an asset apart from goodwill if it (a) arises from contractual or other legal rights, or (b) is separable. A *Separable Intangible Asset* is one that is capable of being separated or divided from the acquired entity and sold, transferred, licensed, rented or exchanged. One category of intangible asset cited by FAS 141 is *Technology-Based Intangible Assets* which are assets related to innovations or technological advances.

Technology-Based Intangible Assets: These include:

Patented Technology: technology intangible assets (e.g., chip manufacturing methodology) that are protected legally by patent or copyright or by contractual or other legal rights

Computer Software: computer programs or systems (e.g., Microsoft Office) that are protected legally by patent or copyright or by contractual or other legal rights

Databases: if they include original works of authorship which are entitled to copyright protection, but not if they were created as consequence of a firm's normal operations (e.g., customer list)

The Bottom Line: Valuation of technology assets is a complex and dynamic issue. Still, given the high ratio of IT assets to other assets in today's organizations, we must make the effort to fine tune the ways that we are evaluating such assets currently.

THE CHANGING ROLE OF THE AUDITOR

There have been significant legislative and professional responses to the series of corporate corruption and auditing failure such as Enron, Global Crossing, WorldCom, Adelphia, Tyco, and others. The conviction of Arthur Anderson LLP on obstruction of justice charges for document-related misconduct regarding Enron's case is also unprecedented. This response has changed the role of both the internal and external auditor.

Legislative Forces: There are two newly legislated acts regarding internal controls for organizations: the Sarbanes-Oxley Act of July 20, 2003 and the USA PATRIOT Act.

Sarbanes-Oxley: *"The Sarbanes-Oxley Act is a landmark U.S. law designed to improve corporate responsibility and accountability, enhance financial reporting and disclosures, and ensure auditor independence"* (Hammer and Markham, 2004). On January 22, 2003, the Securities and Exchange Commission (SEC) voted to adopt section 401(a) of the Act. This act and the SEC adoption have shaken corporate America in terms of tightening the requirements for accounting oversight, internal controls, statement preparation, and statement attestation. We will discuss this act's effect on auditing in this section and its specific effect on internal controls in the next section. The Sarbanes-Oxley Act and SEC's further proposals have the following important requirements:

Public Company Accounting Oversight Board (PCAOB): This nonprofit body, subject to SEC oversight, includes members appointed by the SEC. Whereas the prior Public Oversight Board was supported by fees collected from the auditors whom it regulated, the new PCAOB is funded by mandatory feeds paid by all public companies.

Duties of the PCAOB include (a) registering and inspecting public accounting firms, (b) establishing auditing, quality control, ethics, independence, and other standards relating to preparation of audit reports, (c) conducting investigations and disciplinary proceedings, (d) imposing appropriate sanctions, and (e) reviewing annually those accounting firms that conduct more than 100 audits a year, and every three years for those accounting firms conducting fewer than 100 audits a year.

Auditor Service Prohibitions: To ensure auditor independence, auditors are prohibited from providing certain services to their audited clients. Those services include:

- Bookkeeping or other services related to accounting records of financial statements
- Financial information systems design and implementation, appraisal or valuation services, fairness opinions, or contribution-in-kind reports
- Actuarial services
- Internal audit outsourcing services
- Management functions or human resources
- Broker-dealer, investment advisor services, or investment banking services
- Legal and expert services unrelated to the audit, and any other services that the new PCAOB determines, by regulation, to be impermissible

Other Auditor Requirements: The lead auditor and the reviewing partner may serve for no more than five years on any audit, and cannot return to audit services with the same client sooner than five years. There also is a prohibition on destroying audit documents which are less than five years old. Most importantly, the audit committee is responsible for the appointment and oversight of the auditors; auditors report to the audit committee, not to management. Finally, audit committee members must not be in receipt of money from the firm for any service other than for being a director.

Executive Considerations: The act is addressed not only to auditors, but to company executives as well. The Chief Executive Officer (CEO) and Chief Financial Officer (CFO) of each public firm are explicitly required to state that the financial statements and disclosures are a fair presentation of this firm's operations and financial position. These executives have to reimburse their firm for bonuses that were based on statements that were required to be restated due to material noncompliance with reporting standards. Officers and directors also are prohibited from trading on stock during pension blackout periods. There must be disclosure and explanation of all material off-balance sheet transactions, arrangements, and obligations. Finally, each annual report must contain a section on internal controls to include a statement of management responsibility for and an assessment of the effectiveness of these controls.

USA Patriot Act: The full name for the USA PATRIOT Act is Uniting and Strengthening America by providing Appropriate Tools Required to Intercept and Obstruct Terrorism Act.; it was enacted in October 2001 as a direct response to the terrorist attack on the World Trade Center. The Act imposes new requirements on recordkeeping and financial reporting for a wide range of organizations including federally insured banks, private bankers, uninsured commercial banks, US branches of a foreign bank, registered securities broke or dealers, investment bankers, operators of a credit card system, the US Postal Service, persons involved in real estate closings and settlements, casino or gaming establishments, travel agencies, currency exchanges, among others. The act includes compliance requirements such as the following:

Protection Policies: There must be policies, procedures and controls for (a) verifying customer identification, (b) filing required reports including currency transaction and suspicious activity reports, (c) creating and maintaining required reports in response to law enforcement requests, and (d) integrating due diligence and enhanced due diligence programs for respondent and private banking accounts.

Compliance Officer: There must be a **Compliance Officer** with responsibility for assuring day-to-day compliance with respect to (a) properly filing reports and creating and retaining required records, (b) updating the program to reflect current regulatory requirements, and (c) providing appropriate employee education and training.

Education/Training: There must be education and training for appropriate personnel concerning their responsibilities; this training includes detection of suspicious transactions

Independent Audit: An independent audit must be conducted with a scope and frequency commensurate with money laundering risks posed by the business. The audit must be conducted by either an outside party or by an officer or employee of an entity other than the compliance officer,

Documentation: The act's required control program must be in writing and approved by either the board of directors or senior management. In addition, the written program must be submitted to the Treasury Department upon request.

Internal Auditors: Internal auditors should have a more significant role in their organizations. It was reported that many organizations are considering having internal auditors report directly to the CEO or the audit committee. FirstEnergy Corporation, as a response to the new law, pinpointed many internal control issues to be addressed including verifying the effectiveness of the control assessment process, meeting the financial and education needs of the audit committee, documenting policies and processes for compliance purpose, and reviewing the audit committee's relationship with external auditors

Effect on Accounting and Auditing: These acts purport to enhance the effectiveness of auditors by reducing the conflict of interest, increasing transparency of financial reporting, assigning corporate leadership the responsibility of risk management, and attesting to the effectiveness of their internal control systems.

Professional Forces: The accounting profession also is trying to tighten professional standards relating to accounting responsibilities in general and auditing responsibilities in particular.

SAS 99: Among these efforts is SAS 99, the new statement on auditing standards issued by the Auditing Standards Board (ASB) of the American Institute of Certified Public Accountants (AICPA) in October 2002. This standard is considered to be the cornerstone effort of AICPA to combat financial frauds through accounting standards and procedure. SAS 99 has the following major provisions that affect how we look at internal controls:

Risk: There should be professional skepticism about risk and discussions among engagement teams regarding risk. These discussions should include the client's industry and operation as well as opportunities for fraud. The discussions should involve external auditors, internal auditors, management, the audit committee legal council, forensic auditors, and other personnel who are not directly involved in the financial reporting process.

Preliminary analytical procedure: Preliminary analytical procedures at the planning stage should be considered together with information at a detailed level. Auditors should pay attention to unusual methods for revenue recognition, special or complex transactions, and particular circumstances surrounding unusual transactions. Auditors also must compare the client's financial ratios (e.g., profitability, bad debt expense) with previous years and industry averages.

Audit responses: Three audit responses are required relating to risks of material misstatement:

The first is the *Overall effect* on how the audit is conducted (e.g., assigning more experienced auditors and specialists or adding an element of unpredictability for audit procedure). The second is *Identified risks* involving the nature, timing, and extent of the auditing procedures such as obtaining more reliable evidence, changing the timing of a substantive test from an interim date to period-end, using a larger sample sizes, or performing procedures at untypical locations.

A third response is *Fraud involving management override of controls*: Auditors should address the risk of management override of controls by utilizing both traditional and non-traditional business channels to reveal the reasonableness of the override decisions. Finally, a response is required for *Material Misstatements* due to fraud. In this case, auditors should (a) obtain additional evidential matter to make a definitive decision, (b) consider the implications for other aspects of the audit, (c) discuss the matter with a person at least one management level above where the problem is detected, and (d) suggest that the client consult with legal counsel.

Auditors also should withdraw from the auditing engagement if there are implications about management's integrity and cooperation in investigation.

Other Professional Activities: AICPA also has launched a series of activities to specify anti-fraud criteria and controls for public companies. For example, this association has established an Institute for Fraud Studies, cosponsored by the University of Texas at Austin and the Association of Certified Fraud Examiners. In addition AICPA has:

- mandated anti-fraud training for management, boards of directors, and audit committees
- recommended ten percent of Certified Public Accountant education to be on fraud detection
- suggested that attestation standards for Certified Public Accountants be extended to include the client's internal control system and criteria
- communicated with educators and textbook authors to incorporate anti-fraud topics in programs and text materials
- hosted fraud summits to discuss fraud detection

Effect on Accounting: The accounting profession has realized that its professional standing and image are under serious challenge after a series of high-profile financial fraud cases. Our profession is working hard to restore the public's confidence by revising standards and cooperating with other involved institutes. This, of course, will change expectations for how accountants should perform and behave.

THE CHANGING NATURE OF INTERNAL CONTROLS

Internal controls prevent, detect and correct incidents of error, fraud, or sabotage. Such controls are the core of organizational asset protection and transaction integrity. Yet, the same tool set of internal controls we have used in the past may not be sufficient in today's integrated, open business environment.

Definitions: The following definitions are important to understanding the design and oversight of internal controls in organizations. A **_Threat_** is any possible event that could be detrimental to an organization. A **_Risk_** is the likelihood (probability) of a specific threat occurring. We first identify the possible threats and then we assign risk values (e.g., high) to each threat. We then design internal controls which will cost-effectively reduce the risk of and detect occurrence of threat events.

Risk Management: The Sarbanes-Oxley Act requires each public company to have a risk management policy and program. To begin with, a risk assessment team should be formed consisting of system developers, accountants, auditors, lawyers, record managers, members of the audit committee, and representation from top management. The assessment team has to evaluate the security risks of different information assets based on their values, vulnerability, and impacts if security is breached. There are three categories of IT asset risk: low, medium and high. Risk categorization of IT assets is based upon the following characteristics:

- Relative value of the asset to hackers
- Relative complexity of the technology involved
- Possibility that stored records will be involved in litigation
- Level of possible media coverage should the asset be subject to fraud or destruction
- Relative financial consequence (impact) of fraud or destruction
- Whether or not internal or external records are at risk

Table 6-1 shows high, medium and low risk categorizations of IT assets based upon these characteristics.

Table 6-1 Risk Categorization of IT Assets

Categorization	Low Risk IT Assets	Medium Risk IT Assets	High Risk IT Assets
Asset Value to Hackers	Little	Some	Will Gain High Profile status
Complexity of Technology	Simple	Small Adaptations	Very Complex or New Use
Records Involved in Litigation?	Little Possibility	May be Used	High Probability
Level Possible Media Coverage	Occasionally Harsh	Frequent Unfavorable	Intense with Widespread Public Distrust
Financial Consequence	Minimum or Low	10 to 25% of Budget at Risk	More than 25% of Budget at Risk
Records at Risk	Internal Administrative	Internal or External of Low Importance	External or Vital

CobiT Objectives: The IT Governance Institute has published a document *CobiT – Control Objectives for Information and Related Technology*. This document includes a control maturity model, critical success factors and a control framework. This model was used by KPMG Peat Marwick, LLP for assessing information system vulnerabilities.

Maturity Model: The control maturity model describes the following steps in assessing an organization's current control practices: (a) identify the functions or departments to be measured, (b) identify the current score (0 to 5, with 0 being no control and 5 being the best practice) to the IT control environment, (c) identify the level of IT control desired for the area, (d) calculate the difference between the current control level and the desired control level for each area, and (e) decide how resources should be allocated to meet control needs.

Control Objectives: The Control Objectives section in CobiT describes 34 high-level control objectives and 318 detailed supporting objectives. All of the objectives have indicators to measure relative success. The hierarchy of high-level control objectives, detailed control objectives, and key performance indicators allow different levels of management to "buy-into" the vital concepts of risk management and control. Table 6-2 shows some common control objectives for electronic transactions.

Table 6-2 Common CobiT Control Objectives for Electronic Transactions

Control Objective	Description	Control Objective	Description
Data and Processing Integrity	All transactions processed and all records updated completely	Access Control	Users allowed into system are only allowed to data/privileges with pre-approved need
Data and Processing Reliability	All transactions processed and all records updated accurately	Interception Control	Communications interception by unauthorized parties prevented/ violations detected
Data and Processing Availability	Systems have minimum periods of time when not available for use	Output Control	Products distributed only to authorized parties who have need for product
Session Authentication and Non-Repudiation	Users are who they say they are and cannot repudiate transactions	Backup and Recovery Control	Transactions/file contents replicated; stored off-site
Confidentiality and Privacy	Customer/employee data available only to those with approved need to know	Conformance to General Control Practices	Organization-wide control culture seeded by continuous training

Other Professional Efforts: In response to the proliferation of e-business on the Web, different professional bodies have developed new tools and standards to assess risks. For example, the American Institute of Certified Public Accountants (AICPA) and the Canadian Institute of Chartered Accountants (CICA) issued a new guideline SysTrust Principles and Criteria for System Reliability in 1999 to ensure that a system generates reliable information in an online real-time environment. In addition, the same professional bodies addressed the importance of assessing Internet Service Providers (ISP) by issuing the *WebTrust-ISP Principles and Criteria for Internet Service Providers in Electronic Commerce* in 1999. This guideline provides assurance that ISPs follow a recognized set of principles in conducting e-business and assist their customers in obtaining a WebTrust Business-to-Consumer Seal of Assurance for their Web sites.

An Integrative Model for Internal Controls: Figure 6-1 presents an integrative model for internal controls in the Internet environment. This model has the following elements:

Management Directives, Philosophy and Policies: This is the overall guiding force for internal controls. It is important for top management to establish a corporate culture and environment that discourage fraud and unethical activities. Research studies have confirmed that employees will engage in altruism, courtesy, sportsmanship, civic virtue, and conscientiousness if top management has firm expectations of ethical behaviors from all employees including themselves. Internal control systems should include not only control practices for information systems, but also behavioral controls by imposing a clear, consistent, and material reward and penalty system that encourages ethical behavior and reporting of unethical behavior incidents.

General controls deal with overall organizational security regardless of the type of IT hardware or software used. It includes such policies as (a) separation of duties, (b) independence of auditors from personnel to be audited, (c) hiring and training procedures to ensure qualified and ethical employees, (d) job rotation for key processing functions to prevent fraud opportunities, and (e) proper project management to ensure development of auditable systems

Figure 6-1 Integrative Model for Internet Internal Controls

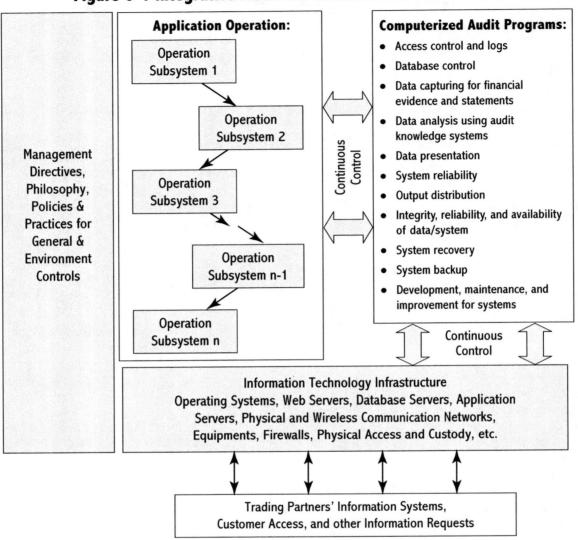

Application Operation:

Operation Subsystem 1

Operation Subsystem 2

Operation Subsystem 3

Operation Subsystem n-1

Operation Subsystem n

Continuous Control

Computerized Audit Programs:

- Access control and logs
- Database control
- Data capturing for financial evidence and statements
- Data analysis using audit knowledge systems
- Data presentation
- System reliability
- Output distribution
- Integrity, reliability, and availability of data/system
- System recovery
- System backup
- Development, maintenance, and improvement for systems

Management Directives, Philosophy, Policies & Practices for General & Environment Controls

Continuous Control

Information Technology Infrastructure
Operating Systems, Web Servers, Database Servers, Application Servers, Physical and Wireless Communication Networks, Equipments, Firewalls, Physical Access and Custody, etc.

Trading Partners' Information Systems, Customer Access, and other Information Requests

Some of these general controls need to be altered when an organization evolves from a manual to an automated setting. For example, separation of duties in a manual processing environment refers to separating the three basic functions of transaction processing including authorization, recording, and custody of assets. A computing environment includes the unavoidable concentration of transaction processing steps into a single system with no human intervention.

System development is yet another example. We can separate personnel engaging in different phases of the development cycle: analysis, logical design, physical design, coding, testing, implementing, training, and maintaining. The separation of duties in the development cycle can prevent mistakes from carrying over and collaboration on fraud activities. Table 6-3 shows how certain internal controls must be modified for the processing environments of manual, automated, and Internet.

Table 6-3 Changing Nature of Internal Controls

Internal Control	Manual System	Change Under Automated System	Change Under Internet System
Separation of Duties	Job design	More difficult — computer combines tasks	Now some outsourcing to 3rd parties
Customer Authentication	Physical identification	Same — no customer entry	Passwords with biometrics
File Protection	Locked file cabinets	Passwords; Access control programs	Passwords, access control and data encryption
Physical Access	Locked desks	Locked computers	Firewalls and intrusion detection systems
Logical Access	Physical oversight	Passwords; Access control programs	Same as automated
Programming Control	None	Computer Audit Software	More complex, thus imported software
Auditing	Manual System	Auditor needs computer knowledge	Must audit e-partners and 3rd parties

Environment controls refer to physical controls that safeguard data and systems such as (a) site access control using an identification badge, (b) password and biometric authentication, (c) backup sites that mirror data and processing of computing systems; and (d) recovery procedures for dealing with natural disasters and human sabotage.

Infrastructure Controls: These controls deal with the horizontal foundation (infrastructure) for all information system control practices. For example there are virus detection systems, intrusion detection systems, the SET standard for Internet payment security, Internet security protocols, data encryption, and certified seals of approval such as AICPA's WebTrust and SysTrust assurance

Computerized Audit Programs are software packages or modules which assist auditors in performing their oversight responsibilities. Such programs in the Internet environment (a) operate continuously rather than periodically, (b) audit technology infrastructure as well as transaction applications (e.g., accounts receivable), (c) use specialized modules designed specifically for auditors, (d) audit both input-process-output of applications and information flow from one subsystem to another, (e) include Web-enabled, Web-supported, and Web-delivered audit activities, and (f) ensure that the audit process is in compliance with the evolving Generally Accepted Electronic Auditing Standards (GAEAS). Computerized Audit Programs include the following modules:

Access control can utilize techniques such as passwords, firewalls, digital signature and envelopes, IP address authentication, and access control.

Database control applies database integrity constraints, triggers, and user privileges to safeguard database resources.

Data capture modules collect users' encrypted digital envelopes, use the auditor's private key to open the digital envelopes, check the digital signatures using the user's public key, and store the messages in the envelope in the auditor's audit knowledge base for further analysis.

Data Analysis Modules apply different detection rules and algorithms to the auditor knowledge base in order to identify abnormalities.

Data Presentation Modules allow the auditor to browse, navigate, and review audit outcome summaries and other documents.

While computing systems present many new challenges to auditors, they also introduce many new opportunities. Audit-through-the-computer techniques reveal program processing logic using common techniques such as embedded audit routines, integrated testing facilities, and parallel simulation. Because of the enormous processing capabilities of computers, auditors now can use computers to do a 100 percent audit rather than applying sampling. Auditors also can trace transaction processing around the clock and apply artificial intelligence methodologies to identify unusual transactions and potential fraud.

Sarbanes-Oxley and Internal Controls: Section 204 of this act promises to have the greatest impact upon how we have considered internal controls traditionally. The act pushes us towards the following practices (Hamerman and Markham, 2004):

<u>Internal Control Compliance a Part of Company Culture</u>: Internal control becomes a collaborative process. All line managers and those directly involved with financial processes are part of a team that assesses internal controls. Control assessment capabilities and monitoring must be spread to a wider audience.

<u>Consistency and Standardization of Business Processes</u>: This will strengthen the internal control setting, thus making it easier to comply with this act.

<u>Accountability of Business Managers and Process Owners</u>: Ultimate compliance responsibility lies with the CEO and CFO, but accountability is pushed down through all levels of the organization. For example, there now is considerable pressure on IT managers to certify the accuracy and security of all IT business applications.

<u>Sustainable Compliance</u>: This cannot be a one-time effort. Companies will scramble to introduce make-shift methods for act compliance. As these companies learn from their mistakes, and as automated compliance packages enter the marketplace, more sustainable practices will develop.

<u>Automated Compliance</u>: The Sarbanes-Oxley act does require that internal control assessment and monitoring be automated. Technological applications, however, will help a company to comply with this act's internal controls requirements. These will include graphical representations, project planning, real-time process monitoring, document creation, and records management.

REVENUE RECOGNITION

The Security and Exchange Commission's Accounting Bulletin 101 (SAB 101), issued in December of 1999, specifies the exact conditions as to when revenue from a sale should be recognized for purposes of financial statements. Unfortunately, these conditions often pose compliance difficulties in an e-business environment. In this section we will examine revenue recognition in an e-business setting.

When Revenue Can Be Recognized: SAB 101 sets the following conditions for revenue recognition from the sale of a product or service:

- A sales arrangement exists.
- Delivery of the product or service has occurred.
- The price of the product or service is fixed or determinable.
- Collection for the sale is reasonably assured.

For the traditional brick and mortar (non-internet) firm, these conditions present few problems. In a bookstore, for example, a customer selects a book and pays cash or a cash equivalent (e.g., ATM card). Obviously, (a) a sales arrangement exists, (b) delivery has occurred, (c) the price has been determined, and (d) collection has occurred (is assured). The situation is not nearly so clear in an e-business setting.

Internet Revenue Recognition Dilemmas: Let us now assume that our books are sold over the Internet (a "click" company). In a sense, the same events occur in that books are exchanged for cash or cash equivalents. But the exchange is not done instantaneously as it is in a traditional book store. Also, many Web bookstores are intermediaries that don't stock the books they sell.

The customer order is placed on-line and the intermediary book outlet (e.g., Amazon.com) passes that information to another business that ships the books to the customer. The vital question is, "When in that stream of events should the order-taking firm recognize the book revenue?" Should the Web retailer recognize the revenue when the order is (a) taken, (b) passed to another business, (c) shipped, (d) delivered, or (e) paid for?

FASB's Tentative Approach: The Financial Accounting Standards Board (FASB) has recognized that earnings processes are specific to business models and that, as business models change, new reporting standards are needed. The FASB accordingly in October 2003 issued tentative guidance for revenue recognition for an e-business setting. This early guidance suggests that revenue recognition should arise from the analysis of some combination of performance and liability extinguishment. In addition, performance obligations must be measured at fair market value, a value that often is difficult to assess reliably.

Revenue Recognition Performance is when benefits arise from the company's specific creation of goods and services and transfer of them to customers. Revenues could not be recognized if the company has arranged for others to create goods and services on its behalf. *Liability Extinguishment* defines that revenues can arise as obligations to customers are extinguished. Revenues could occur if the company arranged for others to perform specific processes. We will use the example of Dell Computers to see how revenue recognition can become complex in an e-business setting.

Dell Computers: Figure 6-2 shows Dell's on-line computer sales system. The customer orders a tailor-made computer on-line and production of that computer begins almost immediately. When production is completed, two events are triggered. First, UPS has access to Dell's production schedule; therefore a UPS truck is waiting at the factory door to deliver the computer to the customer. Second, the customer is billed on-line for the product that has not yet been delivered. The situation becomes more complex on delivery.

Dell does not stock monitors for its computers. Dell subcontracts with a Texas firm to manufacture monitors. When alerted by Dell, that Texas firm ships a monitor to a UPS regional assembly location where it (a) it meets the shipment of the computer that UPS picked up from Dell's assembly line, and (b) is combined with that computer shipment and sent to the customer (referred to as "Merge In Transit"). In the future, Dell and UPS plan to extend their partnership to include UPS installing the computer in the customer's home or workplace and training the customer on that computer's use.

Revenue Recognition Problems: Several revenue recognition problems arise from this e-business sales alliance. First, when should Dell recognize revenue from the sale? Second, when should UPS or the monitor provider recognize revenue from their endeavors? Third, how should total revenue be shared by each of the three trading partners?

Figure 6-2 Dell Delivery System

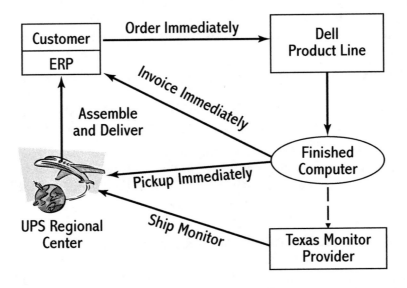

Revenue Recognition Resolution: Let's look at how the tentative guidance that we have received thus far might lead us to resolve Dell's revenue recognition problems.

SAB 101 Guidelines: We shall look at this issue strictly from Dell's perspective, ignoring revenue recognition problems for UPS or the Texas monitor provider.

A sales arrangement exists. The buyer of a Dell computer has selected a computer configuration and agreed to price, delivery and service conditions.

Delivery of the product or service has occurred. If these three entities were to bill the customer separately, then Dell could transfer (sell) the computer to UPS for an agreed price and recognize the revenue at that point. But Dell sends to the customer a single billing and reimburses UPS and the Texas monitor provider after it receives or is promised customer payment. Therefore, Dell cannot recognize revenue until after delivery occurs and Dell is notified of that status.

The price of the product or service is fixed or determinable. This condition is met because Dell includes shipping and handling charges in the up-front statements of computer costs.

Collection for the sale is reasonably assured. We shall assume that customer authentication and credit checks are performed when the customer places an order online. Thus, collection of the sale is reasonably assured.

In summary, as long as only a single billing is sent to a customer, Dell must wait until it receives an UPS notification of delivery from UPS. Dell could pre-pay UPS for its services or pay only after delivery is made. The Texas provider could sell the monitor to UPS when it is shipped to the UPS delivery center, thereby allowing it to recognize revenue at that time.

FASB Guidelines: Let us see how the FASB guidelines fit the Dell revenue recognition problem.

Revenue Performance: Dell could recognize revenue only for its specific creation of goods and services. Under this criterion, Dell cannot recognize revenue on the monitors provided by the Texas firm even if those monitors are purchased by Dell upon completion and the Texas firm is warehousing them for Dell. In addition, Dell could not recognize revenue for UPS services.

<u>Liability Extinguishment</u>: Under this criterion, however, UPS's delivery of the computer extinguishes an obligation to the customer. So Dell can recognize as revenue the UPS portion of the sale because Dell had arranged for others (UPS) to perform the delivery process. The resolution is less clear under this criterion for the Texas monitor provider.

The Bottom Line: This perfunctory analysis of Dell's revenue recognition problem stresses two important points. First, revenue recognition in today's e-business landscape is complex; more concrete guidance is in development for our accounting standards. Second, determination of proper revenue recognition cannot be done at the overview level such as that provided by Figure 6-2. We must look deeper into the processes to answer questions such as:

- What is the arrangement between Dell and the Texas monitor provider?

- Is this provider paid after the monitor is completed, after it is shipped to UPS, or after the customer pays for the total computer package?

- Does UPS buy the computer upon acceptance from Dell's production line or merely perform Dell's shipping responsibilities?

The accountant should ensure that contracts between trading partners such as Dell and UPS specifically address revenue recognition issues. The accountant also should keep a wary eye on the horizon to detect evolving changes in revenue recognition standards.

TAXING THE INTERNET

Internet sales are not taxed to the same extent as are traditional sales. There currently is a world-wide movement to study the taxation of Internet sales. We discuss in this section the issue of whether or not Internet sales should be taxed and current efforts to do so.

Why Tax the Internet? There are three arguments for taxing Internet sales.

<u>Seller Inequalities</u>: The current situation causes inequalities. Physical stores have to add federal, state and local taxes to the prices that they charge to consumers for products while Internet sales outlets do not. Therefore, it is difficult for physical stores to compete with the prices offered by their Internet counterparts.

<u>Buyer Inequalities</u>: It is estimated that 80 percent of Internet sales are made to consumers in the top 20 percent of income brackets. One of the reasons for this inequality may be that consumers in relatively lower income brackets either (a) can't afford the same level of Internet access as higher income consumers, or (b) lower income consumers don't have the same Internet training opportunities, thus rendering their Web efforts less successful than higher income counterparts. Whatever the reason, the result is that higher income consumers are better able to take advantage of lower (tax free) Internet product prices.

<u>Tax Income Loss</u>: Taxing authorities are seeing decreased revenues as sales continue to migrate from taxed physical stores to non-taxed Web sites. The U.S. General Accounting Office has estimated that such sales tax losses could range from $1 billion to $4 billion in the next few years. Some estimate that this tax revenue loss could be as much as $29 billion by 2011.

Internet Taxing Efforts: No nation currently levies taxes on electronic transactions. However, this "moratorium" may expire soon. There are initiatives by countries and U.S. states to close this revenue gap. There is a United Nations effort to attempt to standardize how electronic transactions can be taxed internationally. The Organization for Economic Cooperation and Development (OECD) has a subgroup devoted to Internet sales taxation.

Internet Taxing Problems: One of the reasons why Internet sales have not yet been taxed has to do with the unique problems imposed by Internet transactions. These problems include (a) identifying the taxpayer, (b) determining the jurisdiction in which income was earned, (c) gathering information about the transaction, and (d) establishing a method for collecting the taxes. These taxing needs are rather straightforward when transactions occur within the same country or same state, but Internet transactions that cross jurisdictions can cause taxing problems.

Identifying the Taxpayer: A recent Australian study found that the taxpayer could not be identified in 15 percent of the Internet transactions studied. The reasons for such non-identification included sender anonymity and spoofing (assuming another person's identity).

Determining the Jurisdiction: There is a legal question as to whether or not the alleged taxpayer is a legal resident in the country attempting to impose the tax. E-mail addresses (URL) such as ".org", ".com", and ".net" do not identify jurisdiction. In addition, a Web site does not have a physical or perhaps legal presence as would a buyer in a physical store.

Gathering Transaction Information: Electronic records can be altered or destroyed more readily. So the question is posed as to whether or not these electronic documents are reliable tax records.

Collecting the Tax: The Internet selling company must have familiarity with the tax laws that apply to the transaction. Yet, buyers may reside in multiple locations. Who collects the tax levied on a California Internet sale for a seller that has a main office in Germany?

What is Happening Now: Despite these problems with electronic transactions, there seems to be wide-spread agreement that Internet sales will be taxed in some form or another in the future. There is international consensus that no new *Internet-specific* taxes will be levied. However, that consensus includes the proviso that soon e-business sales will be taxed in the same manner and to the same degree as conventional commerce sales.

THE WORLD ACCORDING TO ROB

Robert (Rob) Taylor, Accounting Manager for Getronics, says:

In your alliances with Dell and Cisco, do you have any problems with revenue recognition?

Rob says, "Not on the hardware; all of our revenue recognition is done at time of shipment. Most of the products that we are buying from Dell or Cisco are brought into our own warehouse facilities. We do the modifications and ship the equipment out to our clients"

Getronics does some drop shipment contracts. For example, Dell computers are acquired and shipped directly to the client without being handled by Getronics. "This adds some complexity to the accounting system," Rob says. "You have to have some notification or understanding as to when equipment was shipped from Dell's facility and then you need to record it as a goods receipt on your books. Then you have to record the transfer to the client. This never seems to be easy."

SUMMARY

This chapter examined five traditional accounting responsibilities to demonstrate how application of these responsibilities must be tailored to meet the demands of increasingly technological, Web-oriented business settings. Hopefully, our discussion has strengthened our contention throughout this textbook that we need not abandon our traditional accounting purviews or mind-sets. We merely must adapt our skills and practices to better fit the e-business world of our future.

KEY TERMS

Acquisition Cost	High Risk Asset	Reliability
Book Value	Infrastructure Controls	Replacement Cost
CobiT	Integrity	Risk
Compliance Officer	Interception Controls	Sarbanes-Oxley Act
Computerized Audit Program	Liability Extinguishment	SAS 99
Current Value	Low Risk Asset	Separable Intangible Assets
Data Analysis Module	Market Value	Threat
Data Capture Module	Maturity Model	USA Patriot Act
Data Presentation Module	Medium Risk Asset	Value in Use
Environmental Controls	Public Accounting	Vulnerability
General Controls	Oversight Board (PCAOB)	

REVIEW EXERCISES

1. Describe three important reasons for valuing IT assets.
2. What are the differences between:
   a. Market Value and Book Value?
   b. Acquisition Value and Replacement Value?
3. Why is Value in Use an important concept? Why do you believe it is not used more?
4. What services are prohibited to be provided by external auditors under Sarbanes-Oxley?
5. What are the major provisions in SAS 99?
6. Describe four (4) CobiT control objectives for electronic transactions.
7. Regarding internal control systems, what are the new responsibilities to management in public companies as required by the Sarbanes-Oxley Act?
8. What are the differences between a general control and:
   a. an environment control?
   b. an infrastructure control?
9. Describe three differences between low-risk and high-risk IT assets.
10. Describe three common CobiT control objectives for electronic transactions.
11. How do physical access controls change when evolving from a manual to an Internet AIS?
12. What are the characteristics for computerized audit programs?
13. What is a Separable Intangible Asset? Why is it important?

14. Define Revenue Recognition Performance.

15. Give an example of Liability Extinguishment.

16. What are the four conditions necessary for a company to be able to recognize revenue?

17. What are the reasons proposed for taxing the Internet?

18. Why is it difficult for taxing authorities to determine the jurisdiction of an e-business transaction?

19. Why is it so difficult for taxing authorities to collect taxes on Internet transactions?

CRITICAL THINKING EXERCISES

1. Survey the accounting staffs of ten companies in your geographic area to determine the methods they use to value IT assets.

2. Ask these same staffs what effect the Sarbanes-Oxley act has had on their internal control environment.

3. You have been assigned the task of informing management of the IT Value in Use for your organization. How would you approach this task?

4. Reference Figure 6-2. Draw this figure for a Web-based company other than Dell. Describe that company's revenue recognition problems.

5. Your class will be divided into two groups for a classroom debate. One side will argue for taxing the Internet. The other side will argue against taxing the Internet. (NOTE: both sides should perform some Web searches for information on this topic before the debate.)

REFERENCES

Casabona, P. and M .Grego; *"SAS99 – consideration of fraud in a financial statement audit: A revision of statement on Auditing Standards 82"*; **Review of Business** 24:2, 2003, 16-21.

Dunn, C., G. Gerard and J. Worrell; *"Evaluation of network operating system security controls"*; **Issues in Accounting Education**; 18:3, 2003, 291-301.

Elifoglu, I.; *"Navigating the "information super highway: How accountants can help clients assess and control the risks of Internet-based E-commerce"*; **Review of Business** 23:1, 2002, 67-72.

Financial Accounting Standards Board; **Statement of Financial Accounting Standards** No. 141; June 2001.

Financial Accounting Standards Board; *"Project Updates – Revenue Recognition"*; October 31, 2003; http://www.fasb.org/project/revenue_recognition.shtml

Financial Accounting Standards Board; **Statement of Financial Accounting Standards No. 141**; June 2001

Hammerman P., and R. Markham; *"Sarbanes-Oxley Solutions – Invest Now or Pay Later"*; **Forrester Research Inc.**, March 2004

Holmes, S.; J. Strawser, and S.Welch; *"Fraud in the governmental and private sectors"*; **Journal of Public Budgeting, Accounting & Financial Management**; 12:3, 2000, 345-370.

Latshaw, C.; *"Fraudulent financial reporting: The government and accounting profession react"*. **Review of Business**; 24:2, 2003, 13-16.

Linsley, C.; *"Auditing, risk management and a post Sarbanes-Oxley world"*; Review **of Business**; 24:3, 2003, 21-27.

Silets, H. and C. Van Cleef; *"Compliance issues in the wake of the USA PATRIOT Act"*; **Journal of Financial Crime**; 10:4, 2003, 392-405.

Swartz, N.; *"The cost of Sarbanes-Oxley"*; **Information Management Journal**; 37:5, 2003, 8.

Thompson, J. and G. Lange; *"The Sarbanes-Oxley Act and the changing responsibilities of auditors"*; Review **of Business**; 24:2, 2003, 8-13.

Yu, C., H.Yu, and C. Chou; *"The impacts of electronic commerce on auditing practices: An auditing process model of evidence collection and validation"*; **International Journal of Intelligent Systems in Accounting, Finance & Management**; 9:3, 2000, 195-216.

The authors wish to thank Dr. Suzanne Ogilby, California State University Sacramento, for her contributions to this chapter.

technology deployment planning

> "Think before you aim. Speed, while important, is a big problem if the direction is off."
>
> *— Stephan Kindt*

INTRODUCTION

The headline in the July 6, 1996 Sacramento Bee read, *"California Pulls Plug on a Troubled System"*. California's Department of Welfare Services had contracted with Lockheed Martin to develop a Child Support Collection system. After eight years and $111 million in wasted spending, the project was terminated. What had gone wrong?

Lockheed had failed to provide the agreed upon project team and had instead used less experienced analysts and programmers. This and other factors had led to the development of a flawed system that did not fully meet client needs. In addition, Lockheed had failed to test system components adequately. Many of these components never worked properly.

State government had added to the risk of project failure by (a) expanding and changing the original project scope, (b) ignoring early warnings of trouble, (c) failing to monitor and control exploding project costs and (d) making incremental payments to Lockheed without proof of delivery. In some cases, Lockheed had been paid twice for the same work.

Yet, the basic problem had been in the conceptual design of how to handle child support payments in a large state such as California. The State and Lockheed had tried to customize the system to each of the many California counties. What had been needed was an enterprise level (state-wide) system. Since that time, legislation has been enacted to take collection away from counties and move it to state level. A new collection system has been designed and deployed.

This incident demonstrates that deployment of technology often is a complex and risky undertaking. That is why almost half of all major technology deployment projects end up seriously over budget, significantly delayed, or both. This chapter describes the organization of, tasks associated with, and factors critical to technology deployment. Entire textbooks have been devoted to this topic. We seek a balance between summarizing a broad body of knowledge while still presenting details necessary for accountants to fulfill their responsibilities within this critical undertaking. Our discussion follows the sequence of (a) Technology Deployment, (b) Technology Deployment Models, (c) Conceptual and Detailed Design, (d) Software Development, (e) Software and System Testing, (f) Rollout Preparation, and (g) Application Rollout.

RELEVANCE TO ACCOUNTING

The accountant has several potential roles in the deployment of technology applications. One role is as a user of the newly deployed system. Another role is as a member of the technology deployment team. A third accounting role is to advise management on such subjects as cost-benefit justification of the technology initiative or measuring the success of the system once implemented. Finally, the accountant may be called upon to assess a deployed technology as an internal or external auditor.

TECHNOLOGY DEPLOYMENT

Technology Deployment is the planning, design, building and implementation of applications using information technology. There are many reasons why an information system application may be required including:

Technological Deterioration: Technology systems hardware can physically deteriorate, but that rarely is a problem today. We develop new technologies so rapidly that old technologies tend to be replaced before they physically deteriorate.

Technological Obsolescence: Technology vendors frequently issue new versions (releases) of hardware and software. These vendors then decrease or eliminate support of older versions, thus making these older versions technologically obsolete.

Business Obsolescence: A system that seems technologically current may not be meeting current business needs. For example, a firm may discover that its competitors are now accepting customer orders over a Web site (e-marketing). That company may then choose to replace its smoothly operating, off-line customer ordering system with a Web version in order to keep up with its competition.

User Expectations: Increased user expectations often drive technology replacement. For example, many state governments are in a quandary because, despite lagging state revenues, their customers are expecting the same rapid responses as they receive from the private sector's e-business (Web) applications.

Outside Influences: A company may be acquired by or merge with another company. Often the acquired company is forced to replace its technological applications in order to be consistent with that of the parent company. In other cases, new government regulations may force changes.

Accounting: Technology, particularly hardware, often is depreciated (written off the books) in a period of five years or less. It is easier for an IT department to justify an application replacement when the old application "doesn't exist", at least in an accounting sense.

Technology Deployment Planning: The decision to deploy a new or revised technological application cannot be taken lightly. Technology deployment is expensive in terms of resources such as funds and manpower. It also is unsettling to day-to-day company operations. Management must decide which of many application needs should be addressed next using an applications portfolio approach. The *Applications Portfolio* is an inventory of IT system needs prioritized by each system's direct contributions to the organization's strategic goals. The portfolio is approved by top-management and constantly revised. The number of projects included in the IT Portfolio will be subject to numerous factors such as market conditions, business health, recent losses, IT department capacity, or potential company growth.

A specific IT initiative will be selected as the next application to be deployed through the following process (Figure 7-1).

Figure 7-1 Front-end Systems Planning

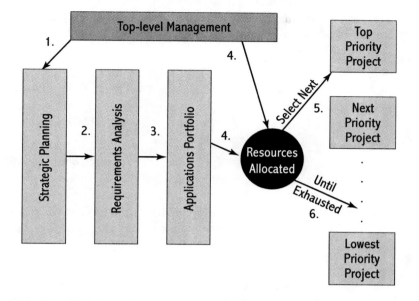

Strategic Planning: The organization determines its mission, objectives required to achieve this mission, and how each department can contribute to these objectives.

Requirements Analysis: An organizational-wide inventory is conducted to determine what technology applications exist, how these contribute to established objectives, and what new applications are needed to reach the firm's objectives. These new or to-be-upgraded applications are prioritized according to relative enhancement of organizational objectives. This becomes the Application Portfolio.

Resource Allocation: Management allocates a certain portion of available resources (e.g., budget) to deploying Applications Portfolio initiatives. There may be resources allocated to three or four technology initiatives; there only may be enough resources allocated to accommodate the highest priority initiative in the portfolio.

Project Planning: The highest priority technology initiative is pulled from the portfolio and that technology deployment project is begun.

The Underlying Infrastructure Evolution: Another major yet often hidden factor in building the Applications Portfolio is that deployment of a specific technology application may be dependent upon the firm's overall technology infrastructure. For example, deployment of a Web-based, e-marketing or e-procurement system may not be feasible if the firm has not first (a) automated all business applications, (b) invested in the technology infrastructure to internally integrate these applications using a centralized database approach, (c) and upgraded that infrastructure to be able to electronically communicate with external parties.

The *Infrastructure Evolution* is the natural hardware progression that a typical firm follows to reach an e-business posture.

Automation: A company automates its internal applications one at a time in stand-alone modes of operation. These applications don't talk (pass data) to one another. Enough hardware is purchased only to support specific applications. There is not much need for a centralized technology infrastructure since the applications are independent and don't share data.

Internal Integration Infrastructure: The firm wishes to integrate internally with one central database and applications (e.g., ERP) that pass data back and forth. Before this internal integration can proceed, however, integration hardware (e.g., database servers, mainframe computers) first must be deployed to establish the required technology infrastructure for this progression.

Internal Integration: The internal integration then is implemented and the firm unites its internal applications. Over the next several years, this infrastructure is patched and upgraded to keep it functional with the firm's growing business needs. After some time, this infrastructure becomes technologically obsolete. Yet, since it still operates effectively and would be expensive to replace, it becomes **Legacy Hardware**: technologically obsolete hardware which still functions effectively as a company's infrastructure backbone.

External Integration Infrastructure: Now the firm decides to electronically link to its customers (e-marketing) or to its suppliers (e-procurement). But the legacy hardware comprising the company's infrastructure is too slow and unwieldy to effectively operate at the speeds and complexities required in the e-business world. The company then must undergo the expensive process of replacing its legacy hardware with the latest technologies including message servers and networks.

E-business External Integration: Now the company has the requisite infrastructure to begin development of an integrated, external e-business enterprise. Note that considerable investment in infrastructure technology is required *before* cost-saving and benefit-producing business software applications can be deployed.

Staged Obsolescence: Some technology applications that were deployed in the 1980s were still operating effectively at the turn of this century. The Y2K (Millennium) problem caused many legacy software applications to be significantly upgraded or replaced. E-business needs are forcing the replacement of more legacy hardware. If a firm waits until a crisis such as Y2K occurs, then all of its hardware and software may have to be replaced at once. This creates an enormous drain on resources and a traumatic change environment for technology users. The replacement or upgrade of infrastructure hardware and software ideally should be staged over a multi-year period.

Staged Obsolescence is the planned replacement of hardware, software, and infrastructure over a multi-year period of time. The firm must continually review and alter this staging plan to align it with changing business and technology conditions. The accountant will play a key role in determining appropriate depreciation write-off periods and resource allocation strategies for this staging plan.

Whatever may be the reasons, the firm is continuously faced with the problem of having to deploy technology applications. Several alternatives are available for such deployment.

TECHNOLOGY DEPLOYMENT MODELS

Discussion of deployment models is the topic of entire textbooks. We will deal only with those portions of this topic for which the accountant may play a significant role. A technology deployment project can be organized in several different ways.

Alternate Deployment Models: There are two classes of deployment models interestingly termed "heavy" and "light" methodologies;

Heavy Methodologies: These are the traditional development models that are include every feature that anybody wants. The system typically is not delivered until all features are completed. This deployment model's primary objective is the building of a technology application that will last for a long period of time. Unfortunately, today's rapid rate of technological obsolescence makes this objective difficult to attain. Because of this "built to last" objective, this approach requires an extensive amount of project and system documentation. That is where the term "heavy" comes from.

Heavy methodologies often are referred to as "development dinosaurs" because they cannot react quickly to today's rapidly changing technological and business landscapes. We will discuss the Systems Development Life Cycle (SDLC) as an example of a heavy methodology.

Light Methodologies: Light methodologies are adaptive rather than predictive. The models assume that all application requirements will *not* be known in advance but will appear as the deployment project progresses. Light methodologies are more sensitive to promised application delivery dates and are geared to delivering a partial, working solution on time rather than a full solution late.

These models focus on less external documentation (e.g., system flow charts) and more on documentation within programming source code. This is done with the view that 80 to 90 percent of all application changes are for relatively minor program patches (maintenance programming). Therefore, documentation should be focused on the program rather than the system. There are several light methodologies in use. We will use the Scrum model as an example of a light development methodology.

System Development Life Cycle (SDLC): The System Development Life Cycle (SDLC) is a traditional heavy model for breaking down a technology project into distinct and manageable stages. Each stage is the responsibility of a set of people with distinguishable skills (e.g., programmers, systems analysts). Each SDLC stage also has a planned (a) start date, (b) end date, (c) output product (deliverable), and (d) resource allocation (budget).

The number of SDLC stages varies with different organizations. Hughes Aircraft used to divide its IT projects into 15 separate stages while its competitor TRW used only nine. It only is important that the number of SDLC stages be internally consistent.

We have chosen an SDLC of six stages (Figure 7-2); each of these stages is divided into several sub-stages, or phases. Note the dotted arrows on this figure. This shows that the SDLC is not always a serial process; at any stage, we may recycle back to a previous stage for rework. For

Figure 7-2 Systems Development Life Cycle (SDLC)

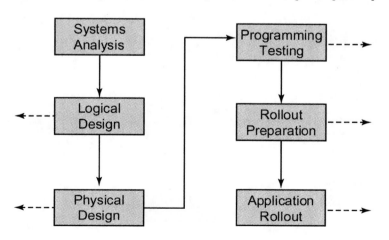

◄ - - - - - Return to Prior Stage if Necessary

example, during the Logical Design stage, we may discover that the alternative that we have chosen in the analysis stage actually will be far more expensive than we projected. We may then have to halt our logical design work so that we can redo our feasibility analysis to determine if this alternative really is our best choice. This recycling often is referred to as the ***Waterfall Model***. Now, we shall look at each SDLC stage in more detail.

Systems Analysis is the discovery, description, and development/selection of alternatives for solving a problem. Accountants typically play a greater role in this stage than in the succeeding, more technical stages. This stage is similar to contacting a housing developer to determine what type of house you require given your specific budget and family needs. There are five phases within this Systems Analysis stage.

Problem Detection: Reasons emerge for having to deploy a new technology application. Application problems can be detected reactively through such means as department requests or user complaints. Application problems can be anticipated proactively through careful construction and continuous update of the Applications Portfolio.

Current System Description: The current technology system is described in entities such as inputs, output, storage, interfaces, and performance.

Requirements Analysis: Optimum system requirements are determined. A user may be asked, for example, *"If there were no cost or other constraints, what would be the ideal system you would like to work with?"* This ideal system often is described in performance terms such as *"We need to decrease our Accounts Payables Outstanding by 15% in order to match the industry average."*

Alternative Development: The Current System Description and the Requirements Analysis have created a gap between what we have now and what we really want (Figure 7-3). We now must create alternatives for narrowing that gap. For example, in a Customer Ordering system, three alternatives might be implementing a Point of Sale (POS) off-line system, building a Web site to conduct e-marketing, or both.

Feasibility Analysis: The alternatives created are compared as to their increases in functionality, deployment time and costs, and expected future benefits. The "best" alternative solution is selected and the Logical Design stage of the project begins.

Figure 7-3 Systems Analysis Stage

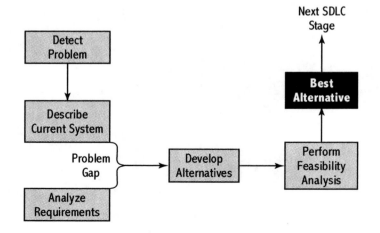

Logical Design is the high-level description of what the new technological solution will look like. It is analogous to an architect rendering a drawing or a scale model of your new house. High-level documentation (e.g., screen layouts) is produced for proposed new system output, input, files, connectivity, and internal controls.

Accountants play an important role in this stage by ensuring that the planned internal control structure is adequate to minimize fraud and errors and facilitate subsequent auditing. For example, it is at this stage that the accountant may stress the need for application systems to include embedded audit modules.

Physical Design is the transformation of logical design specifications into the detailed computer specifications necessary to make the new technological system work. This is similar to converting the architect's drawings of your new house into a specialized blueprint that construction workers can use to physically build your house.

Programming and Testing includes writing the software programs that will operate the technology application and testing the accuracy and interconnectivity of these programs. Often this stage is included as a part of the Physical Design stage. We have chosen to make this a separate stage because it (a) consumes a significant proportion of SDLC time and resources, (b) is critical to subsequent application success, and (c) is a technical area typically avoided by accountants. The accountant, however, can significantly enhance this stage by ensuring that it is structured properly, contains checks and balances, and is sufficiently documented to facilitate subsequent auditing and application enhancement.

Rollout Preparation is a series of tasks that must be completed before the application can be delivered to its users. This is analogous to construction workers putting the finishing touches on your house so that you can move in. It includes such phases as user training, computer site preparation, development of operating procedures, and data conversion. The accountant can play a major role in this stage by determining how the new system will be introduced to the day-to-day work environment. The accountant must help ensure that the competed technology application will be reliable, functional, and efficient when it is transferred to user departments.

Application Rollout is the actual transferring of the newly designed technology application into the operational control and responsibility of the user. The typical firm's increasing levels of geographic expansion and technological integration have dramatically increased the difficulties of placing the newly developed application into the hands of using clients and making it work properly and smoothly.

The Scrum Light Methodology: Scrum is an example of an "advanced" deployment approach emanating from the classic failures of traditional heavy methodologies such as the SDLC. This approach, marketed by VMARK, is based upon the assumption that technology deployment is an undefined process – that no one model such as the SDLC will work in every situation.

Scrum Approach: The Scrum project is separated into manageable chunks that are small enough to be completed in a few months. Scrum substitutes small project teams for the typically large SDLC teams. This allows for more parallel (and thus faster) project processing. However, the teams continually synchronize interfaces between their separately developed system modules. The Scrum approach assumes that technology applications are never complete; they require continuous change.

Scrum Goals: Scrum has the following goals:

• Always have a product that can be shipped immediately even if not complete

- Continually test the product as it is being built rather than after it is built. In this way, the early shipped product has been tested.
- Continually adapt the product to technical and marketplace changes

  Scrum Project Phases: Scrum has the following project stages (Figure 7-4).

Planning and System Architecture: In this stage, (a) project controls are established, (b) project teams are organized, (c) the technological application (product) is broken in small parts (called chunks), and (d) chunk priorities are established.

Sprint: The software product is developed by teams of six or less specialists including a developer, a documentation specialist, and a quality assurance (testing) specialist. Each team develops a "mini-sprint" which applies project management principles to its chunk. Each team's "Sprint" continues until the project chunk is completed or the time has come to deliver the total application product to the client, even if that product does not include all of its planned features.

Closure and Consolidation: This stage includes (a) integration of the separately developed product parts into one integrated system, (b) total system testing, (c) user training, and (d) management-level systems documentation.

Figure 7-4 SCRUM Sequence

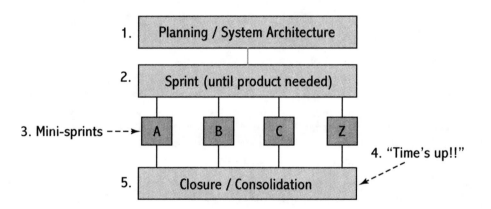

LOGICAL AND PHYSICAL DESIGN

It is beyond the scope of this book to present the specific tasks that comprise designing an information system at both the logical (conceptual) and physical (detailed) levels. We have chosen to concentrate instead on two topics germane to accountant participation in and oversight of the development process.

Principles of Well-designed Systems: Well designed technology applications have certain characteristics which can be planned for and measured. These application characteristics determine how system and program construction is organized and linked. An auditor can evaluate a computerized application by determining the relative presence of these characteristics without that auditor having to inspect detailed program code.

Modularity: The system is separated into small *Program Modules* which perform specific functions independently except to accept data from and send results to other modules.

Cohesion: *Functional Cohesion* exists when a specific program unit contains all and only those tasks contributing to the generation of a single information function or product. For example, an Invoice Printing module's sole task might be to print only invoice data that are accepted from the Invoice Generation module. If both modules are combined into one, the functional cohesion principle is violated.

Decoupling: A well designed program structure would have **Decoupled Modules** that were independent of one another so that, when one module is repaired, there is minimum disruption to other modules. An automobile engine has decoupled parts so that, for example, when you have to replace spark plugs, the internal engine is unaffected.

Reusability: Design of small, decoupled program modules increases the probability that modules can be reused in the future without reprogramming. For instance, if we had to completely redesign the Invoice Generation module, we might be able to reuse the program code for the Invoice Printing module without any rework. We could do this because the modules were decoupled and had functional cohesion. Module reusability reduces the time and costs of technology deployment

Scalability: A system or program module has **Scalability** when it can accommodate differing levels of activity. For example, a system developed at Intel must work effectively (be scalable) for that firm's smallest and largest worldwide installations.

Adaptability: A system or program module has **Adaptability** if it can be altered easily to fit changing business or technology conditions. For example, programs which are not documented well may be difficult to modify in the future. The new programmer may not be able to understand the program logic well enough to adapt it to new conditions; that new programmer may have to scrap the old module and start all over again.

Usability: IBM used to have a motto which stated, *"If the auto industry had changed at the same rate as the computer industry, then a Cadillac would cost $10, get 1,000 miles per gallon, and fit on your thumb."* That is quite impressive, but a Cadillac the size of one's thumb would be hard for a human being to drive; it would not be very usable.

Usability in technology applications generally is measured by the strength of the **Human Interface**: the computer screens, navigation paths, and error handling routines that an application user must deal with in order to process a business transaction. If this human interface is not designed well, then the technology application will be as useful as a thumb-sized Cadillac.

Prototyping: *Prototyping* is the process of quickly building a model of the final software system in order to elicit system requirements from and actively involve ultimate system users. Prototyping can be used in conjunction with hard or light deployment models.

Why Prototyping: There are many reasons why prototyping may be chosen in a technology deployment project, including:

Understanding System Unknowns and Risks: Prototyping particularly is appropriate when the application to be deployed is new to the organization. A prototype model provides the analyst with a vehicle to understand the problem environment. It allows the analyst to "surround" system unknowns and to better gauge system risks and costs.

Analyst / User Communication: In the typical non-prototyping environment, users are presented with a complex collection of detailed, technical diagrams. All of these are difficult for the non-technical user to understand. Prototype models are system requirements expressed in terms of the user's everyday world. A prototype includes the keyboarding, navigation paths, and report extractions that relate to what users actually do or will do.

User Involvement: One of the most significant predictors of ultimate application success is user ownership of that system. Prototyping allows users to become involved early and consistently throughout the development project. Users suggest changes and see those changes made almost immediately. Prototyping can stretch user's imaginations and can elicit more creative input, thus resulting in a more forward looking system. This type of user involvement breeds a sense of user ownership – that this is *their* system rather than one thrust down upon them from above.

Earlier Error Detection and Correction: Experiences at AT&T, TRW, and IBM have shown that some 30 percent of system requirements will change *before* initial system delivery. The longer it takes to discover these changes, the more expensive it will be to correct them. This is shown in Figure 7-5, which has been derived from assembly line situations such as in the auto industry.

This time to cost relationship in application systems development is de to the fact that there is more interlinking of modules as the project proceeds; the system becomes exponentially more complex. A change in one module may require changes in several other modules. Prototyping allows errors and requirements changes to be detected earlier in the SDLC. Experiments have shown that prototyping can decrease program size and effort by 40%.

Earlier and More Extensive System Training: Prototyping allows user training to begin earlier in the development project. Prolonged exposure to change has been shown to decrease significantly users' resistance to that change. Early project training using prototype models can facilitate the implementation process.

Prototype Types: There are three different versions of prototypes that can be developed: *Patched-up*: The **Patched-Up Prototype** is pieced together from existing code. The process of patching in engineering is called **Bread Boarding**. Generally, patched-up models are developed when these is an abundance of reusable code.

Iterative: This type of prototype becomes the final system after a series of evolutionary changes based upon user feedback. Often, this type of prototype is referred to as a **First-of-a-series Prototype** or a **Pilot Prototype**.

Throwaway: The **Throwaway Prototype** becomes a model of the final system; it is abandoned for coding (construction) purposes. It resembles an architect's drawing of a building that must be converted to a technical blueprint before construction can begin. While this type of prototype is "thrown away" for system design purposes, it can be used for training and demonstration. Often this type of prototype is referred to as a **Non-operational Prototype**.

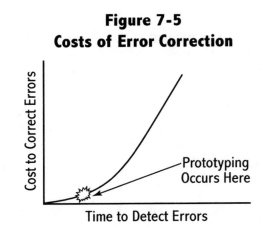

**Figure 7-5
Costs of Error Correction**

SOFTWARE DEVELOPMENT

The software development stage includes converting logically and detailed designed inputs, outputs, files, processes, and their interactions into program code that drives the operational application system. The accountant typically does not have the detailed knowledge to participate actively in software development. Nevertheless, it is important that the accountant ensures that there is adequate planning and execution of these tasks so that subsequent auditing and program maintenance are facilitated.

Profiling the Applications Programmer: It is dangerous for us to stereotype the typical applications programmer. Yet, it is helpful to better understand the conditions under which this programmer operates so that we can see how the accountant's mindset can come into play. The typical applications programmer:

- is under enormous pressure to complete assigned tasks on time and within budget
- is creative in nature and anxious to proceed to the next problem to be creatively solved
- seeks perfection and is frustrated when things don't go right (and they rarely do)
- is an individualist who prefers to work alone rather than in teams
- is proud of his or her work and does not easily accept criticism of that work

The accountant's penchant for structure and measurement can enhance the program development stage by acting as a reasoned curb to the programmer's desire to move forward perhaps too quickly.

Programming and Fraud: Unscrupulous programmers can build into an application's coding routines that facilitate fraud. Three of the most common techniques for doing this are the Round-down, Salami, and Trojan Horse.

Round-down: Interest calculations typically are rounded off to two decimal places. If the third position to the right of the decimal point is greater than five, the second figure (cents) is increased by one; otherwise, the second figure remains the same. All digits to the right of the second figure then are truncated. The programmer can write code that (a) fails to do any rounding, (b) extracts the leftover figures to the right of the second digit, (c) posts these one-thousands of dollars to a bogus internal account, and (d) sends a payment from the internal account to a bogus vendor location.

This malicious code is hard to detect since the books balance. While the amount of dollars extracted from a single customer account is very small, the total sum accrued over thousands of transactions for thousands of days can be quite large. Interestingly, the first reported instance of round-down discovery was by an auditor who did not know how to program and thus did not inspect the actual program code. She became suspicious of some apparently bogus vendor accounts and traced back payments to the bogus internal accounts. She then elicited the aid of programmers in her firm who then discovered the malicious code.

Salami: This malicious code allows tiny slices of money to be stolen over a period of time by changing programmed business rules. For example, all production costs can be increased by a fraction of a percent. The increased portion then can be posted to a bogus account.

Trojan Horse: This malicious code involves unauthorized computer instructions being inserted in an authorized program; these instructions perform illegal operations at predetermined times or for a predetermined set of conditions. For example, the malicious code can be activated when a transaction is input with a specific vendor or employee identification number. That vendor or employee then is overpaid. This type of malicious code is difficult to detect since the fraud is perpetrated intermittently rather than in a regular pattern. The Alaska Court System once uncovered a unique Trojan Horse where a contracted programmer built in code that would disable the application about every six months. Then the courts would have to rehire this contractor to fix the problem.

Figure 7-6 Audit Hooks

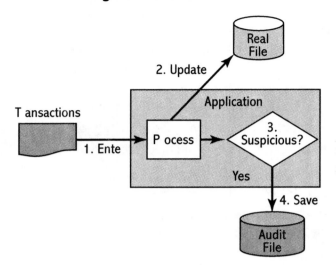

Fraud Prevention Programming:
Accountants can use their roles on technology deployment teams to encourage the insertion of modules that can reduce the risk of fraud occurring and facilitate such occurrences being detected. This is much like having a home security system installed in the infrastructure of a house under construction. Two types of fraud prevention programming that can be built into a technology application.

Audit Hooks are software modules that continually monitor transactions to highlight those that are suspicious. Auditors or others input specific parameters (tolerances). If transaction data exceeds any of these parameters, the transaction is copied to a special audit file (Figure 7-6). For example, payroll transactions that include more than 55 weekly hours may be flagged for closer inspection.

Embedded Audit Modules (EAM) are software embedded in host application systems (e.g., Receiving). The auditor selects predetermined records transaction types which, when detected, are stored in a special file for further analysis (Figure 7-7). EAMs can be used to later conduct substantive tests of balances and control tests. These tests detect whether or not transaction input and record update included proper authorization, was accurate and complete, and was posted correctly to the right account.

Programming Standards: A primary design goal is to maximize the ease of future programming changes (program maintenance). This means that different programmers at some future time must be able to understand the logic and sequence of currently developed programs. This goal sometimes requires sacrificing current program efficiency in order to optimize program change.

The most effective means of emphasizing future ease of change is to establish and enforce programming standards including:

- a modular system design that allows future program modification with minimal interruption to other program modules

- the same programming language structure in all modules

- consistent documentation that is easily understood by other programmers and internal auditors This documentation can include hierarchical charts, program flow charts, compiled listings and results, or sample output based on test data.

Figure 7-7 Embedded Audit Modules

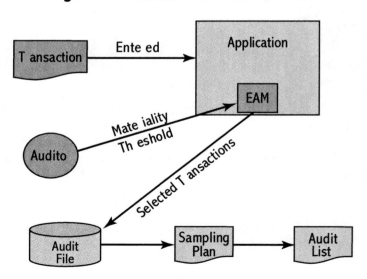

The Accountant's Role: The accountant need not inspect detailed program code to determine if a technology application's programming was done effectively. The accountant need only examine the structure and planning of the programming efforts to see if those efforts include the principles described in this section. Our experiences have taught us that poorly planned programming results in poorly executed programming.

SOFTWARE AND SYSTEM TESTING

It is essential that thorough testing be done to program modules because the effort required to change an application can be several times greater after implementation than before. It is rare that the accountant is actively involved in actual testing during the technology deployment project. However, one of the auditor's responsibilities is to review how testing was done; this includes inspection of methodology and test data. Therefore, it is important for the accountant to prepare for this by actively ensuring that the structure of the testing process reduces the risks of subsequent application failure or ineffectiveness.

Testing Dimensions: Four quality dimensions are tested (Table 7-1).

Functionality: a software system's external quality, to include:

Correctness: Are system outputs accurate and complete?

Reliability: Do functions perform consistently without failure?

Integrity: Are results consistent with user expectations?

Engineering: a system's internal quality, to include:

Efficiency: Are functions performed in minimum times with minimum lines of code?

Testability: Can modules be tested and audited easily?

Documentation: Has the system been documented to allow easy future modifications?

Structure: Is the software system organized logically to facilitate tailoring and training?

Adaptability: a system's future quality, to include:

Flexibility: Can the system be adapted to the needs of a diverse and changing cast of users and business situations?

Reusability: Can modules be reused in other systems?

Maintainability: Does the organization of the system facilitate future changes?

Usability: a system's ease of use, to include:

Learning Time: Can users learn to use the system quickly?

Performance Speed: Does the system maximize transaction throughput?

Table 7-1 Testing Quality Dimensions

Testing Dimension	Dimension Includes		
Functionality	Correctness	Reliability	Integrity
Engineering	Efficiency	Testability	Documentation
Adaptability	Flexibility	Reusability	Maintainability
Usability	Learning Time	Performance Speed	Error Handling

Error Handling: Does the system provide users with adequate and helpful guidance to detect and correct errors?

Risk-based Testing: Complete testing rarely is possible. Suppose you wish to test the accuracy of each IF..THEN..ELSE statement in a program and that there are 15 such statements. In the simplest case, where each statement has only two states (True or False), the number of tests needed is 2 raised to the 15th power, or 32,768 tests. The number of tests required will grow exponentially with increased system complexity. Therefore, you seldom have sufficient resources to test every system possibility.

We can use *Risk-based testing* which applies limited testing resources to the most probable and important sources of failure through the following process (Figure 7-8):

- Identify those modules having the highest probability of failure (probably the most complex modules).

- Within these modules, identify those with the highest risk of loss when failure occurs (usually those that have more user visibility or dependency).

- Position each module at its appropriate grid in Figure 7-8.

- Following the arrow path in Figure 7-8, fully test the riskiest module, then the next riskiest, and so on until testing resources are exhausted. For example Program D has the greatest combination of user impact and programming complexity.

- Recognize that this risk-based strategy may result in some less risky modules not being tested.

A San Diego based bank used a risk-based testing strategy which resulted in 12 percent of the less important and complex programming modules *not being tested at all*.

The Test Plan: A testing plan is prepared before testing is begun. This plan includes:

<u>Success Criteria</u>: When to stop testing (e.g., when all critical and 90% of non-critical modules have passed tests successfully)

<u>Testing Procedures</u> to include (1) type approach (e.g., top-down), (2) testing stages (e.g., regression), (3) who will perform testing, and (4) retesting procedures (How/Who)

Figure 7-8 Risk-based Testing

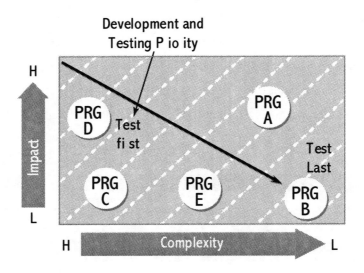

Test Data to be used

Assumptions: For example, *"We do not have the time available to test all modules fully. Therefore, we have organized the modules in the following priority sequence."*

Testing Strategies: Testing can be planned with two different strategies (Figure 7-9).

Bottom-up: Testing begins at the lowest level program modules. These are the action modules – the ones that actually do transaction processing tasks such as record update. Then testing proceeds to the next highest level (parent). This testing approach continues in an upward direction until the entire software system is tested as a unit.

Top-down: The top-most (main menu) module is programmed and tested first. All child modules (level 2) are "stubbed out;" they contain a message such as "Module under construction - press any key to return to the last screen." The next level of modules (children) is comprised of intermediate menus that are programmed and tested independently with their respective children modules stubbed out. Then these intermediate menu modules are "hooked onto" the main menu (parent) module and the entire group is tested as a unit. This top-down approach continues until all program modules have been programmed, tested independently, and then tested as a group. The top-down approach is very compatible with the use of prototype models.

Testing Stages: There are four testing stages within the testing strategy chosen:

Unit Testing: This is done for primitive level modules that perform application tasks. Test data is input to each module to determine how effectively it functions. Typically test data is designed so that there are values (a) within a specified data range, (b) outside that data range, (c) at the boundaries of the range, and (d) at the value zero.

String Testing: Several independently tested modules belonging to the same parent module are tested concurrently. Emphasis is placed on correct passing of data between modules and on a smooth navigation path through the module string.

System Testing: This involves full integration of application system hardware and software. It includes stress testing and regression testing:

- *Stress Testing*: The system is ingested with (a) more data than expected, (b) no data at all, and (c) the expected data load. This is done in a short time frame to see if the application system can handle various levels of data input. System response times and data accuracy are verified.

Figure 7-9 Testing Strategies

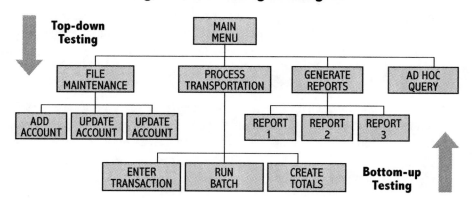

- ***Regression Testing***: The application system undergoes repeated testing under similar circumstances. New results are compared with old results and any differences reconciled.

Acceptance Testing: Ultimate system users or an independent group uses the system guided by documentation provided by the development team. Ideally, the acceptance-testing group tries to "break" the new system by entering data outside the range of normal usage. Acceptance testing should be designed for each of the four software quality spaces of functionality, engineering, adaptability, and usability.

Test Data: Data used to test software modules can be either tester generated or user provided. For tester generated data, the tester may have to "manufacture" certain test data. For example, there may not be any real-world transactions with quantity values of "zero," yet that value needs to be tested. The tester also can employ user provided data - real-world transaction data provided by system users. This allows comparison of new system with current system output.

The Accountant's Role: A technology application that has not had a well planned, systematic testing effort has a high risk of serious problems occurring after deployment. The accountant need not actually perform software or system testing. The accountant need only review the testing process to ensure that it has been planned and executed well.

ROLLOUT PREPARATION

The programmed and tested application system now must be prepared for transfer (rollout) to the customer in several relatively independent phases. The accountant can play a significant role in ensuring that preparation choices are made with an eye more towards user long-term convenience rather than current technical efficiency.

File Conversion: Development of a new application system requires some conversion from the old system file format to the new system format. This conversion can be extensive if the old application system is manual or is using very old hardware or software. The Alaska Court System once abandoned its participation in the development of a statewide computerized criminal justice information system solely because the courts did not have the resources to accomplish the file conversion that would have been required.

File conversion programs are written to automatically transform old system file contents to new system formats. There will be new file requirements that do not exist in the old system; these will have to be added off-line. At a specified period of time, old system file contents are downloaded to an off-line medium such as magnetic tape. The downloaded files and the off-line file augmentations are uploaded to new system hardware using file conversion program.

Training: Training on the developing application system must begin as early as possible. It has been demonstrated that the longer the period of time end-users are indoctrinated to new system changes, the less resistance they will exhibit towards these changes. In addition, early systems training leads to earlier discovery of system faults. Correction of system faults becomes more expensive the further along the project has progressed. The following questions need to be addressed.

Who is the training audience? The foremost audience is prospective system end-users. Information processing specialists also must be trained on how to operate the new system. Finally, managers and executives require at least an overview of the new system.

Who should conduct training? The ideal training team is composed of (a) end-users who know the applications area, (b) information systems specialists who know the technology, and (c) professional trainers who are experts in training methodologies and techniques.

Where should training be conducted? The three choices are (a) on-site in end-user work areas, (b) on-site in separated training facilities, and (c) off-site. On-site training is less expensive, but is subject to interruptions and distractions from the immediate work environment.

When should training be conducted? There is a tendency to postpone training in the face of "more pressing" programming rollout issues and tasks. However, the advantages of early training include (a) better preparation for new system operation, (b) a greater range of personnel undergoing training, and (c) more opportunity for end-user feedback on potential system problems. At the same time, refresher training should be conducted as close to new system operation as possible to refresh earlier learning.

Use of prototype models in the analysis and design phases of the SDLC can facilitate early training. Early prototypes can be used for application orientation and familiarization of managers and users. Successively refined prototype models can be used for training in increased depth. An advantage of using prototype models for system training is the similarity of those models to the user's actual operational environment.

The Bottom Line: Accountants can play a major role in the Rollout Preparation stage since such phases as file conversion, training and documentation are within accounting responsibilities and skill sets. This stage too often is made the responsibility of technicians only. That can create problems when the application is implemented and operated by non-technical workers.

APPLICATION ROLLOUT

All rollout preparations are now complete. It is time to discontinue use of the current application system and begin use of the new system.

System Changeover: The old (current) system must be discontinued and the new system started in operation. This must be done as smoothly as possible to ensure that business processing is interrupted as little as possible.

Changeover Scheduling: Many problems can occur during the changeover process. These problems can adversely affect a wide range of users and customers. Therefore, a changeover schedule is designed and distributed widely. This schedule includes:

User Notification: Far enough in advance to allow orderly user planning.

Activity Phase-down: Transaction activity must be decreased so that only priority matters are handled during the changeover period.

File Conversion: Old files are downloaded from the old system and up-loaded to the new system. New file elements (e.g., new Geographic Area code) are developed off-line and merged into the new file formats.

System Cutover: The old system is discontinued and the new system begins its operations.

Activity Resumption: Transaction activity is resumed at normal levels on the new system.

Changeover Alternatives: Direct Changeover (also referred to as *Big Bang Changeover*) is the simultaneous discontinuance of the old system and full operation of the new system at a given cutoff date. The direct changeover alternative is the least costly and least confusing of the three alternatives since there are not two separate systems operating at the same time. This changeover tactic forces stronger user commitment, since the old system no longer exists to fall back upon if the new system fails. Direct changeover also forces more thorough design and testing, because analysts must ensure that the new system works well since there will be no old system to fall back on. However, this tactic is riskier; if the new system fails, the old system no longer exists.

Parallel Changeover entails operation of both the current and the new application systems for a period of time until everyone is comfortable that the new system works effectively. The parallel changeover alternative is the safest of the three alternatives, providing a safety net should the new application system not work effectively. However, it also is the most expensive tactic, since two full applications systems must be operated at the same time. This approach is the most auditable, since new system output can be compared to old system output.

Staged Changeover is where the old system is discontinued and the new system is initiated one stage at a time. There are two variations of this changeover alternative. The first is the *Pilot Changeover*, which entails implementation of a complete new application system at a single geographic location. Lessons learned at the pilot implementation are used to fine-tune the system before implementation at other locations. The second type is the *Phased Changeover*, where modules of the new application are implemented consecutively rather than concurrently. For example, the Purchasing module is implemented. When it is operating effectively, then the Receiving module is implemented.

Choosing a Changeover Tactic: Figure 7-11 shows changeover alternative tradeoffs.

These tradeoffs are based upon the following deployment characteristics:

Cost Constraints: The parallel changeover method requires two systems to be operated at the same time. This can be very expensive. There would be a tendency to use the direct changeover approach if there are serious cost constraints.

System Criticality: A system is critical if the firm cannot operate effectively without it. An inventory system is critical since its cessation results in lost sales and poor customer relations. The more critical the system, the more the tendency will be to "play it safe" with the parallel changeover method.

System Complexity: The more complex a system, the more likely it will be that problems will occur during implementation and operation. Relative system complexity can be measured through such metrics as number of lines of program code or number of program modules inter-

Figure 7-11 Changeover Tactic Trade-off

CRITERIA	DIRECT CHANGE OVER	?????	PARALLEL CHANGE OVER
Cost Constraints	Serious	←——————→	Relaxed
System Criticality	Low	←————→	High
System Complexity	Low	←————→	High
Application Experience	High	←———→	Low
User Computer Experience	High	←———→	Low
IT Personal Experience	High	←———→	Low
User Resistance	High	←————→	Low

facing with one another. The more complex the system, the more will be the tendency to use the safer parallel changeover method.

Application Experience: The deployment will be riskier and more difficult if the application is new to the organization, either in type (e.g., first inventory forecasting system) or in delivery method (e.g., first Web application). The less the firm's application experience, the more will be the tendency to use the parallel changeover method in order to better orient users to the new experience.

User Computer Experience: The more "computer savvy" are the ultimate users of the application, the more attractive will be the use of the less costly direct changeover method.

IT Personnel Experience: A firm must consider the match between IT personnel skills and those skills required to build the new application. The greater the skills match, the more confidence there will be that the application has been programmed and tested effectively. This confidence leads to an increased tendency to use the faster direct changeover method.

User Resistance: The greater the perceived resistance from users to the new system, the greater will be the tendency to use the direct changeover method. In this way, the resistors quickly will lose the old, comfortable system as a crutch to lean on. The new system will be the only system available. Some factors that tend to increase user resistance are (a) poor IT department application deployment history, (b) strained relations between the IT department and the user community, and (c) lack of user participation in the planning for deployment.

For any given application implementation, one would mark on Figure 7-11 where on each criterion scale the current changeover environment falls. Often a pattern appears (e.g., most marks on the left side of the figure) which will suggest choice of one changeover alternative over the other two. If a clear pattern does not result, often the user community can be consulted to determine (a) which of the criteria are the most important, and (b) its relative comfort with the alternate changeover methods. User participation in the choice of changeover method tends to reduce user resistance. It is critical that selection of the changeover alternative be done early in the development process so that expectations can be fixed appropriately. Choice of changeover alternative can be changed later if necessary.

System Evaluation: The new application system has been installed and is now handling day-to-day operations. There is now a period of fine-tuning and performance evaluation before responsibility for the new system can be transferred to the business unit.

System Fine-Tuning: There will be an initial period when the new system requires fine-tuning. Users expect perfectly deployed application systems much as they expect their new cars or toaster ovens to operate flawlessly. However, deployment of application systems is too complex a process for us to expect perfection. We must condition our users to expect minor flaws with the accompanying promise that such flaws will be fixed expeditiously.

Post-Changeover Evaluation: A comprehensive evaluation is conducted at a specified time (e.g., 6 months) after system changeover. This evaluation determines whether or not the new application system is operating according to expectations and is ready to be transferred to the business unit. Participants in this review include designers, end-users, auditors, and management.

SUMMARY

Today's technology applications have more complex features and are more extensively interlinked to customers, suppliers, customers, and other applications. A poor technology application deployment can have ripple effects that are disruptive, costly, and threatening to the firm's existence and its partners. We must apply our accounting skills and mindsets to reducing the risks of technology deployment failures. We can do so by taking a more active role in the planning for and overseeing of new technology application deployments.

KEY TERMS

Acceptance Testing

Adaptability

Applications Portfolio

Application Rollout

Audit Hooks

Big Bang Changeover Method

Bottom-up Testing

Bread-boarding

Decoupled Modules

Embedded Audit Modules (EAM)

Engineering Testing Dimension

Feasibility Analysis

File Conversion

First-of-a-series Prototype

Functional Cohesion

Heavy Methodologies

Human Interface

Infrastructure Evolution

Legacy Hardware

Light Methodologies

Logical Design

Modularity

Non-operational Prototype

Parallel Changeover

Patched-up Prototype

Phased Changeover

Physical Design

Pilot Changeover

Pilot Prototype

Program Module

Prototyping

Regression Testing

Requirements Analysis

Reusability

Risk-based Testing

Rollout Preparation

Round Down

Salami

Scalability

Scrum

Staged Changeover

Staged Obsolescence

Stress testing

String Testing

Systems Analysis

Systems Development Life Cycle (SDLC)

System Testing

Technology Deployment

Throwaway Prototype

Top-down Testing

Trojan Horse

Unit testing

Usability

REVIEW EXERCISES

1. Describe how the Application Portfolio is created.
2. What is Staged Obsolescence? Why is it important to the firm?
3. Describe three (3) differences between Heavy and Light development models.
4. Describe the Waterfall SDLC model.
5. What is Requirements Analysis? How is it related to describing the current system?
6. What are the stages of the SDLC model used in this chapter?
7. Describe the Scrum process. How does it differ from the SDLC?
8. List four (4) reasons why a firm might use prototyping?

9. Compare and contrast:
   a. Functional Cohesion and Decoupling
   b. Functional Cohesion and Modularity
   c. Scalability and Adaptability

10. What is the Human Interface?

11. What are the four quality dimensions to be tested?

12. What is Risk-based testing? Why is it necessary?

13 What are the elements of Changeover Scheduling?

14. Why would a firm choose the Direct Changeover method?

15. Compare and contrast the Pilot and Phased changeover methods.

16. What factors are important in selecting a changeover method?

17. What is System Fine-tuning? Why is it important?

18. Who participates in the Post-changeover Evaluation?

CRITICAL THINKING OPPORTUNITIES

1. The parent company has demanded that a firm's purchasing application be scrapped and an e-purchasing system be deployed in its place. The project must be up and running within six months. It also must be designed to facilitate fast and efficient future changes. Write a memorandum recommending:
   a. The deployment model that should be used and why
   b. How the project should be organized

2. Survey five to ten firms in your geographical area to determine
   a. the software testing standards and techniques that are being used in technology deployment.
   b. how the firm allocates scarce testing resources.
   c. Do you use prototyping? If so, why?

   Prepare PowerPoint slides to present the results of your survey.

3. Table 7-2 shows the estimated complexity, impact and testing cost estimates for four modules to be tested and deployed... Replicate Figure 7-8 for this situation. What would happen if the testing budget was restricted to $10 thousand?

4. Elgin Marbles is a small firm with typical cash flow problems. The firm is planning to convert its automated off-line customer ordering system to a Web-based e-marketing system. This will be Elgin's first e-business application. Elgin will have to hire or contract with a programmer with Web experience since none of its current IT staff of six employees has internet skills. However, this IT staff has enjoyed a very amiable relationship with the user community. Write a memorandum to Elgin's President recommending which system changeover method should be used. Include reasons for your recommendation.

Table 7-2 Testing Characteristics

Module	Complexity	Impact	Testing Costs ($)
Payables	Medium	Medium	2,700
Receivables	Medium	High	3,400
Inventory	High	High	6,500
General Ledger	Low	Low	1,500

REFERENCES

Carey, J.; *"Understanding Resistance to System Change: An Empirical Study"*; **Human Factors in Management Information Systems;** ed. J. Carey; Ablex, 1988

Hetzel, William; **The Complete Guide to Software Testing;** John Wiley and Sons, 1984

Martin, Merle; **Analysis and Design of Business Information Systems;** 2nd Edition, Prentice Hall, 1995

Martin, M.; *"Prototyping"*; **Encyclopedia of Information Systems**; Wiley, 2003

Martin, M.; *"Systems Implementation"*; **Encyclopedia of Information Systems;** Wiley, 2003

Price Waterhouse World Technology Center; (1997); *Technology Forecast: 1997*; (Menlo Park, CA; Price Waterhouse)

Stahl, Bob; *"The Ins and Outs of Software Testing;"* **Computerworld,** October, 1988

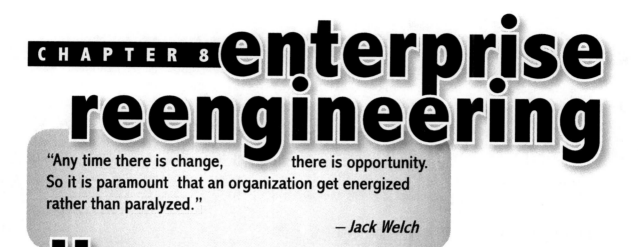

CHAPTER 8 enterprise reengineering

"Any time there is change, there is opportunity. So it is paramount that an organization get energized rather than paralyzed."

— Jack Welch

Have you ever made a traumatic change to your life? Have you moved across country, or started a new job, or even made the decision to start back in school? Such changes are pretty frightening, aren't they? But consider a company making a massive change which, if done incorrectly, may put it out of business – or at least in a worse competitive situation. The following is a true if disguised story.

Sam Watkins, the Vice President for Information Technology at Clear Technologies, was presenting to the Executive Committee a proposal to join a technology industry alliance. This alliance was attempting to standardize the way that all industry partners did business with each other, their customers and their vendors. Sam was confronting a high level of skepticism from members of the committee.

Jason Conrad, the manufacturing vice president, shook his head and said to Sam, "We've got the most efficient processes in the industry. Wouldn't we have to share some of our secrets with our competitors and thus lose our competitive advantage? Sam Watkins replied, "We did a study that showed that only about eight percent of our processes are different, perhaps better, than our competitors. But the other 92 percent are common to everyone in our industry. It's this 92 percent that are the targets for standardization in this alliance. We don't have to share our unique ways of doing business."

Susan Griffith, the marketing vice president, spoke next. "We've got the largest share of the industry market in our industry. Why change? Why should we cooperate when we're top-dog?" Sam answered, "Today's business and technology landscapes are changing so rapidly that, at best, we only have a six month advantage for any of our innovations. If we don't continually change for the better, we'll fall behind rather than be ahead."

Sam sipped from his coffee cup, and then he continued. "More critically, if we don't join this alliance, one of our competitor's ways of doing business may become the industry standard. Industry customers and vendors then will force us to change our ways to those adopted by the rest of our industry so that they won't have to deal with two systems. We'll be behind the power curve. It would be much more preferable if we could we use our influence within the industry alliance to ensure that we are comfortable with any standards that are developed."

Emily Mann, the firms CEO, said, "Well Sam, your arguments are logical. But I'm getting a little tired of all these changes you keep proposing at these meetings. And this particular change scares me to death!" The issue was tabled until the next Executive Committee meeting.

Whether we like it or not, change is necessary in today's revolutionary business environment, and sometimes necessary change may "scare us to death". That's because e-business changes may force an organization to cooperate with and share "secrets" with traditional competitors. Even industry leading companies are faced with this challenge as they discover that today's competitive advantages can last as little as six months. So, as Jack Welch suggests, we cannot afford to become paralyzed by needed changes – we must be energized to implement those changes as effortlessly, quickly and economically as we can.

We will discuss in this chapter the processes and prescriptions for changing (reengineering) an organization at the enterprise level. We will emphasize the role of the accountant in seeking an effective balance between reducing process costs and maintaining effective organizational control mechanisms. The sequence of discussion will be (a) Benchmarking, (b) Enterprise Reengineering, (c) X-engineering, and (d) Business Process Management (BPM).

RELEVANCE TO ACCOUNTING PROFESSION

Reengineering is an alternative solution when a firm is faced with an IT system which is not achieving its performance objectives. The other alternatives are to keep the current IT system as it is (perhaps with some minor "tweaking") or to replace the current system. Each of these alternatives has specific costs and benefits associated with it that can be entered into cost-benefit analysis. The accountant has domain knowledge and often responsibility for cost-benefit analysis.

In addition, reengineering has particular significance for the accountant. That is because much of reengineering stress has been to reduce or eliminate operational redundancy, and thus processing costs. Yet redundancy is a vital ingredient for the accountant. Internal controls add redundancy costs to a processing system. Auditing is a redundant task that, on the surface, adds no value to the firm's product or service. However, we as accountants know that such "planned" redundancy is necessary to protect the firm from potential fraud, disastrous events, or egregious errors.

Thus we must be on constant guard that zealous reengineering efforts do not seek reduced costs at the expense of the firm's long-term welfare. We must guard against, in the words of an old cliché, "throwing the baby out with the bath water". To do so, we must know just what is reengineering.

BENCHMARKING

How do we know that our organization in general, and its ways of doing business in particular, requires substantial changes? We often discover this need through benchmarking. **Benchmarking** is the process of comparing parts of another company's operations so as to improve those parts in your organization. The purpose of benchmarking is to discover and to learn from the best and thus to bring your organization closer to the best level of performance.

Studies have shown that payback to an organization for benchmarking can run into the tens of millions of dollars a year. The key to successful benchmarking is (a) stifling organizational assumptions that "we know best" and (b) finding other organizations that are willing to share knowledge of their processes.

The Benchmarking Process: Benchmarking proceeds in the following sequence:

Select Activities to be Benchmarked: These should be a limited number of critical processes. *Critical Processes* are those processes which, if shut down, would prevent the organization from doing business.

Determine Benchmarking Metrics: Select performance measurements that will allow you to (a) determine that another organization performs better on selected processes, (b) measure any improvement shown when you borrow these best practices, and (c) perform subsequent cost-benefit analyses...

Identify Benchmarking Partners: Find organizations which (a) have similar processes, and (b) will allow you to study those processes.

Study Best Practices: Study in detail how the benchmarking partner performs selected processes. This can be done through on-site visits, securing documentation, or both.

Modify and Plan Changes: Determine how the studied processes can best be imported to your organization. Not all of another organization's methodologies may be pertinent to your firm's culture and circumstances. This determination should include a cost-benefit analysis to convince management of potential benchmarking and process revision payoffs.

Implement Changes: Changes should be implemented in a formal project management setting.

Track Progress: Track and communicate through your selected benchmarking metrics the improvements shown by your imported processes.

Cultivate Ownership: Users who feel that a change is "their change" rather than one force-fed from above will develop a sense of change ownership which can reduce resistance significantly. User change ownership is bred by constant and sincere consultation – by a partnership between users and the change implementation team.

Intel's Operations Service Center: One example of a successful benchmarking project occurred at Intel Corporation in 1999. Intel wanted to rebuild its Operations Service (OSC) which monitors and controls its worldwide telecommunications traffic. The old center was too crowded, was not human-factors designed, and had not been kept up to the latest technological advances. A project team was assembled for the $500 thousand project. The team first conducted a survey of OSC employees during March 1999. This survey determined what center workers felt that the new OSC should include. Benchmarking should not exclude the real possibility that people in your organization may have some of the better ideas.

Then the project team performed a benchmarking study of other companies that had recently built or significantly modified their service centers. The team visited such companies as Lucent Technologies, Cargill, PacBell, and AT&T. None of these companies were direct competitors of Intel. The team documented these company's service center best practices and combined this documentation with the internal employee survey to produce a requirements document for the proposed new operations service center.

Benchmarking and Reengineering: Benchmarking often is a prelude to reengineering. Benchmarking allows comparison of current practices to those performed better elsewhere. A reengineering vendor often brings to the organization knowledge of best practices performed by its other clients. This is a form of benchmarking. ERP software is an example of vendors incorporating into their packages best practices discovered by studying other organizations.

ENTERPRISE REENGINEERING

Hammer and Champy (1991) define **_Reengineering_** as the _"...**fundamental** rethinking and **radical** redesign of business processes to achieve **dramatic** improvements..."_ We have bolded the

Figure 8-1 Organization System Change Alternatives

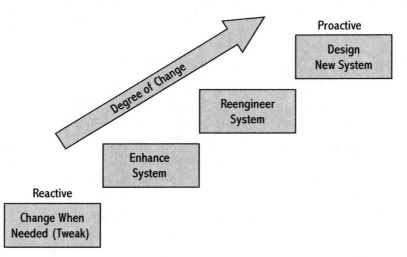

words fundamental, radical and dramatic to emphasize that enterprise reengineering is concerned with significant changes, not minor modifications (tweaking). Enterprise reengineering not only changes how we do things, but what things (processes) we do.

Enterprise reengineering is costly, risky, and unsettling to workers. It requires a long implementation time and considerable worker retraining. Yet, despite these negative characteristics, enterprise reengineering can "turn an organization around."

Reengineering as an Alternative: Enterprise reengineering is but one alternative to effect required change (Figure 8-1).

We can be reactive and make changes only and when they are needed. We can be a little more proactive and seek and import new ideas as enhancements to our ways of doing business. We can be totally proactive and completely replace our processes. Reengineering falls to the left of total replacement on the degree of change progression. Of course, the further to the right that we progress on Figure 8-1, the more change resistance we can expect to encounter. Figure 8-2 shows the State of California's strategy regarding reengineering.

Figure 8-2 State of California's Process Change Guidelines

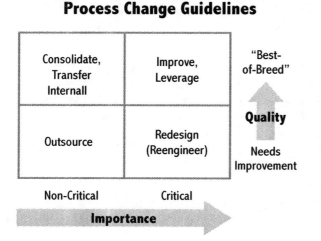

The State's strategy is determined by where a process lies on the two dimensions of importance and quality. Reengineering is called for when the process is critical but needs improvement. The important point is that someone doesn't say, "I've got a great idea. Let's reengineer!" We embark on the reengineering journey only if (a) we are dissatisfied with current, measured performance, and (b) we have selected reengineering as the best change alternative.

The Business Process: The target of reengineering is the business process. We provide here two different definitions of a business process...

Figure 8-3 Business Process

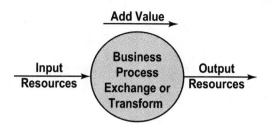

Generic Definition: American Management Systems (AMS) defines a **Business Process** as a set of tasks that directly support the achievement of business objectives by providing a product or service for a customer who is outside the department or in a different organizational unit.

Accounting Oriented Definition: Professor Bill McCarthy of Michigan State defines a business process as a ". . . production function where an enterprise exchanges some input resources for some output resources of greater value to the customer." This definition lends itself to such accounting functions as cost accounting (e.g., value added) and preparing financial statements. Figure 8-3 graphically displays this definition.

Core Processes: Reengineering is expensive and usually is restricted to an organization's core processes. A **Core Process** is a process which is critical to an organization continuing to do business in an effective manner. The test of whether or not a business process is core or not is the question, *"Can this organization continue to operate effectively in the short run if this process stops?"* Obviously, discontinuing the customer order process would cripple the company. Halting the building maintenance process may be unsettling, but the company should be able to continue business as usual – at least for a reasonable period of time.

There are about four or five core processes in any organization. These should be the primary targets of enterprise reengineering. These core processes may be named differently in different types of organizations. Nevertheless, a core process is easy to identify. Tables 8-1 through 8-4 are example of core processes for four different types of organizations – two profit-taking and two not-for-profit firms.

Table 8-1 Financial Core Processes

GENERIC PROCESS	FINANCIAL PROCESS
Product Development	New loans, savings and checking accounts
Sales and Marketing	New accounts, acquisitions
Order Fulfillment	Deposits, loans, withdrawals
Customer Service	Financial planning, inquiries

Table 8-2 Pharmaceuticals Core Processes

GENERIC PROCESS	PHARMACEUTICAL PROCESS
Product Development	R&D testing
Sales and Marketing	Market segmentation, contracts
Order Fulfillment	Contract management, shipping
Customer Service	Claims analysis

Table 8-3 Government Core Processes

GENERIC PROCESS	GOVERNMENT PROCESS
Services Development	Budgeting, policy development
Public Relations	Outreach programs, publications
Service Delivery	Provision of health, other services
Support Function	Ombudsman

Table 8-4 Education Core Processes

GENERIC PROCESS	EDUCATION PROCESS
Service Development	Curricula development
Public Relations	Enrollment management, fund raising
Service Delivery	Degrees, student loans
Support Function	Alumni services

The Reengineering Cycle: The *Reengineering Cycle* is the sequence of steps required to reengineer an organization. It consists of five phases: (a) assess current processes, (b) determine root causes of process problems. (c) identify improvement opportunities, (d) set performance targets, and (e) design future processes.

Assess Current Processes: We first define the reengineering process scope – which core processes we wish to target. We can break each core processes into sub-processes depending on the detail required for our study. Then we document each core process's setting in the entire workplace by describing its (a) where the process is in the product or service flow, (b) who performs the process, (c) interaction with other processes, and (d) the overall work setting (e.g., lighting).

Then we use a charting technique such as Data Flow Diagrams (DFDs) to document each selected process (a) interfaces (handoffs), (b) decision and approval steps, (c) processing times, (d) waiting (delay) time, and (e) the business rules (procedures including internal controls).

Determine Root Causes of Problems: Next we compare each process' documentation (current state) with our expectations of how the process should perform (expected state). The norms that we use for expected performance can be internal performance objectives, often called *Theoretical Maxims*, such as "The maximum time for processing a Purchase Order will be 48 hours." Alternately, we can use exported norms resulting from a benchmarking project.

We must be careful to differentiate between "downstream" problems and the root causes or "upstream" problems. For example, our Purchase Order maximum time may be above the 48 hour theoretical maxim we have established as a performance objective. Yet this degraded performance may not be the fault of Purchasing Department employees, but instead it may be caused by operating department errors and omissions in filling out the Purchase Request (Figure 8-4).

Identify Improvement Opportunities: We now narrow our attention on those core processes that show *significant* differences between actual and expected performance. What is a significant difference is a matter of judgment, but the core processes can be ranked as to difference significance (Table 8-5). Then the processes can be pulled for further analysis one at a time from the top of the ranked list until (a) the list is exhausted, or (b) we run out of project time or allocated funds.

Set Performance Targets: We now set process improvement (performance) targets that we hope to achieve by reengineering. These targets should be aggressive (big change) but not so

Table 8-5 Process Problem Ranking

Rank	Department	Process Objective	% Deviation from Objective
1	Purchasing	Process P.O. within 48 hours	12.3
2	Shipping	Ship merchandise within 24 hours	9.7
3	Accts Payable	Payment within 3 days after Invoice	9.0
4	Accts Receivable	Less than 5% overdue over 90 days	6.9
5	Inventory	Pick stock within 4 hours	5.8

Figure 8-4
Upstream and Downstream Problems

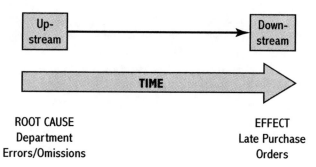

ROOT CAUSE
Department
Errors/Omissions

EFFECT
Late Purchase
Orders

unrealistic that there is little chance of achieving them. A typical target might be, "The maximum time for processing a Purchase Order is 12 hours."

Design Future Processes: We now must redesign our targeted core processes so they can reach the performance targets which we have set. The next section describes ways in which we can redesign these processes.

Designing Future Processes: Following are 12 common reengineering design opportunities.

Line Balancing: Try to balance process flow by eliminating very large and very small processes. Convert single, complex processes into multiple, smaller processes. These smaller processes can be preceded by a process triage function. *Process Triage* is the separation of incoming transaction flow into separate paths leading to separate processes. It is similar to emergency room triage where a nurse separates patients into critical, serious, and not-so-serious categories in order to direct those patients to different levels of patient care.

Line balancing reduces bottlenecks in the transaction processing system caused by large, cumbersome processes. The line balancing technique should reduce transaction cycle time variances, thus making delivery time quotes more dependable.

Internal Process Outsourcing: Transfer the operation of a costly, faulty process to a customer or vendor. For example, order entry can be moved to the customer via a Web-based system. Dell Computer outsourced its delivery function to UPS. There may be a fee charged by the outsourcer, but often that fee is much less than the process operating cost. Outsourcing simplifies the transaction processing system and, depending on outsourcer performance, can decrease cycle times.

Process Elimination: Eliminate processes which don't add value to the product or service. Ask the question, "Would the customer pay extra for this process?" Some candidates for this elimination are routing, sorting, and checking processes. Elimination of such redundant processes reduces costs without necessarily reducing the value (and thus price) of the product or service. This then should lead to increased profits. However, accountants should ensure that the process being deleted is not a critical internal control.

Seamless Database: Establish one central, distributed database rather than several local, autonomous databases. This will allow the organization to both centralize database security and update while still allowing units to exercise local control over operations.

Customer Focus: This technique is an example of adding complexity (costs) to a system in order to increase product or service quality. Make a single point of customer contact (a Case Manager) to avoid separate processes from passing the blame or responsibility for product delivery tardiness to another process ("finger pointing"). This added redundancy can (a) increase customer satisfaction (and thus future sales) and allow more rapid adjustment to changing customer needs.

Process Buffering: Processes typically accept input from a preceding process, perform some task to enhance the product, and then pass the results to a succeeding process. If one of these se-

Figure 8-5 Buffering Processes

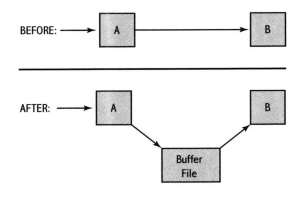

rial processes speeds up or slows down, the other linked processes stack up their output or sit idle waiting for input.

Place a storage function (e.g., data file) between any two processes so that the flow from one process to another is decoupled (Figure 8-5). The sending process can place its output into storage at whatever rate it chooses. The receiving process can draw its input from storage according to its processing speed. This technique is similar to a computer's Print Buffer which prevents the much faster central processing unit (CPU) from being idle while waiting for action from the much slower printer.

Process Concurrency: Make serial processes parallel by duplicating inputs so that they can simultaneously flow to multiple processes (Figure 8-6). A system with parallel (concurrent) processes operates faster than one with serial processes. This can be done by having multiple form copies routed to different locations or using an interactive system where, for example, an entered Customer Order can be accessed by several processes simultaneously.

Care must be taken to ensure that concurrency makes sense. In Figure 8-6, for example, if 20 percent of customer orders are denied because of credit problems, then the warehousing process will have to restock the product already pulled for these customers. If, however, only two percent of customers are denied credit, then this small amount of rework will be more than compensated by reductions in product or service delivery times.

Satisficing: **Satisficing** is seeking a better solution rather than the best (optimal) solution. It entails some sort of sacrifice of a desired objective in order to achieve improvement in another objective. Reduce reconciliation processes. You will lose some accuracy, but you can significantly reduce cycle time and processing system complexity.

Process Consolidation: This technique is the opposite of the Line Balancing technique. Here sequential processes are combined into one larger process. This typically is done with relatively small processes. The result is that the new process is more complex and challenging to workers – a form of job enrichment. This tends to increase worker pride and ownership in a process that no longer is trivial. From a more accounting perspective, this technique also reduces transaction "handoffs" and thus opportunities for errors and fraud.

Figure 8-6 Concurrent Processes

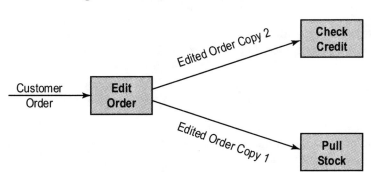

External Process Absorption: This is the opposite of the Internal Process Outsourcing technique. Here we take inputs or outputs to our organization and assume them as internal processes. This is what a vendor does when it establishes a Just-in-time (JIT) inventory contract with one of its customers. The vendor adopts as one of its internal processes the customer's Inventory Ordering.

An organization, by absorbing an external entity as an internal process, can ensure commitment to future dealings and "lock" in the customer as a trading partner. UPS did this with Dell Computers when it absorbed Dell's Shipping process.

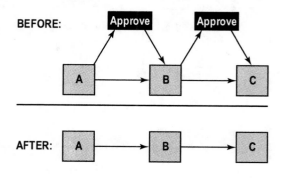

Figure 8-7 Reducing Approvals

Eliminate Redundant Processes: Consolidate similar processes with similar names. This will reduce costs, decrease product cycle times, and decrease system complexity. The State of California did this when it reduced its number of data centers from eight to two.

Reduce Approvals: Eliminate most approval processes. Empower process workers to make these higher-level decisions. Alternatively, develop intelligent agents that can make decisions at the process flow level rather than bouncing transaction flow up and down from worker to supervisor level (Figure 8- 7).

Reducing approval functions may seem a means to allow fraud to run unchecked. Yet, you can establish reasonable compromises that allow reengineering enhancements while still protecting the organization. For example, you can establish procedures which allow process-level (clerical) approval of all Purchase Orders less than $200. Any Purchase Order over that threshold must be approved by a supervisor.

These 12 techniques can serve as a checklist (Table 8-6) for reengineering activities.

The Accounting Dilemma: Reengineering seems a natural ally to accountants since its goals primarily are to reduce costs – an important accounting objective. Yet, over-zealous reengineering efforts also can eliminate planned redundancies (e.g., internal controls) which have been instituted to protect the organization. So accountants may well find themselves in the uncomfortable position of arguing against reengineering changes which will decrease costs. How can we make this argument effectively? Remember our primary risk formula:

Expected Event Loss = Maximum Event Loss x Probability of Event Occurring

Suppose, for example, that a reengineering advocate recommends eliminating a particular approval process with a projected savings of $15 thousand a year. You are fearful of eliminating this approval process completely because it would increase the probability of errors and fraud occurring. The burden of proof is on you to prove that elimination will cost more in errors and fraud committed than the savings promised by the reengineering advocate. You estimate that the maximum loss from an error or fraud event is $200 thousand (worst case scenario). You research industry statistics and your company's internal records to estimate that the probability (risk) of error or fraud occurring is 10 percent. Then:

Expected Error/Fraud Loss = $200,000 x 0.10 or $20,000

Now you can argue that the reengineering advocate's potential savings of $15 thousand a year is less than the expected loss that would be incurred by eliminating the approval process.

Table 8-6 Reengineering Technique Use

TECHNIQUE	TARGET	QUESTION	BENEFITS
Line Balancing	Large Processes	Can we break into smaller processes with triage function?	- Reduce bottlenecks - Reduce cycle time variance
Internal Process Outsourcing	Non-critical Processes	Can we outsource to vendor?	- Reduce costs - Reduce cycle time - Simplify system
Process Elimination	Processes which don't add value to product or service	Can we eliminate processes?	- Reduce costs - Simplify system
Seamless Database	Multiple Files	Can we consolidate files into distributed database?	- Reduce costs - Reduce data inconsistency
Customer Focus	Job Order Processes	Do we need a Case Manager to track jobs through system?	- Increase customer satisfaction - Adapt more quickly to changing customer needs
Process Buffering	Serial Processes with differing processing rates	Can we place buffer storage function between processes?	- Reduce cycle time variance - Reduce process reliance on other processes
Process Concurrence	Serial Processes	Can we duplicate previous process output so succeeding processes can run parallel?	- Reduce cycle time
Satisficing	Reconciliation Processes	Do we need a check on process outputs?	- Reduce costs - Reduce cycle time
Process Consolidation	Processes with similar functions	Can these processes be consolidated into one process?	- Reduce Costs - Increase job satisfaction
External Process Absorption	Vendor or Customer processes	Can we profitably assume this external process?	- Increase influence over vendors and customers
Eliminate Redundant Processes	Processes that have similar names or functions	Can we consolidate these processes into one larger process?	- Save costs - Decrease cycle time - Simplify system
Reduce Approvals	Processes that require higher-level approval	Can we eliminate or reduce management approvals?	- Save costs - Reduce cycle time - Increase job satisfaction

X-ENGINEERING

Business spends $2 trillion a year on logistics. It is estimated that 40 percent of that is spent for paperwork and administration. If these administrative costs could be cut in half, then this could amount to an annual savings of $400 billion. The reengineering efforts of the 1990s made significant gains in reducing administrative costs. Yet, these efforts typically were internal. A company looked within itself to improve its processes. Little effort was made to improve processes across firms and industries, particularly across competitive firms.

The general thinking was that a company's internal business processes were unique and gave the company a competitive advantage over its competitors who used supposedly less effective processes. Now that thinking is being challenged and an external, cross-company form of re-engineering is emerging. This new form has been labeled by some as X-engineering.

According to Champy (2002), *X-engineering* is the "... *art and science of using technology-enabled processes to connect businesses with other businesses and companies and with their customers to achieve dramatic improvements in efficiency and create value for **everyone** involved*" (emphasis added). Surprisingly, the "everyone" includes a company's competitors.

Underlying Beliefs: There are several underlying beliefs that make X-engineering rather unique. These include:

- People will take better care of themselves, at less cost to the company, when given access to company processes.

- People will do the right thing for both customers and the company when given the right information.

- Eighty percent of a firm's business processes are common to other firms.

- Competitors can work together to develop industry standards that benefit everyone.

- A competitive advantage resulting from an innovative process will last less than one year.

X-engineering versus Reengineering: X-engineering, as its predecessor reengineering, (a) has a business process focus, (b) makes it possible to greatly improve internal process efficiencies, and (c) requires radical rethinking and fundamental change. X-engineering, however, goes beyond reengineering internal efforts. X-engineering provides an external focus which promises vast improvements in operations and processes *across* organizations – among companies and their suppliers, partners and customers.

Proprietary and Common Processes: Most of a firm's business processes are not unique. Some of these common processes can be performed better and less expensively by other companies. These processes should be outsourced thus allowing organizations to concentrate on the proprietary processes that it does uniquely. *Proprietary Processes* are those processes which are unique to an organization and provide competitive advantage.

Common Processes, on the other hand, are those business processes that are not proprietary to the organization. X-engineering proposes that those common processes which are not outsourced must be shared and standardized so that they can be integrated with suppliers, customers, and trading partners. This requires common process transparency to everyone, even an organization's competitors.

This process transparency can create the following dramatic sequence of events within an industry or industry sector:

- Everyone sees what the organization has to offer – their prices and terms.

- Consumers can "shop around" for the best product with the most service at the lowest price.

- The consumer can do this directly or through an intermediary such as Expedia.com.

- The smallest customers will demand everything that is offered to the largest customers.

- The pressure will be on all companies to reduce costs and decrease delivery cycles in order to meet this type of demand.

An X-engineered System: All industry players actively collaborate to select common process best practices and to standardize these processes in order to establish common rules for business interchange. This results in lower industry costs and greater customer value. Performance is improved for *all* supply chain members. There is emphasis on technology use and a customer self-service mode. A full x-engineered system provides performance and quality feedback to all collaborative partners.

One example of an x-engineered system is RosettaNet, a consortium of all players in the information technology sector. RosettaNet has established standard rules of transaction processing

Figure 8-8 RosettaNet Participants

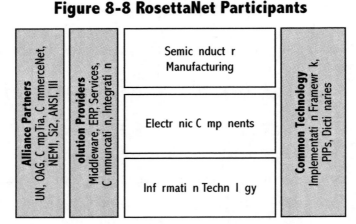

and interfacing within that sector. The types of firms that comprise RosettaNet are shown in Figure 8-8. The X-engineering effort represents a large leap of faith for many firms. *"Cooperate with our competitors? Are you crazy? They'll steal us blind."* However, as Doug Busch (Vice President for Information Technology at Intel) has said, "If you don't join in setting industry standards, then eventually you'll be forced to adopt somebody else's standards."

BUSINESS PROCESS MANAGEMENT (BPM)

Business Process Management (BPM) is software enabling the design, analysis, optimization, and automation of business processes. BPM, in conjunction with Web Services, is judged by many to be the fastest evolving business technology with implementation expected to peak within the next five years.

BPM Functions: BPM separates common process logic from the business applications (e.g., purchasing) that use these common processes. Thus, process logic is standardized and can be reused. In addition, adoption of BPM allows import to an organization of common process best practices as incorporated in the BPM software. Business Process Management (a) manages relationships between shared process participants, (b) integrates internal and external processes so that they coexist seamlessly, (c) monitors process performance, and (d) redesigns current processes around the Internet

Current BPM Expectations: A recent Sterling Commerce survey found that respondents had three primary expectations when considering BPM. First, 32 percent of respondents wanted to automate repetitive tasks in order to reduce process cycle times. Second, 25 percent of the respondents wanted to manage and monitor process performance and process related tasks and people. Finally, 20 percent of the respondents sought the ability for non-technical personnel to change business rules and the operating logic of enterprise software.

A BPM Example: Sterling Commerce is a world-wide B2B service provider. It is a wholly owned subsidiary of SBC Communications. Sterling markets a scalable BPM product called *Sterling Integrator* which has the five functions of (a) process modeling, (b) process monitoring, (c) process operations, (d) process Web automation, and (e) integration.

Process Modeling: Sterling's BPM approach defines a process differently than found elsewhere in this chapter. A Sterling Integrator process is "an ordered string of services". The Integrator Process Modeling function includes 80 different services, both internal (e.g., posting) and external (e.g., send message). Non-technical personnel can use a visual flowcharting tool to design a

Ingersoll-Rand X-engineering (Ulfelder, 2003)

Ingersoll-Rand is an $8 billion company that manufactures industrial equipment. The company is in a highly competitive industry so it always is seeking ways to reduce supply chain costs. In the past, it has focused its purchasing efforts on its 20 largest suppliers who accounted for 80 percent of its procurement expenditures. During the 2001 economic slump, Ingersoll-Rand intensified its efforts to drive down costs. It began paying attention to smaller suppliers because that area hadn't been scrutinized before. What Ingersoll-Rand discovered was quite revealing.

Major suppliers had been reducing prices, but some of the smaller suppliers had been increasing their prices by as much as ten percent. Yet, inflation was practically nonexistent. Smaller suppliers also had poorer on-time delivery records than did large suppliers. This caused premium last-minute shipping costs, stock shortages, and production line stoppages. Ingersoll-Rand performed a benchmarking study of other firms and found that almost all of these firms were having the same problems with small vendors.

Ingersoll-Rand resolved this problem by forging an alliance with SupplyWorks, which provided supply chain software, and Robertson transportation. This alliance formed a procurement outsourcing business called the 21st Supplier. The goal of this new business was to reduce company's costs of doing business with small suppliers. 21st Supplier client's trade doing business with many smaller suppliers for doing business with one larger intermediary (Figure 8-10). 21st Supplier targeted as customers all manufacturers with annual sales over $500 million.

Its first customer was Hussman Corporation, a $600 million company. Hussman experienced the following improvements by outsourcing its small supplier purchasing process to 21st Suppler:

- Small supplier procurement costs were reduced by five to 15 percent.

- Freight charges were reduced.

- Inventories were cut due to tighter cycle times.

- Small supplier performance improved due to improved 21st Supplier performance measurement and incentives.

- Stock shortages and line stoppages were reduced.

This case study is an example of several topics discussed in this and other chapters.

Figure 8-10 the 21st Supplier

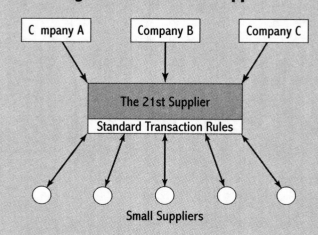

Small Suppliers

Reengineering: Companies such as Hussman outsourced their small supplier procurement functions.

X-engineering: There was a three-firm alliance to improve small supplier procurement.

New Business Model: A new distribution channel was added to the supply chain model.

Standardization: Smaller suppliers were forced to conform to the same business rules.

business processing system. The resulting design can be prototyped with ultimate process users to refine the initial design. Then the Process Modeler can generate XML programming code.

Process Monitoring: The Process Monitor can examine information flow as a business process executes. It also can inspect system workload at any point in time, in order to discover bogged-down or idle processes. Monitoring can provide general or drill-down detailed views.

Process Operations: The operations function provides many technical system optimization features such as efficient memory management. More importantly to accountants, this function facilitates auditing, problem diagnosis, and full recovery from system failures.

Process Automation: This function produces the XML code to generate Web-based processes. The function also invokes translation services consistent with standards such as ebXML. A Business Process Engine controls all services to be called including security or communication services.

Integration: This function provides a translation capability between internal applications and dealings with other enterprises. It supports ERP, CRM, SCM, and e-procurement. It also supports EDI, XML and ebXML. The integration function will allow update translation to any Data Base Management System. This translation allows an organization to "plug in" the Sterling Integrator to almost any current process configuration.

The Sterling Commerce integrator is but one current example of a Business Process Modeling approach which can better enable an organization's reengineering efforts.

THE WORLD ACCORDING TO ROB

Robert (Rob) Taylor, Accounting Manager for Getronics, says:

You recently reengineered your Accounts Receivable system. Why did you do this?

"We felt it was a priority to improve cash flow by speeding up invoicing and collecting. We also wanted to find ways that we could work with our vendors to potentially extend payment terms. In theory, if we could get a customer payment in 35 days and get 45 day payment terms on vendor payments, then we could be either cash positive or cash neutral on most transactions."

How did you do the reengineering? "We got senior management buy-in to bring in an outside consultancy firm. The consultants brought in concepts and ideas. We put a team of people together to review with them how we do receivables. Then we came up with ways to improve our processes."

What is an example of one of the improvements you made? "We put in what we call a "pre-collection" process. After an invoice is sent, we have an accounts receivable collector who makes a call to the client to ask if the invoice has been received and if there are problems with it. This allows us to catch problems right now rather then, say, at the end of the 30 day collection period.

We don't do this for all invoices — just those over a certain dollar amount."

What have been the results of this reengineering effort? "We've improved our days accounts receivables outstanding by roughly 15 days. I think the average now in North America is about 33 or 34 days."

SUMMARY

For the accountant, enterprise reengineering often represents a balancing act between reducing costs and establishing adequate internal controls. The accountant should be prepared to perform cost-benefit analyses which compare reengineering savings with the expected losses that will be incurred by eliminating redundant controls. The accountant must ask these questions for every proposed "best practice".

- What can go wrong with this change?
- What is the proposal's impact on cost accounting, internal controls, fraud prevention, asset protection, and auditing?

One characteristic that is evolving in the new global and electronic economy is that profit margins will shrink because more competitors are able to enter the marketplace. Shrinking profit margins certainly will increase the zeal to reengineer the organization to decrease costs, reduce cycle times, and thus increase competitive postures. The accountant increasingly will become the sentinel that halts rash or reactive organizational change by forcing participants to consider the rational bottom line.

KEY TERMS

Benchmarking	Proprietary Process
Business Process	Reengineering
Business Process management (BPM)	Reengineering cycle
Common Process	Satisficing
Core Process	Theoretical Maxim
Critical Process	X-engineering
Process Triage	

REVIEW EXERCISES

1. What is Benchmarking and why is it important?
2. How does enterprise reengineering differ from the day-to-day changes required in any organization?
3. What are the Generic and Accounting-oriented definitions of a Business Process?
4. Define three Core Processes for a:
   a. coffee shop (e.g., Starbucks)
   b. Automobile manufacturing plant
5. Describe the Reengineering Cycle.
6. What is a Theoretical Maxim and why is it important?
7. What is Process Triage and when is it used?
8. What are the differences between the reengineering tactics of Process Elimination and Satisficing?

9. What are the differences between Reengineering and X-engineering?

10. Describe two Proprietary Processes and two Common Processes for a:

    a. university
    b. coffee shop (e.g., Starbucks)

11. What is BPM and why is it important to a firm's reengineering efforts?

12. Briefly describe the five functions of Sterling Commerce's Integrator BPM software.

CRITICAL THINKING EXERCISES

1. Survey companies in your geographic area to find examples of the use of Benchmarking.

2. Design three aggressive Performance Targets for:

    a. scheduling of classes in your academic department (e.g., Accountancy)
    b. on-line bookstore product delivery
    c. an Accounts Receivable department

3. Research the Internet to find descriptions of four competitive companies in the same industry. Describe and justify what you believe to be Proprietary and Common processes for these companies.

4. Write a memorandum to the IT Manager of your university suggesting how your university could utilize X-engineering to improve student experiences.

5. Contact five to ten different company managers in your geographic area. Solicit and document their answers to the questions:

    a. "Are you using or do you plan to use Business Process Management (BPM) software?
    b. "What are the reasons why or why not you are using or plan to use BPM?

REFERENCES

Champy, J.; **X-Engineering the Corporation**; Warner Business Books, 2002

Hammer, M. and J. Champy; **Reengineering the Corporation**; Harper Business, 1993

Martin, M.; **Analysis and Design of Business Information Systems**; Prentice Hall, 1995

Martin, M; R. Ching and J. Podlipnik; "*Achieving Breakthrough Performance*", **Proceedings of the Decision Sciences Institute**, San Francisco, 1998

O'Leary, D.; **Enterprise Resource Planning Systems**; Cambridge University press, 2000

Ulfelder, S. "*Managing the Other 20%*", **Computerworld**, March 2003.

CHAPTER 9 information technology performance measurement

> "Whenever you measure anything, you change what you are measuring."
>
> — *C. West Churchman*

Have you ever wondered why a soccer player was given a particular uniform number? Have you pondered over what the Gross National Product (GNP) number really means – or why stock prices go crazy when General Motors is slightly below its quarterly earnings projections? We seem to be a society that is possessed by numbers. We put a number on everything we see and experience. Consider the following true story:

Srinvasa Ramanujan, the famous Indian mathematician, was lying ill in a hospital. A friend came to visit him. This friend was saddened by Srinvasa's weak and despondent state and thought that some small talk might be a diversion. So the friend remarked, "I rode here in taxicab 1729. This seems to me rather a dull number. I hope it was not an unfavorable omen. "No," Srinvasa replied weakly, "it is a very interesting number; it is the smallest number expressible as the sum of two cubes in two different ways."

If the mathematician had been an historian, he might have interpreted 1729 as an important date in history. If the mathematician had been an accountant, he might have framed his explanation in terms of balance sheet dollars. Numbers only have meaning in the context in which they are considered. For example, a firm's dollar investment in inventory may have meaning for the accountant preparing financial statements. That figure, however, has little meaning for the inventory clerk who must decide how many physical units of stock must to be reordered and how much the shipping weight will be.

Modern society seems enthralled with a perceived need to describe everything in numbers. For example, the success or failure of a television program is based far more on the Nielson Rating (sample of the number of households watching) than it is on the quality of the program itself. The popularity of presidential candidates is reduced to numbers rather than "Good", "Bad" or "Indifferent". That is probably because there seems to be readier agreement on what a number represents than on words such as "beautiful" or "evil". Numbers can hide true meaning and can mean different things to different people. We must be careful to measure only that which needs to be measured and to ensure that our measurements are widely understood. This is true particularly when we measure the performance of information technology functions.

The measurement of an organization's information technology (IT) endeavors has not kept pace with that of other parts of the business system. IT is relatively new compared with other organizational areas. In addition, IT's more technical nature has made many measurement specialists fearful of entering this arena. Finally, there has been an aura of experimentation surrounding IT – "we can't be measured the same as others because we're just learning how to use technology."

Yet, as technology becomes more ubiquitous and more centric to organizational missions, we no longer can afford to ignore the need to measure the effectiveness of the IT department in the same way that we measure performance in other areas. Whether we like it or not, our accounting standards dictate that we are responsible for measurement of organization performance, and that includes the IT function. This chapter presents concepts and tactics that can be employed in the measurement of an organization's IT operations. The discussion follows the sequence of (a) Performance Measurement Concepts, (b) Balanced Scorecard (BSC) Models, (c) the BSC in an IT Environment, (d) Measurement Pragmatics, and (e) an Intel Case Study.

RELEVANCE TO ACCOUNTING

Measurement of organizational performance has been a responsibility of the accounting profession for quite some time. This measurement, however, too often has been restricted to dollars since that is the dimension which dominates our financial statements. The last twenty years has seen a movement towards a more comprehensive and less dollar-dominated approach to measuring an organization's health. The accounting profession must lead the way to exploring all forms of organizational performance measurement, including the complexities associated with IT operations.

PERFORMANCE MEASUREMENT CONCEPTS

This section includes conceptual guidance that can be used to establish a performance measurement system in an organization in general and its technology operations in particular. Many of these concepts also are applicable to economic justification of information technology (IT) systems. Economic justification can be considered as merely is a subset of performance measurement – a subset which gauges *anticipated* rather than *past* performance.

Definitions: There are a few basic terms that must be defined at the outset.

Metric: A number that quantifies a characteristic of some entity (e.g., process or product).

Raw Metric: A metric that can be observed directly such as the number of processing.

Derived Metric: A metric computed or derived from raw metrics, usually in the form of a ratio or index. Examples include errors per day or IT dollars spent per employee.

Indicator: A representation of metrics that provides insight into the health or status of a process or activity. Indicators typically are comparisons between metrics such as the budgeted versus the actual amount spent on an IT project or data entry error trends over time.

Intangible: An entity that is difficult to quantify, such as employee knowledge.

Surrogate Metric: A metric that does not measure an entity directly, but is used because a direct (raw) metric is too difficult or costly to acquire. For example, polling all customers as to their attitudes towards a firm's products may be too costly. The firm may instead use a small panel of customers as a surrogate measure of total customer attitudes.

Why Do We Measure? We undertake organizational measurement for a variety of reasons. First, we wish to gauge the health of the organization both from an external (stockholder) and internal (auditing) perspective. Measurement is implicit in our efforts to continually improve our operations until we reach desired goals. Measurement also can be used to indicate current or projected problems so that we can correct them before they reach crisis proportions.

In the larger sense, measurement can be used, intentionally or not, to control and change human behavior. As C. West Churchman noted, "Whenever you measure something, you change what you are measuring." Suppose you are driving down a freeway at a speed far in excess of the legal limit. Then you spot a state trooper's car in your rear view mirror. What do you do? You probably will slow down. The state trooper's possible measurement of your speed has changed your speed. We never must forget that measurement has a pronounced effect upon an organization's workers; measurement changes how they behave. If we are careful, we can use this fact for positive results. If we are not careful, results may be contrary to our goals.

When Do We Measure? There are three distinctly different settings in which we exact measurement of IT performance: before an IT initiative (project) is begun (feasibility analysis), while that project is in progress (project management), and after the project is completed and the application is operating on a continuous basis.

How Do We Measure? There are four increasingly powerful *Measurement Scales* by which we can measure an entity. The *Nominal Scale* uses a unique number to identify a specific entity; for example, employee identification number may not be used for computational purposes, but merely as a unique employee identifier much as the number on a soccer player's uniform. The *Ordinal Scale* takes us one step further by assigning meaning or relative ranking of entities. Thus, customers may be asked to measure their preferences for five flavors of jelly by marking their first choice of strawberry as a "1", their second choice of grape as a "2", and so on.

The *Interval Scale* measures not only relative placement, but the magnitude of difference between entities. For example, suppose our customers were to rate the five jelly flavors on a scale of 1 to 10 with: 1 representing "I hate this jelly flavor", 10 representing "I crave this jelly flavor" and the numbers 2 through 9 representing gradient preferences between the two extremes. Our total customer preference scores might show that Strawberry jelly was most preferred (average ranking of 9.23), Blackberry jelly was next (average ranking of 7.15), and Grape jelly was third (average ranking of 7.02).

Note the large average ranking gap between Strawberry and Orange Marmalade, and the small gap between Orange Marmalade and Grape. Use of an interval scale gives us more information than ordinal scale which did not show magnitudes between flavors (Figure 9-1).

The *Ratio Scale* is derived by dividing one interval measure

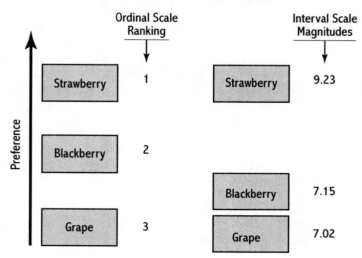

Figure 9-1 Differences between Ordinal and Interval Measurements

Semi-Tough Sheds

The Semi-Tough Shed Company makes storage sheds which are used at construction sites, schools, and residential homes. The company markets four different types of sheds: Tudor, Hard-Hat, Plain-Jane, and Shanty. Each shed has a unique product number.

The Product Number is an example of a Nominal Scale; the numbers have no special meaning except to uniquely identify each product. This is similar to the numbers on soccer player's uniforms. The Sales Price, however, has comparative value because it uses an Interval Scale. For example, the Tudor product costs more than twice as much as the Shanty product.

Table 9-1 Semi-Tough Products

Product	Tudor	Hard-Hat	Plain-Jane	Shanty
Product Number	16	8	22	7
Sales Price ($)	525	307	234	125

The information from Table 9-2 was extracted from a Semi-tough brochure. The Sales Ranking uses the Ordinal Scale. What is hidden by this scale, however, is the fact that there is a significant sales quantity gap between the number one ranked (Plain-Jane) and all the other products. Table 9-3 uses an Interval Scale to show this gap.

Table 9-2 Semi-Tough Marketing Statistics

Product	Tudor	Hard-Hat	Plain-Jane	Shanty
Sales Ranking	4	3	1	2
Stockage-to-Sales Ratio	0.9	2.3	7.3	17.1

Table 9-3 Semi-tough Annual Sales (thousands of dollars)

Product	Tudor	Hard-Hat	Plain-Jane	Shanty
Sales	197	206	432	223

The Stockage-to-Sales statistic of Table 9-2 uses a **_Ratio Scale_**. This statistic is computed by dividing Annual Sales by the Average Number of Units Stocked in Semi-Tough warehouses. A lower number reflects a less costly stockage position. This statistic can be compared with past performance (over time), across Semi-Tough products, and with industry averages.

Note that product performance on the two measurements of Table 9-2 is not consistent. For example, the Tudor product is ranked last in Sales while it has the best performance on Stockage-to Sales Ratio. This reflects Semi-Tough's practice of constructing most of its more expensive Tudor sheds only after receiving an order; very few of these sheds are pre-constructed. Conversely, while the Plain-Jane shed has the top Sales ranking, it also has the worst Stockage-to-Sales ratio of the four products. This relatively poor performance is the result of falling sales and an over-aggressive pre-stockage policy.

by another. Thus we can compare an interval metric over time (raw metric divided by time unit) or in kind (raw metric divided by metric goal). Much financial analysis uses ratio scales (e.g., earnings per share).

Measurement Constraints: Our measurement approach (system) will be influenced by four factors. First, GAAP provides some guidelines of what needs to be measured. Second, measurement should be a shell provided by an organization's strategic goals. Third, the organization's culture may dictate how measurement is perceived, accepted, and implemented. For example, companies such as Intel have a measurement culture; from the point of hiring, Intel employees expect that their performance will be monitored and rewarded based upon a specified set of metrics.

Finally, the measurement approach largely will depend on the organization's current measurement capability – the depth, for example, of its cost accounting system. American Management Systems (AMS) often will include the implementation of a measurement structure as a part of its IT contracts with customers. In this way, AMS can determine what performance increases are associated with the IT enhancements it has introduced to the customer organization.

Measurement Guidelines: The following guidelines will help in building an effective performance measurement system:

Measure critically: The 20 percent most prevalent transactions (e.g., customer orders) will account for 80 percent of that system's total volume (Martin, 1995). Similarly, some 20 percent of the things we could measure will represent some 80 percent of the system's significance or value. Don't clutter the measurement system with non-significant metrics.

Critical measurements are linked to the organization's overall strategies. A measurement such as Cost per Production Unit may be appropriate for Wal-Mart whose marketing strategy is to offer the lowest price to its customers. However, that metric may not be as appropriate to Mercedes Benz whose marketing strategy is based on high-end quality rather than lowest price.

Show a preference for dollars: A metric should not be discarded merely because it cannot be converted to dollars. At the same time, however, you should try to convert as many metrics to dollars because this unit of measurement is one of the few organizational concepts that everyone seems to use and understand.

Be specific and action oriented: Poor performance on an indicator should point directly to actions necessary to improve performance. For example, an overall measurement of data entry error rate does not suggest a specific corrective action. However, data entry error rate stratified by time-of-day, data entry operator, or transaction type will be tied more directly to corrective actions that can be taken.

For example, the Alaska Court System discovered that data entry error rates increased significantly in the afternoons after operators had been performing their tasks for five or six hours. There was a slight improvement in this error rate after the lunch break (Noon to 1 p.m.), but the rate began rising again by 1:30 p.m. The error rate was reduced by assigning data entry operators to other non-keying tasks after 2 p.m. Productivity did not suffer because the data entry hours lost were offset by the decrease in error rework that would have been required.

Beware of combined indices. For example, we have seen Employee Satisfaction defined as an index which combines average performances on such indicators as employee turnover, absenteeism, number of complaints, and the results of periodic employee surveys. The problem with this indicator is that, if it exceeds tolerances, the firm does not know upon which of these sub-entities (e.g., absenteeism) to concentrate. Assume that absenteeism is a problem, but that there is a lower than expected number of customer complaints. The absenteeism problem may be obscured by an index which is increased because of good performance on the complaint portion.

Be timely: Measurements that are published several months after events have occurred are too late to allow quick resolution of smoldering problems.

Reward carefully: Rewarding those who meet or exceed goals can be an incentive for better performance. However, punishing those who don't reach the standards can be an incentive for false reporting.

Limit reporting: A periodic reporting of all metrics of a performance measurement system may result in management information overload. Limit reporting to only exception indicators (those whose current values outside a tolerance range) or those specifically requested by managers (Figure 9-2).

There are three types of performance measurement reports that should be produced; all of them are subsets of the entire set of measurement indicators available.

Exception Reports: This includes indicators which are now or are forecast to be below the established performance tolerances. It signals areas where corrective action is needed.

On-Demand reports: This is a one-time report which includes specific indicators requested by a specific person. For example, a marketing manager may be planning a trip to the Boston office and requires marketing performance indicators for the Northeast sector of the United States.

Tailored reports: This type of report is periodic (e.g., monthly). However, the specific measurement indicators included in this periodic report differ from manager to manager according to their specific needs. For example, a DVD Recorder product manager may wish to see only those production indicators associated with that specific product line.

Use ratios as much as feasible: Ratios are powerful; they allow us to compare across time and function because ratios essentially are dimensionless. For example, the ratio Sales per Employee allows us to compare companies of different sales magnitudes. Other examples are Revenue per Employee, Revenue per Customer, and Cost per Transaction. These types of ratios often are referred to as **Anchor Measures**, because our means of comparison will not drift over time or range of activity.

Measure benefits as well as costs: Costs are much easier to measure than are benefits. This is because a firm of even modest size has a relatively deep cost accounting system that can track costs. Benefits are more difficult to quantify, but they may be as or more important to management than costs. Yet, avoid trying to put numbers on essentially un-measurable entities such as

Figure 9-2 Limiting Measurement Reporting

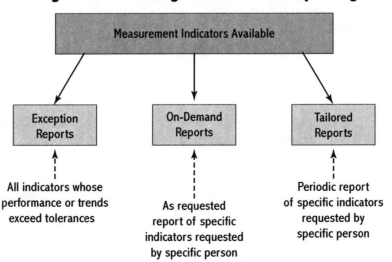

future sales, technology impact, or future shareholder confidence. If you can't measure well, don't measure! Rely instead on qualitative assessments (e.g., excellent, good, poor).

BALANCED SCORECARD (BSC) MODELS

There are many performance measurement models used to gauge the health of business organizations. This chapter focuses upon the Balanced Scorecard (BSC) model. It is estimated that some 75 percent of corporate value is derived from intangibles such as employee knowledge or customer information. Yet, most performance indicators used in a typical business firm are financial in nature. Financial data is easier to collect because we are obligated to use it for other purposes. Yet, collection of primarily financial data is not consistent with today's business realities.

We have seen numerous examples lately in which a company's financial status may have little predictive value. In addition, use of dollar indicators my not be as relevant to lower levels of the organization where units such as "number of items" or "miles driven" are more closely tied to assigned processes . Finally, the predominance of financial indicators indicates a reluctance to attempt to measure the more difficult to quantify, but equally critical non-dollar aspects of a company.

The Balanced Scorecard (BSC) is one approach which attempts to stretch the organization beyond the financial perspective. This model has been used in business for some time. It only is recently, however, that BSC has been applied to an information technology (IT) setting.

Balanced Scorecard (BSC) Perspectives: The BSC model has four perspectives:

<u>Customer</u>: How do customers view our company?

<u>Financial</u>: How do stakeholders view our company?

<u>Internal Business Processes</u>: How can our company improve internal operations in order to improve service to our customers?

<u>Learning/Growth</u>: What should our company do to remain successful in the future?

The BSC prescribes for each of these perspectives a mission, objectives, and measurement indicators. Table 9-4 includes examples of this BSC structure.

Table 9-4 Balanced Score Card (BSC) Example

Perspective	Mission	Objectives	Measures
Customer	Deliver best added value to customers	1. new products 2. partnerships with customers	1.% new to total products 2. # joint development efforts
Financial	Assure added value for stakeholders in long and short run	1. survive 2. prosper	1. ROI and cash flow % 2. % market share
Internal	Efficiently produce and deliver products and services	1. production excellence 2. delivery excellence	1. cost/price per unit 2. average order process time (days)
Learning/ Growth	Innovate, improve and learn to the maximum	1. technological leadership 2. product focus	1. months to develop new products 2. #old/#new products

There are several characteristics of note in this BSC example. First, only two of the eight measures are dollar oriented. Second, each perspective's mission and objectives are tied directly to the organization's overall mission and objectives. Finally, six of the measures are ratios and the other two are in units of time. This allows easy comparison over time, between organizational units, or with other companies. Figure 9-3 summarizes the process for developing a BSC measurement system.

Mission, Goals and Strategy: These are how the IT department will implement corporate missions, goals and strategies.

Objectives: These are specific objectives that implement the mission. For example, an objective of "Introducing new products" is one way of realizing the mission of "Delivering the best added value to customers."

Measurements: These are the actual measurements selected to gauge whether or not objectives are being met. For example, "Percent of new to old products" is one way to measure whether or not the "Introducing new products" goal is being met.

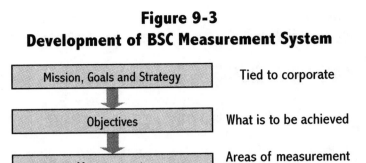

Figure 9-3
Development of BSC Measurement System

Mission, Goals and Strategy	Tied to corporate
Objectives	What is to be achieved
Measurements	Areas of measurement and standards
Evaluation	How, when, where
Corrective Action	Incentives and accountability

Evaluation: Evaluating BSC is similar to that used in other measurement models. You:

(a) compare indicator results over time and with industry standards or averages, (b) compute future projections to prevent today's problem from becoming a crisis, (c) report immediately indicators that have exceeded tolerances, (d) report the remainder of the indicators on a fixed, periodic basis, and (e) tie performance to bonuses and promotions.

Corrective Action: These are the incentives or pressures to improve performance on areas falling below objectives.

Outcome Metrics versus Performance Drivers: An effective BSC should include a mixture of outcome metrics and performance drivers. An *Outcome Metric* measures productivity directly. For example, the Number of Weekly Transactions Entered measures productivity of data entry operators. Outcome metrics are dependent variables; they measure what happened, but not why. They fail to capture what event occurred "upstream" that caused the outcome metric to behave as it did.

A *Performance Driver* is the "why". It causes the outcome metric to behave as it does (Figure 9-4). It is similar to the cost accounting definition of a cost driver. For example, one performance driver for Number of Weekly Transactions Entered would be Number of Training Days per Data Entry Operator. The more an operator is trained, the more transactions that operator to process each week. Figure 9-4 shows the relationship between performance drivers and outcome measures.

Table 9-5 Performance Driver and Outcome Metric Mixture

PERFORMANCE DRIVER	RELATIONSHIP	OUTCOME MEASURE
Average Help desk Response Time	Quicker the response, more satisfied the customers	Index of User Satisfaction
% Budget Spent on IT Research	IT research leads to faster deployment of new technology	% Applications Younger Than 5 Years
Educational Budget as % of IT Budget	Trained IT workers are quicker and more efficient	Average Days Late in Delivering Software

Figure 9-4 Relationship between Performance Drivers and Outcome Metrics

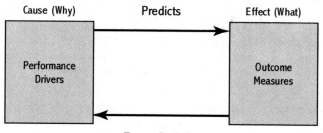

THE BSC IN AN IT ENVIRONMENT

One specific approach for information technology operations will be used to demonstrate how the Balanced Scorecard model can be used in an IT setting (Grembergen, 2000). The BSC perspectives used in this approach were IT User Orientation (Customers), Corporate Contribution (Finances), Operational Excellence (Internal Processes), and Future Orientation (Learning/Growth). Note that a company need not follow slavishly BSC nomenclature or even structure. Indeed, the Intel system discussed near the end of this chapter uses the BSC merely as a starting point.

IT User Orientation: This perspective considers customers as being the intra-company end users. In this example, the IT department also markets its services outside the company.

Mission: to be the preferred supplier of IT (as opposed to outsourcing) and to exploit business opportunities maximally through IT.

Objectives:

- preferred supplier of applications and operations
- partnerships with users
- user satisfaction

Measurements:

Objective	Preferred Supplier	Partnerships with Users	User Satisfaction
Measurements	- % applications managed by IT - % applications delivered by IT	- Index of user involvement in developing new applications - Frequency of IT Steering Committee meetings	- Index of user satisfaction - Index of applications and system availability - Index of system user friendliness

Corporate Contribution: This perspective considers how the IT department contributes to the profitability of the firm.

Mission: obtain reasonable business contribution for IT investments

Objectives:

- control IT expenses
- sell IT products/services to 3rd parties
- obtain business value for new IT projects
- obtain business value for IT function

Measurements:

Objective	Control IT Expenses	Sell IT Products to 3rd Parties	Obtain Business Value for New IT Projects	Obtain Business Value for IT Function
Measurement	- IT budget $ per company employees - IT budget $ per # work-stations	- $ outside sales of IT products - $ outside sales of IT services - Ratio of outside to inside sales $	- Average project ROI % - % projects delivered within budget	- % IT overhead and administrative $ to total $ - IT budget as % of total company budget - Index of % IT to total company budget to industry average

Operational Excellence: This perspective looks within the IT department for improving efficiency. Many of these measures are counterbalanced by measures in the other three perspectives so that "cost-cutting" does not hamper overall effectiveness.

Mission: efficiently deliver IT products and services

Objectives:

- efficient software development
- efficient operations
- acquisition of PCs and PC software
- problem management
- training users
- management of IT personnel

Measurements:

Objective	Efficient Software Development	Efficient Operations	Acquisition of PCs and PC Software
Measurement	- Average days late delivering software - % code reused - Visible and invisible backlog - % maintenance activities	- % mainframe unavailability - % network unavailability - Response time (hours) by user type - % jobs done within set times	- Average delivery lead time (days)
Objective	Problem Management	Training Users	Management of IT Personnel
Measurement	- Average help desk response time - Help desk calls per # employees	- % users that have received education - Quality index of education given	- % people hours charged to projects - IT staff satisfaction index

Future Orientation: This perspective considers investments made in the IT department that will better position the company to take future advantage of its technological resources.

Mission: develop opportunities to answer future challenges

Objectives:

- permanent training/education program for IT personnel
- IT personnel experience
- age of applications portfolio
- research into emerging technologies

Measurements:

Objective	Permanent Education of Staff	IT Personnel Expertise	Age of Applications Portfolio	Emerging Technologies Research
Measurement	- # education days per person - Education budget as % of IT budget	- # years experience per person - Age pyramid of IT staff	- # applications by age category - % applications younger than 5 years	- % budget spent on IT research - # IT research jobs in progress

The above list is not intended as a prescription, but merely as a suggestion of how to develop a BSC for IT. Notice how the IT department is required to develop a mission statement for each of the BSC perspectives. Hopefully, these mission statements will be consistent with overall organizational mission statements. Then each perspective mission leads to several objectives and each objective leads to one or more measurements. These measurements include outcome metrics (e.g., IT staff turnover rate) and performance drivers (e.g., frequency of IT Steering Committee meetings). Many of the indicators are ratios (e.g., % budget spent on IT research).

The Balanced Scorecard model is only one of various forms of measurement that can be implemented. It is top-down driven, comprehensive, and unifying in that it forces all parts of an organization to measure their functions in the same manner. The BSC provides an excellent starting point in establishing a performance measurement system. Most IT departments today do measure performance, although that measurement may not be in the form of the Balanced Scorecard Model.

MEASUREMENT PRAGMATICS

The Balanced Scorecard is but one of many approaches to measurement of IT functions. Regardless of the measurement approach used, there are several pragmatic measurement elements to be considered. These include (a) the hierarchical structure of the system, (b) performance goals and tolerances, and (c) trend measurement.

American Management Systems (AMS)

American Management Systems (AMS) is one of the world's largest consulting firms. It is organized into vertical market segments such as government, technology, etc. AMS enters into contracts to act as a systems integrator in development of large technology applications. For example, it developed a new Collectables application for the Franchise Tax Board (FTB) of the State of California. In this instance, as well as in many other development engagements, AMS entered into a Performance-based System Development Contract. This type of contract has the following features:

• AMS and the client agree on measurable objectives for the newly designed application upon its implementation. For example, one objective of a collectables system might be to "Increase the dollar amount of taxes collected by 15%."

• AMS is not paid any consulting fees until and if all agreed upon objectives have been met.

In the FTB case, the implementation of the new collectables took over a year during which AMS was not paid any fees or reimbursed for any expenses by the State of California. Indeed, payment was not made until FTB had achieved all the agreed upon system objectives. Therefore, it is important to AMS to ensure that the client has a deep enough performance measurement system to be able to compare before and after system performance. In that way, AMS can prove that contracted system improvement goals have been met.

Therefore, AMS often includes as a part of their development plan the building or enhancement of a client Performance Measurement System. This measurement system also can be used by the client for ongoing performance measurement after AMS has concluded its engagement.

Hierarchical Structure: An effective performance measurement system should use a hierarchical, top-down structure. There should be a few critical indicators at the top of the structure, each with a defined goal and measurement tolerance. If a top-level indicator is within tolerance, then we move on to the next crucial indicator. If this indicator fails the tolerance test, then we **Drill Down** to lower-level, more detailed indicators so that we can gain more insight into the indicated problem. This "drill down" process is shown in Figure 9-5.

Performance Goals and Measurement Tolerances: Each measurement indicator should have a performance goal and a measurement tolerance. A **Tolerance** allows reasonable fluctuations from expected performance (e.g., new personnel) before we decide that there is a problem. For example, we might set a goal for Data Entry Accuracy Rate of greater than 90 percent. We also might set the tolerance level at minus 3 percent. In this way, any short term fluctuations between 87 and 90 percent would not be cause for alarm. However, if data entry performance drops below 87 percent or remains below 90 percent for a prolonged period of time (e.g., 3 measurement periods), then we might become concerned.

Typically, such goals and tolerances are set by a group of IT staff and users. The group may consult past history or perform benchmarking studies of other firms or the industry in general. Alternately, goals may be set according to benefits promised for newly developed IT systems. The IT department, for example, may have projected that a newly developed customer ordering system would reduce order entry error rates to 5 percent. This 5 percent figure then might become an objective for the operating system.

Trend Measurement: Problems encountered in the technology arena typically require more time to solve than do many other business problems. Therefore, timely prediction of measurement indicator trends is critical so that IT problems can be corrected before they become crises. Early detection allows more lead time to correct the problem before it becomes a crisis (Figure 9-6).

There are many methods for computing performance measurement trends. This chapter describes only the three methods of moving averages, exponential smoothing, and adaptive exponential smoothing.

Moving Averages: A **Moving Average** simply is a computed mean taken from a data set over a number of periods. When data is collected for a new period, the oldest period of data is eliminated and a new average is computed. Moving averages adjust for temporary variations in a measurement indicator. The longer the collection period (e.g., 12 months), the less sensitive is our adjustment to current indicator levels. The primary disadvantage of this trend technique is that the system must store several periods of data. However, this becomes much less a problem in this era of data warehousing and inexpensive storage. Figure 9-7 demonstrates moving average computations.

Exponential Smoothing: This trend model is a surrogate for the moving average, but it doesn't require as much storage space. Exponential smoothing requires storage of

Figure 9-5 Hierarchical (Drill-down) Structure

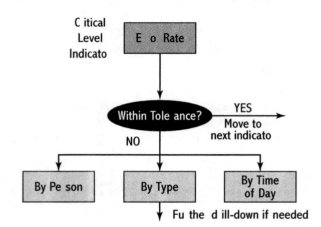

Figure 9-6 Need for Trend Measurement

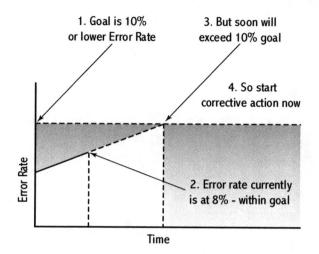

1. Goal is 10% or lower Error Rate

3. But soon will exceed 10% goal

4. So start corrective action now

2. Error rate currently is at 8% - within goal

Error Rate

Time

only one value for past history. The exponential smoothing formula is:

$$X = (1 - a)Y + aZ \text{ where:}$$

- X is the Newly Stored Trend Value

- a is the Smoothing Constant (0.1 to 1.0)

- Y is Last Period's Stored Trend Value

- Z is this period's value for the measurement indicator

The higher the **Smoothing Constant**, the greater is the weight that is placed on current period data. Typically, smoothing constants are in the range of 0.1 to 0.3. Suppose this month's Data Entry Error Rate (Z) is 12 percent, last month's computed Trend Value (Y) is 8 percent, and our Smoothing Constant (a) is 0.2. Then, the New Trend Value (X) is computed as follows:

$$X = (0.8 \times 0.08) + (0.2 \times 0.12) = 0.88$$

Note that this month's value is four percent higher than the stored trend value of eight percent. Yet, this formula results in less than a one percent rise in the newly stored trend value. However, if error rate continues at the 12 percent level, the trend figure will *eventually* rise to this new level.

<u>Adaptive Exponential Smoothing</u>: The problem with exponential smoothing is that, depending on the smoothing constant chosen, it will take a long time before the system recognizes a significant change in a data pattern. Adaptive exponential smoothing provides an adjustment to the regular smoothing model if new patterns persist. For example, a new IT system might be implemented with a much easier and less error-prone data entry capability.

The adaptive exponential smoothing technique first tests to see if the indicator values have exceeded the established tolerance for a given number of periods (e.g., three months). If that has happened, then the trend system recognizes a new data pattern. The system then sets the smoothing constant at a very high value (e.g., 0.9) for several periods to imbed the new pattern. This, in effect, erases past data history. Then the system resets the smoothing constant to its previous lower level.

Figure 9-7 5-Month Moving Average Computations

2nd 5-Month Moving Average = 33/5 or 6.6

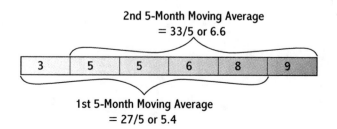

| 3 | 5 | 5 | 6 | 8 | 9 |

1st 5-Month Moving Average = 27/5 or 5.4

INTEL CASE STUDY

Intel is a company with a strong culture of performance measurement. Its measurements are used as a partial basis for individual and department bonuses, and for promotions as well. One specific measurement system within Intel is the "CIO Dashboard", an internal IT department measurement system which is a subset of the larger corporate measurement system. The CIO Dashboard is web-based so that all employees have immediate access to the latest performance information. The CIO Dashboard is a modified balanced scorecard system. Figure 9-9 shows the introductory screen.

Note that the four typical BSC perspectives of Financial, Customer, Operations and Future (people/ environment) are shown. A fifth perspective of programs is added. There are three to five top-level performance indicators for each of these perspectives. For example, the Financial Perspective is segregated into the categories of Spending, Capital, Headcount, Product/Service Cost and IT versus Intel Revenues.

Legends (annotated arrows) are shown next to these indicators to show current status. Green (G) denotes a satisfactory condition. Yellow (Y) denotes a cautionary condition. Red (R) indicates an unsatisfactory condition. The direction of the arrow indicates the direction of the indicator's trend. In some cases lower level indicators may have mixed trends. In these cases, the numbers in the boxes show the number of lower level categories in each status. For example, look at Product/Service Quality within the Operations perspective (Figure 9-2). The numbered boxes indicate that, of the 13 lower level measurement indicators within Product/Service Quality, 11 are favorable, 2 are cautionary, and none are unsatisfactory...

The Dashboard is a hierarchical, drill-down system. Clicking on one category will lead you to another screen displaying more detailed measurement indicators within that category. For example, if you click on the "Site IT Customer Experience" indicator of Figure 9-9's Customer perspective, the "Sub-board" shown in Figure 9-10 will appear with more detailed indicators within "Site IT Customer Experience".

This performance measurement system also has a third drill-down level. An example of a third-level containing more detailed information including graphics. Confidentiality constraints prevent us from presenting the more detailed aspects of this Intel performance measurement system. However, this case clearly illustrates the structure of a "best practices" measurement system.

Figure 9-9 Intel CIO Dashboard Introductory Screen

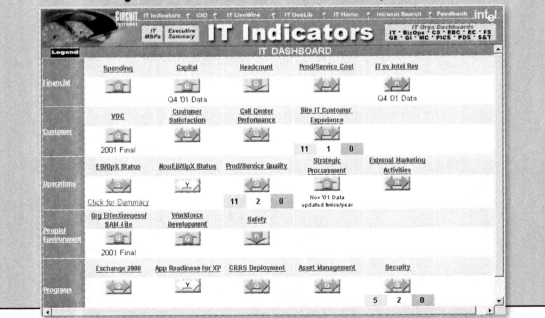

Figure 9-10
Site IT Customer Experience Sub-Dashboard

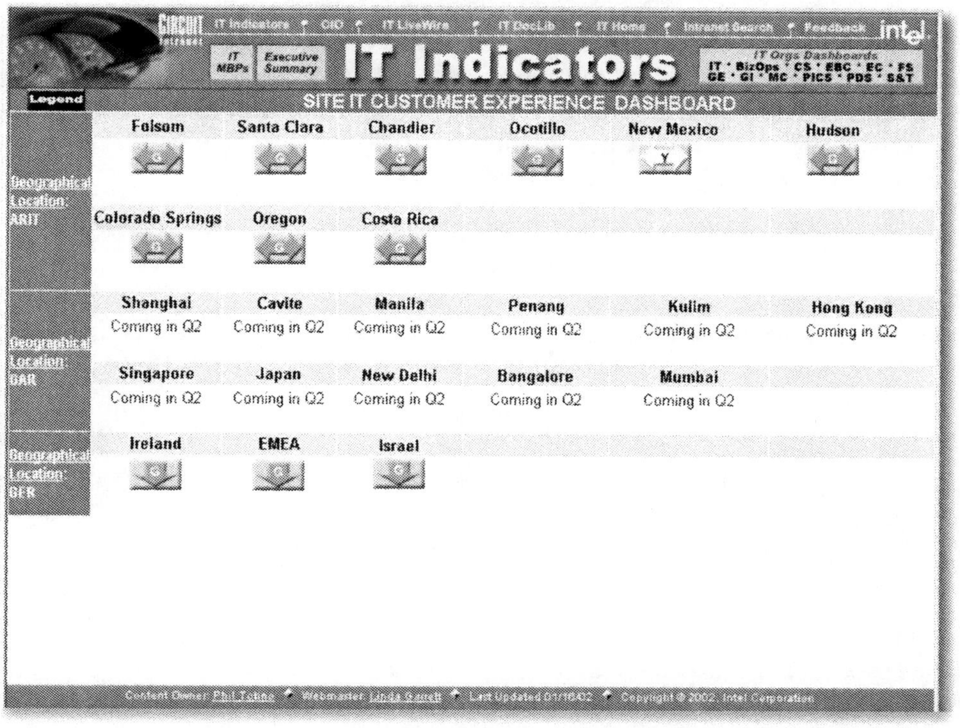

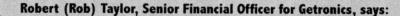

Robert (Rob) Taylor, Senior Financial Officer for Getronics, says:

How do you, as an accountant, use performance measurements? "I can look at our Profit and Loss Statement (P&L) and I can trace revenue back to a purchase order or a customer order. I can track the cost of purchase orders or payroll records."

So, rather than using a formal Performance Measurement System, you look at P&L performance instead? "Yes. We have performance measures in other areas such as project management. But most of my work is from looking at the P&L, drilling down into the details, then zooming back up. We can run a P&L report anytime in the day. Then I can drill down to as many as seven different levels to give me the base document if I want it. A lot of our information is scanned in automatically, say purchase orders, so I can look at the actual document."

You mentioned project management performance measures. Do you, as an accountant, actually measure project performance? "Not directly, but I attend the monthly project status meetings where we all review each project by comparing its performance to a number of numerical goals. For instance, one of the goals is that the project has to have at least a 30 percent margin of revenue over costs. If a project's losing money, that's my business and I get involved at these meetings and afterwards."

SUMMARY

Many of the specific measurements used in this chapter (e.g., invisible backlog) are not expected to be in the accountant's normal knowledge domain. In addition, measurement of IT functions would seem to be the purview of IT people who might not welcome interference from "outsiders". While all this is true, this author suggests that accountants must be involved in the IT measurement process because:

- Our accounting standards indicate that organizational performance measurement of any type is within the realm of our responsibilities.

- An IT performance measurement system cannot be separated from a total organizational measurement system; accounting is one profession that includes a holistic view of the organization.

- Poor IT performance leads to a wasting of organization funds; funds management certainly is within the accountant's domain.

We predict that the future role of the computer-savvy accountant will include an even larger responsibility for performance measurement in general, and technology performance measurement in particular.

KEY TERMS

Adaptive Exponential Smoothing	Exponential Smoothing	Moving Average	Ratio Scale
Anchor Measures	Indicator	Nominal Scale	Raw Metric
Derived Metric	Intangible	Ordinal Scale	Smoothing Constant
Drill-Down	Interval Scale	Outcome Measures	Surrogate Metric
	Metric	Outcome Metric	
		Performance Driver	

REVIEW EXERCISES

1. What is the difference between a raw metric and a derived metric?

2. Give an example of a surrogate metric in your university environment.

3. You wish to compare different brands of DVD players. Give an example of how you would use the nominal, ordinal, interval and ratio measurement scales in your comparison.

4. Give an example of an anchor measurement you might use to compare IT department performance to other companies in the same industry.

5. How does the Balanced Scorecard (BSC) model differ from typical cost accounting methods?

6. A company uses the measurement "Number of Data Entry Errors" to evaluate the effectiveness of data entry operators. What problems do you have with this measurement?

7. Define both an outcome metric and a performance driver for each of the following situations:

a. How your personal automobile operates

b. Receiving Section effectiveness

c. Accounting clerk effectiveness

8. Describe how a BSC model is "top-down driven".

9. Give an example of a performance goal and a measurement tolerance for each of the following situations:

a. Your grade-point average

b. Employee attendance

c. Computer system availability

10. What are the advantages and disadvantages of using exponential smoothing instead of a moving average?

11. What are the advantages and disadvantages of adaptive exponential smoothing as compared with other trend models?

12. Why is performance measurement of IT performance relevant to the accounting profession?

CRITICAL THINKING OPPORTUNITIES

1. Contact a business organization in your area. Select one department for that organization (e.g., Accounts Receivable). Extract one example of measurements that department uses for each of the nominal, ordinal, interval, and ratio scales.

2. Somewhere Inc. does not have a performance measurement system for its IT department. The Vice President of IT has resisted any suggestions for implementing such a system because it is "too costly" and "IT is too difficult to measure."

a. Write a memorandum to this Vice president explaining why a performance measurement system would enhance the IT department.

b. As an accountant, how would you justify to this Vice President why this matter is of concern to you when you are not assigned to the IT department?

c. Should you involve Somewhere's Chief Executive Officer in this matter? Why or why not?

3. Somewhere's Vice President of IT has been impressed by your memorandum of problem 2. She has asked you to help her implement a performance measurement system within the IT department.

a. Briefly describe in ten steps or less how you would stage the implementation of this system.

b. Assume that this implementation would take one year. Design a graphic schedule (e.g., Gantt chart) of your implementation plan.

4. Reference Figure 9-4. Describe three (3) sets of performance drivers and that outcome measures that could be used to measure employee performance in the department you surveyed in opportunity 1.

5. For each of the measurements that you described in opportunity 4, describe what this department *might* use for a measurement goal and a measurement tolerance.

6. Given the data shown in Table 9-6 (page 158):

a. Compute a 6-month moving average for the last two periods.

b. Compute an exponential smoothing value for the last two periods (assume a smoothing constant of 0.2).

c. Compare the results of your two calculations as to their ability to detect potential problems early.

d. What value would adaptive exponential smoothing have added to this situation?

7. Reference the Intel CIO Dashboard performance measurement system described in this chapter. Construct a similar hierarchy for a Purchasing department using:

a. three (3) top level indicators

b. two (2) 2nd level indicators for *one* of the top level indicators

c. two (2) 3rd level indicators for *one* of the 2nd level indicators

Table 9-6 Entry Error Rate History (in %)

Month	Jan	Feb	Mar	Apr	May	Jun	Jul	Aug
Rate	7	9	9	13	14	12	15	15

REFERENCES

Churchman, C. W.; **Challenge to Reason**: McGraw-Hill; 1968

Fadiman, C. and A. Bernard; **Bartlett's Book of Anecdotes**; Little, Brown and Co., 2000

Grembergen, W.; *"Measuring and Improving Information Technology through the Balanced Scorecard"*; **Electronic Journal of Information Systems**; Volume 1, Issue 1, Paper 3, 2000

Martin, M.; **Analysis and Design of Business Information Systems**; Prentice Hall, 1995

Menasce, D. and V. Almeida; **Scaling for E-Business: Technology Models, Performance, and Capacity Planning**; Prentice Hall, 2000

enterprise system justification

> "In any decision situation, the amount of relevant information available is inversely proportional to the importance of the decision."
>
> — *Michael Minerath*

Have you ever tried to put a dollar value on a good friendship, or a beautiful summer day, or even a child's happy laughter? Of course not! Yet we accountants continually are pressed to put dollar values on assets and events that defy numeric measurement in general and dollar measurement in particular. Consider, for example, the following real-life conversation.

Norm and Rafael were producing a "business case" for a project they were hoping to get approved. They met with Ned, their Director of IT Development. Norm said to Ned, "We're trying to do an ROI and we're stuck. We just can't make any sense out of it. We'll never get this project approved; it takes me too long a period for this project to recognize a return on its investment."

Ned mulled his beard for a moment, then he replied, "What's the success criteria necessary to proceed on this project and how will you measure that success? Are dollars the only thing that's important here?" Norm countered, "A project has to have an ROI."

"Why?" asked Ned. "In how much time does a project have to show a return? What if it doesn't have an immediate ROI? Can it still be successful? Aren't there other goals besides an ROI? Are you itemizing those other goals in you project request?" Rafael shook his head and asked, "What do you mean? What other goals?"

Ned answered, "Maybe you should consider your task a 'project justification' instead of an 'ROI'. While an ROI should be part of justifying an IT project, there are other critical factors that should be considered. Why don't you try submitting more facets of the project that are important and that make you think the project should be approved, with suggestions as to how the facets can be measured? Measure things like expected quality improvements, increased customer satisfaction, better competitive value, increased efficiencies, or faster delivery timelines."

Rafael looked at Norm, but Norm just shook his head. Then Norm said, "That sounds good, but how do you convert all of those things into dollars so that they'll fit in an ROI spreadsheet?"

Why this great concern over justification of this IT project? A surprisingly large number of IT investments become runaway projects; these projects finish substantially over budget, over schedule, or both. Yet, surveys consistently show that formal justification of IT initiatives is not always done by IT departments; if it is done, it most often is done once at the beginning of a project. The use of formal return-on-investment analysis for IT projects seems to follow closely the business cycle. When the economy is healthy, companies seem to place less emphasis on cost-cutting and more emphasis on strategic (qualitative) initiatives. When the economy sours, companies stress cost reduction which is more amenable to ROI analysis.

For some companies, IT projects represent over 50 percent of capital investments. Given this fact and the high rate of IT runaway projects, it is understandable why executives are placing proposed IT investments under closer scrutiny. This chapter presents a comprehensive view of the difficulties posed by and the opportunities available in justifying enterprise-level IT systems. The sequence of discussion is (a) Budgeting and Enterprise System Justification, (b) Business Cost-benefit Strategies, (c) an IT Return-on-investment Model, (d) Intangible Factors, and (e) Justification Success Factors.

RELEVANCE TO ACCOUNTING PROFESSION

There is continuing controversy over whether ROI analyses should be used for proposed IT investments and how such analyses should be conducted. The accountant's role in such ROI analyses is important because (a) cost-benefit (ROI) is within accounting domain knowledge, (b) accountants often are called upon to help the IT department prepare such analyses, and (c) accountants often are called upon to be independent reviewers of ROI analyses prepared by the IT department.

BUDGETING AND ENTERPRISE SYSTEM JUSTIFICATION

There is a close interrelationship between justifying an enterprise level system and budgeting for its implementation. The successful justification will require adjustments to the IT department's budget. IT department budgets may act as a constraint on whether or not an enterprise system will be justified. Let us use an example to illustrate the separation of justification from budgeting. Suppose a company's IT department has prepared a Return-on-investment (ROI) analysis (sometimes called a Business Case) which shows that a $600 thousand investment in a Web-based Purchasing system would pay for itself in three years. There are several scenarios of how this system justification could relate to the project budget.

Partial Budget: Management may decide to reduce the project scope and budget only $450 thousand for the project.

Staged Budget: Management may decide to authorize a budget of only $50 thousand for the Requirements Analysis phase of the project. Then, based upon the knowledge gathered during this phase, the IT department will prepare a new ROI for the remainder of the project. Then management will decide whether or not to increase the project budget.

Staged, Competitive Budget: Management may authorize a limited budget for several competing projects to complete an initial project phase. Then management may choose one or more "survivor" projects for continued funding.

Situational Budget: Project budget priorities are set initially but are continually reviewed and changed as new business situations arise. For example, one IT consulting firm has only 42,000 man-hours per year approved for IT development and enhancement projects. The firm's budget was based on priorities for projects known at the time of budgeting. Throughout the year the firm must make adjustments within that fixed number of hours to accommodate unexpected and sometimes critical new requirements and opportunities. If the priority is deemed higher for a new project than for an originally budgeted project, the older project is scrapped in order to accommodate the new project. So, we will attempt to separate the budgeting process from the system justification process in this chapter, recognizing that it is not always easy to do so.

BUSINESS COST-BENEFIT STRATEGIES

What cost-benefit strategies should be used in business to justify enterprise-level IT systems? Academic textbooks suggest that the predominant model used would be return-on-investment (ROI) analysis, also referred to as the **Business Case**. ROI analysis has been used successfully in business for a considerable period of time. Yet it appears that use of ROI analysis for IT projects is not as prevalent as some might expect. A 2001 study by Marcoccio Consulting (Computer World, 3/18/02) revealed that only 23 percent of surveyed businesses required detailed ROI analyses for all IT projects. This figure had increased from 9 percent the year before, and the consulting firm predicted that the figure would increase to 65 percent by the end of 2002. Apparently, difficult economic times spur more use of ROI analyses.

Another study was conducted by Computer World at its Premium 100 conference in March 2002. 300 attendees were surveyed on their use of ROI analysis for IT proposals. The question posed was, *"Do you measure project ROI six months after the work is completed?"* The results were that (a) 68 percent responded "rarely" or "never", (b) 65 percent responded that their IT employees didn't have sufficient ROI tools or knowledge, and (c) 75 percent responded that their firms did not collect deep enough data to support ROI analyses for IT projects.

Why the relative lack of use of ROI models for IT proposals? Some would argue that IT investments are unique, or at least different from most other business investments. Others would argue that this merely is a self-serving excuse on the part of IT departments.

There is, however, a middle-ground between these two opposing positions. This position uses certain logical precepts to decide if, when and how ROI analysis is to be used. Five such approaches are (a) IT Risk Management, (b) Stratified ROI, (c) ROI Scenarios, and (d) Evolving ROI, and Berry's Value Triangle.

IT Risk Management: One approach is to proactively concentrate on IT threats rather than waiting for a specific IT system proposal. In this approach, we first separate IT contingencies into categories of risk. It is assumed that some type of IT system event will need to be funded in order to counter serious risks. For example, a purchasing application may be at risk of becoming obsolete and a reengineering effort requires organizational resources to counter that risk. IT systems then are evaluated by comparing projected risk-countering costs with projected losses based upon the probability (risk) of the IT event occurring. A unique feature of this approach is that it focuses upon possible future events, rather than proposed IT systems. An IT system may have several future threatening events, and a threatening event may encompass several IT systems. This approach is compatible with the accountant's calculation of expected loss.

$$\text{Expected Loss From Threat} = \text{Maximum Loss if Threat Occurs} \times \text{Risk of Threat Occurring}$$

IT risk management can be done on the entire spectrum of IT systems (**System Portfolio**) or on a case by case basis. The following description applies to the spectrum approach. The following steps are executed:

Determine IT system threats: Perform an inventory of all IT systems. For each system, determine what future events pose threats to that system (may impact system effectiveness). It is important to select an appropriate time horizon in which to forecast these threats. Five years probably is too long, given the dynamic natures of the business and technology landscapes. One year may be too short a horizon.

Figure 10-1
IT Risk Matrix Example

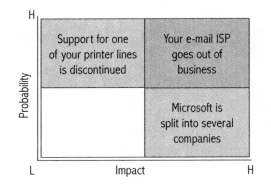

Classify IT threats: Place each IT threat into a matrix based upon relative probability (risk) of that adverse event occurring and the impact upon the organization should that event occur. Figure 10-1 shows examples of such adverse events in an ***IT Risk Matrix.***

Prioritize IT threats: Figure 10-2 shows a suggested action scheme based upon priority categories. Notice that quantification (e.g., ROI analysis) is only required for category 2 threats. Category 1 items will have to be taken care of regardless of economic projections; therefore, ROI analysis may be irrelevant for this category. Category 4 items have a low probability of an adverse event requiring system modification or replacement, and a low impact if that event occurs. So we don't have to worry so much about them. We can place them in a future action file and retrieve them when they are re-prioritized or more resources become available.

Quantify the expected loss for all category two IT threats: For example, assume that there is 30% likelihood that the enterprise accounting package won't be supported in two years. Further assume that the cost of completely replacing that system is a million dollars. Then the risk value is 0.3 times $1 million, or $300 thousand.

Prioritize category 2 threats: This prioritization simply may be based on risk value. Alternately, we may consider factors such as cash flow requirements, IT budget, IT skills inventory, customer preferences, or any other considerations consistent with organizational culture and strategic emphasis.

Adjust for interdependencies: Two or more IT system threats may be closely related. For example, discontinuance of an accounting package may make inoperative certain portions of an inventory application. In such a case, both threats may be packaged together.

Identify alternatives: Discover alternatives that will reduce or eliminate each threat (e.g., purchase new accounting system).

Select best option: Use a business case (e.g., ROI analysis) to choose between risk avoidance alternatives, or to accept the expected threat as calculated.

Figure 10-2 IT Risk Categories

2. Quantify and Prioritize	1. Top Priority
4. Don't worry about	2. Quantify and Prioritize

Probability (vertical axis, L to H), Impact (horizontal axis, L to H)

Revisit process: This should occur every six months, or even sooner in a dynamic organizational environment.

IT risk management presents one option where formal cost-benefit analysis is used for only certain categories of IT systems, and only after these systems undergo prior review to see if this analysis is appropriate. However, critics of this approach suggest that it is too risk-averse – that it fails to include proactive projects that do not address specific threats but may add value to the firm. For example, where would the following projects fit in the Risk Management matrix?

- Capture an electronic image at POS workstations which will save $2.2 million a year.
- Add Wealth Management services to a customer Web site which will add $1 million in new sales.

Perhaps a workable strategy to creating an IT development portfolio might be to (a) have one group use the more reactive Risk Management approach, (b) have a second group use a more proactive approach to look for non-risk oriented IT opportunities, and (c) force the two groups to find a middle ground between these two approaches.

Stratified ROI: Some firms require different levels of economic analysis depending on the nature of the IT project under review. One approach used by one of one of our author's consulting clients is not to use ROI analysis for certain IT projects, to use an abbreviated form of ROI analysis (Light ROI) for other projects, and to use extensive ROI analysis (Full ROI) for the remainder of the projects. The ROI decision is based upon specific project characteristics.

Light ROI: This type of cost-benefit analysis is a "rough estimate." Analysts don't spend too much time on extracting precise dollar estimates or on attempting to quantify intangible factors. The simple Payback Period metric is used and the results of the analysis are conveyed by internal memorandum to IT department managers.

Full ROI: Analysts spend a great deal of time on refining cost and benefit figures. They try to quantify as many intangibles as possible. The metrics used consider the organization's cost of capital – the **Opportunity Costs** of the organization not being able to use IT project investment dollars for some other endeavor. Thus, metrics may include Discounted Payback Period, Net Present Value, or Internal Rate of Return. Often, **Sensitivity Analysis** is performed, varying opportunity costs and time horizons to evaluate differing future scenarios. A full business case is prepared and sent outside as well as inside the IT department. If the IT project is approved, a cost-benefit tracking and reporting system is established to force ROI revisions as the project evolves.

Selection Criteria: The example used here is for a major technology firm. This firm determines the level of ROI analysis to be used by considering three criteria (Figure 10-3):

- Is the project investment amount within the IT department's budget? (Can it be approved internally without outside review?)
- Can the project be competed in less than one year (the budget cycle)?

Figure 10-3 Major Technology Firm ROI Decision

Condition	Decision Rule					
	1	2	3	4	5	6
Is project within IT budget?	Y	Y	Y	N	N	N
Can project be completed in < 1 year?	Y	N	N	–	Y	N
Are there mission-matching benefits?	–	N	Y	N	Y	Y
Action:						
Scrap Project		X		X		
No ROI required	X					
Light ROI			X		X	
Full ROI						X

- Does the project offer benefits that match specific company mission statements or goals?

Notice that use of full ROI occurs only in a few cases. Another firm with which one of our authors works uses a similar approach, but refers to Light ROI as Fast-track analysis. This firm even sets a maximum amount of time and analyst hours that can be devoted to this type of quick analysis.

ROI Scenarios: Different versions of ROI analysis can be used to portray different future scenarios. For example, the IT department may wish to present best-case and worst-case scenarios for a proposed IT project. The best-case scenario might only use the Payback Period metric. The worst-case scenario might use more conservative metrics such as Net Present Value (NPV).

These metrics could be made more conservative by using discounting formulas as described later in this chapter. If the worst-case scenario is acceptable to management, then the project is approved. If the best-case scenario is unacceptable to management, then the project is rejected. An acceptable best-case and unacceptable worst-case situation requires deeper analysis and management negotiation on intangible factors.

Evolving ROI: One of the reasons that there are so many IT project cost and time overruns is that often the initial cost-benefit analysis is performed only once. This typically is at the very beginning of the project process. For all but the simplest projects, there are too many "unknowns" involved, particularly if the project involves complex tasks such as integration with other software or use of new technologies. In such cases, the true depth of project effort cannot be discerned until the project is underway. The project itself is a learning process. Therefore, ROI analysis done at the beginning of the project and never repeated is destined to be erroneous. Figure 10-4 demonstrates this phenomenon.

The solution to this problem is to require ROI analysis after each project phase. Continued funding of the project may be contingent on the latest ROI figures. Indeed, the project may receive funding authority only in stages. For example, one firm approved one project in phases with new cost-benefit analyses and go/no-go decisions at the end of each phase. The project included the phases shown in Table 10-1.

One commonly used argument against this approach is that abandonment of an IT project in "midstream" is a waste of the resources already expended – the sunk costs. This may seem to be a compelling argument in some firms, but does not make much sense economically. A State of Alaska Personnel system was abandoned after 18 months and $1.5 million dollars expended. It was not logical or cost-beneficial to continue expending resources on an unfinished personnel system that was not going to work regardless of the amount of resources expended.

Berry's Economic Value Pyramid: Another stratified approach to ROI analysis is Berry's Economic Value Pyramid (Berry, 2002). Berry divides proposed IT investments into three categories (Figure 10-5):

<u>Strategic Initiatives</u>: These are IT systems that promise benefits that increase a firm's long-term financial posture. Such projects have the potential to, for example, increase market share, reduce order or cash cycle times, or increase

Figure 10-4
System Unknowns and ROI Accuracy

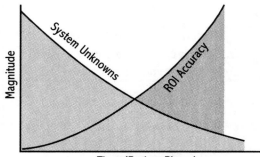

Table 10-1 Project Approval Phases

PROJECT PHASE	PROJECT DELIVERABLE	BUDGET
Scope	Deliver scope and level-1 pricing	$200K
Specification	Deliver specifications and revised pricing	$350K
Implementation - Beginning - Test - Rollout	Begin implementation phase Delivery to customer for testing Rollout to production	25% of pricing 50% of pricing 25% of pricing

revenues. Customer Relationship Management (CRM) and Supply Chain Management (SCM) systems are examples of strategic initiatives.

<u>Tactical Initiatives</u>: These are IT proposals that focus on internal business process applications (e.g., Purchasing). Such initiatives promise to decrease costs directly or indirectly through increased productivity.

Figure 10-5 Berry's Economic Value Pyramid

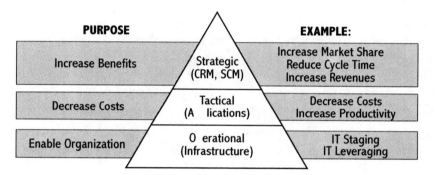

<u>Operational Initiatives</u>: These are IT proposals that enable the firm to develop strategic and tactical initiatives. Such initiatives include the firm's technology infrastructure such as intranets and extranets. These initiatives do not directly increase revenue or decrease costs. Operational initiatives allow a firm to have the capability to consider IT Staging or IT Leveraging. The triangle shape reflects the fact that there are more operational initiatives than there are tactical and then strategic initiatives.

Berry then uses this triangle as a guide as to when and to what extent ROI analysis should be used for these three categories of initiatives (Figure 10-6). ROI analysis is not recommended for Operational Initiatives because such initiative's benefits are (a) long range and difficult to specify in dollars, and (b) diffused and shared throughout the firm and thus difficult to quantify centrally. Moderate ROI analysis (e.g., light ROI) is recommended for tactical initiatives while full ROI analysis is recommended for strategic initiatives.

Figure 10-6
Economic Value Pyramid and ROI Strategies

Enterprise-level IT proposals can be segregated into categories, whether by risk or some other logical distinction. Then different ROI tactics, including not using ROI analysis at all, can be applied to the different categories. Given that variable approach, what specific approach should be used when ROI analysis is dictated?

IT RETURN-ON-INVESTMENT (ROI) MODEL

While IT system economic justification may not be unique, it does require increased attention to characteristics that may not be as prevalent in other firm investment opportunities. This section includes a model for economic justification of enterprise-level information technology systems. Following are basic definitions of terms and elements that will be used:

Definitions:

IT Portfolio: An inventory of IT system needs prioritized by each system's contributions to the organization's strategic goals (Martin, 1995). The number of projects included in the IT Portfolio will be subject to numerous factors such as market conditions, business health, recent losses or potential growth.

Technology Leveraging: Using an IT system or component (e.g., database) for beneficial purposes other than originally intended. For example, a database initially designed for internal company use might be used outside the company to attract a new trading partner. As another example, bank data intended for tracking and auditing financial transactions increasingly is being leveraged for marketing information such as branch use trends, product use trends, product costs, customer relationships, and other such information.

Technology Staging: Building IT infrastructure in order to seize future, but not yet defined opportunities. This might be building a Web site for brand recognition prior to formally considering migration to business-to-customer (B2C) e-commerce sales. Alternately, it might be building an extranet in order to explore eventual business-to-business (B2B) e-commerce integration opportunities.

Justification Model: We can build a practical model of an IT ROI analysis by considering (a) benefit dimensions, (b) project value, (c) ROI metrics, and (d) the problem of marginal costs.

Benefit Dimensions: Figure 10-7 demonstrates the benefit dimensions that the ROI analysis process must try to capture.

The highest priority IT project is selected from the IT portfolio. This project will follow one or more of the following ROI paths:

Direct Benefits: Some IT systems, often critical in nature, will demonstrate direct, demonstrable and swift dollar returns. ROI analysis is rather straightforward for these systems.

Figure 10-7 ROI Benefit Dimensions

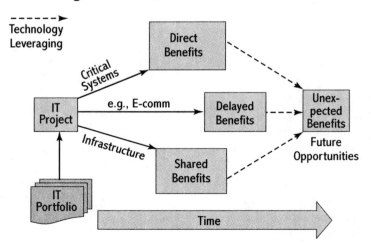

Delayed Benefits: Some IT systems (e.g., e-commerce) will show demonstrable returns only after a lengthy gestation period. Here, ROI analysis becomes more difficult because (a) future benefits are more uncertain and thus more difficult to quantify, and (b) the ROI analysis must be conducted over a longer, riskier time horizon.

Shared Benefits: Some IT systems (e.g., infrastructure) have benefits that are diffused through many users and many departments. It is difficult to gather all of these benefits (many of which are intangible) into one consolidated ROI analysis.

Unexpected Benefits: All IT systems, regardless of which ROI difficulty path is followed, may be subject to technology leveraging – the unexpected use of a system for a beneficial purpose for which it was not originally intended. For example, American Airline's SABRE system was not perceived originally as a vehicle for committing connected travel agents to book flights on American, but the system eventually evolved in this direction. It is very difficult to use ROI analysis to demonstrate this type of benefit.

Project Value: Figure 10-8 shows how these categories of benefits combine to create IT project value. **Project Value** is additional revenues expected from the IT system minus additional costs accrued through implementation and operation of the new system. This is computed over the planning horizon of the ROI analysis (e.g., 5 years). Direct benefits can be directly input to the ROI computations. Caution must be exercised, however, not to project direct benefits too far into the future (e.g., beyond 3 years). The business and technology landscapes change too rapidly to guarantee direct benefits too far into the future.

Delayed benefits may be too uncertain to be represented by firm dollar figures. These benefits may best be handled as indirect or intangible benefits. Unexpected benefits really may not be unexpected at all, but be the product of someone's hunch or vision. Still, visions are hard to convert to the dollar figures that ROI analysis demands. So this type of benefit should be considered only as a weaker intangible factor. The same can be said for opportunity benefits – unexpected future benefits that may come along and for which we happen to be prepared. It is difficult to project the real value of such "possible" opportunities.

ROI Metrics: There are several metrics that can be used in return-on-investment analysis. Some of the most common metrics are:

Break-even Point (BEP): This metric calculates the point where the new IT system is generating positive cash flow, regardless of whether or not the original front-end investment dollars have been fully recovered or not.

Figure 10-8 Project Value

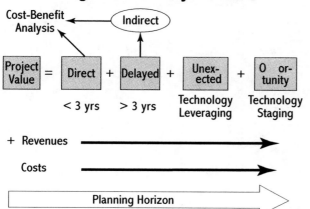

Payback Period (PP): This metric computes how long it will take for increased revenues and reduced costs to equal (pay back) the original investment (seed money) required to implement the new system. This is the simplest of the ROI metrics. It also has the advantage of not requiring the analyst to select a planning horizon (e.g., 5 years) in which to frame the analysis. The analyst simply computes how long it will take to balance the investment; then management must decide if the computed period is too long.

Discounted Payback Period (DPP): This metric augments Payback Period by adjusting future revenues and costs by the opportunity costs incurred by the firm from not using this project's investment resources for some other business alternative(s). The metric uses a compound interest formula where the interest rate is the firm's expected return-on-investment (ROI) on the other alternatives or, alternately, the ROI the firm can expect doing "business as usual."

Present Value $=$ $(1 / ((1 - ROI)$ **n)) * Value in Year n

As with the simpler Payback Period metric, the analyst need not select a planning horizon for the analysis. The use of opportunity costs (often referred to as the time value of money) stretches out the period that would be computed using the simpler Payback Period metric. Thus, Discounted Payback Period is the more conservative metric.

Net Present Value (NPV): This metric is similar to Discounted Payback Period with one critical difference. The analyst must select a planning horizon for the analysis. This planning horizon often is a function of organizational policy. For example, the finance manager may dictate that he will not approve any IT investments that do not pay for themselves in four years. Once a planning horizon is selected, the analyst sums the discounted cost/benefit totals for all years in that horizon to arrive at a single dollar figure. If that figure is positive, then the project will pay for itself within the planning horizon.

Internal Rate of Return (IRR): This metric is similar to Net Present Value except that, instead of a dollar figure being computed, the cost/benefit gains of the proposed project are divided by the initial investment required to derive the project ROI. The project ROI then is compared to normal firm ROIs from everyday business or the ROIs from competing projects. One must solve for the IRR using the following formula:

$$0 = \frac{R(\text{year 1})}{(1 + IRR)} + \frac{R(\text{year2})}{(1 + IRR)**2} + \frac{R(\text{year 3})}{(1 + IRR)**3} + \cdots \frac{R(\text{year n})}{(1 + IRR)**3} - \frac{\text{Initial}}{\text{Investment}}$$

There are several Web calculators which can be used to derive this metric. Some companies such as Intel are skeptical of using this metric because the results can be" misleading". The metric seems to favor small versus larger value projects.

ROI Calculation: Table 10- 2 shows estimates for a new IT system at Nitram Industries.

The pattern shown in Table 10-2 is typical for IT projects. The new system is built during the first year-and-a-half, thus causing the project to show negative cash flow (Row 3). Then the new system is implemented sometime in the middle of year 2. From that point on, the new systems shows positive revenue/cost gains over the current system. It is sometime before the end

Table 10-2 Nitram Purchasing System Benefit Projections (in thousands of $)

TYPE SYSTEM COST	CALCULATION	YEAR (n)				
		1	2	3	4	5
1. Current System		25	28	34	45	57
2. New System *		55	38	14	15	16
3. Difference	1 - 2	-30	-10	+20	+30	+41
4. Cumulative Difference	Sum (1 – 2) n	-30	-40	-20	+10	+51
5. Discount Value **	ROI = .16	.85	.73	.62	.53	.46
6. Discounted Difference	3 * 5	-25.5	-7.3	+12.4	+15.9	+18.9
7. Cumulative Discounted Difference	Sum (3 * 5) Over n	-25.5	-32.8	-20.4	-4.5	+14.4

* Total of $72 thousand spread over 18 month deployment period

** Based on an average; Nitram Return-on-Investment (ROI) for the past three years

of year 4 that the cumulative effect of new system gains (Row 4) creates a positive return on the project's initial investment.

ROI metric calculations for this scenario are as follows:

Break-even Point (BEP): This is calculated on the Difference (Row 3). Notice that this Difference changes from negative to positive sometime before the end of year 3. Assuming that yearly expenses are spread uniformly throughout year 3, the BEP is:

$$\text{BEP} = \text{Year } 2 + \frac{10}{(10 + 20)} \quad \text{(distance to travel from -10 at end of year 2 to zero)} \\ \text{(total distance to travel from -10 to +20)}$$

or 2.33 years

Payback Period (PP): This is calculated in the same manner as for the Break-even Point, but the Cumulative Difference (Row 4) is used instead. The Cumulative Difference transforms from a negative to a positive amount sometime after year 3. The PP is:

$$\text{PP} = \text{Year } 3 + \frac{20}{(20 + 10)} \quad \text{(distance to travel from } -20 \text{ at end of year 3 to zero)} \\ \text{(total distance to travel from } -20 \text{ to } +10)$$

or 3.67 years

Discounted Payback Period (DPP): The firm's total return-on investment for the past three years has averaged 16 percent. We use this average ROI in lieu of i in the traditional interest formula (Row 5). We compute the DPP the same way as the BEP and PP, except we use the Cumulative Discounted Difference (Row 7). The DPP is:

$$\text{DPP} = \text{Year } 4 + \frac{4.5}{(4.5 + 14.4)} \quad \text{(distance to travel from } -4.5 \text{ at end of year 4 to zero)} \\ \text{(total distance to travel from } -4.5 \text{ to } +14.4)$$

or 4.24 years

Net Present Value (NPV): A time horizon needs to be selected in order to compute the NPV. Nitram's Comptroller insists that all investment proposals must show a positive return by the end of the 5th year. So our planning horizon is 5 years. We see that the Cumulative Discounted Value (Row 7) at the end of year 5 is 14.4. Thus **NPV = 14.4**

Internal Rate of Return (IRR): We solve for IRR using the Difference (Row 3) as follows:

$$0 = \frac{-10}{(1 + \text{IRR})} + \frac{20}{(1 + \text{IRR})^{**}2} + \frac{30}{(1 + \text{IRR})^{**}3} + \frac{41}{(1 + \text{IRR})^{**}4} - 30$$

or 33 percent

Which Metric Should Be Used: Assuming that a company chooses to use ROI analysis, the choice of ROI metric will be dependent on the answers to several questions:

- Will "Light ROI" be used? If so, the simplest metric of Payback Period should be used.

- Does company policy specify a planning horizon for which ROI analyses must be framed? If not, NPV and IRR will require the analyst to select an arbitrary planning horizon. The use of Payback Period or Discounted Payback Period might be more appropriate.

- Does the company have a conservative investment culture? If so, use of the relatively optimistic Payback Period metric might be inappropriate.

- Is this a not-for-profit organization? If so, use of all but the Payback Period metric may be complicated by the fact that the organization does not realize a return-on-investment in the normal sense of that term. Still, even a not-for-profit firm has alternate (opportunity) uses for investment funds. After all, ROI has as much to do with cost-cutting as it does with revenue enhancement. That is why the US federal government uses a 10 percent ROI in its analysis, despite its non-profit history.

- What is the organization's policy? ROI metrics are used to compare alternate projects often submitted for consideration from different functional areas (e.g., Marketing, Production). Such comparison requires that all ROI analyses use similar metrics.

- The Break-even Point probably is the least useful of all the ROI metrics. It can be used as a tie-breaker when two alternatives perform at about the same level for one or more of the other metrics. The BEP also can be useful when a company finds itself with surplus investment funds until year X (e.g., temporary tax relief). Then the company may insist that an investment's BEP occur before Year X.

Marginal Costs: A continuing controversy in cost-benefit analysis is the concept of marginal costs. A marginal cost is a true out-of-pocket cost; it does not include the accountant's classification of overhead costs. For example, suppose that one of the IT department's justifications for a proposed IT project is that it "will free up 15 percent more clerical hours." This would be considered a marginal benefit (negative marginal cost) only if that increased productivity will lead to actual cost reductions such as reduced personnel hiring hours (e.g., lay-off workers) or not having to hire people in the future (*cost avoidance*). If, however, the hours saved merely are used by personnel for other tasks (no reduction of personnel costs), then this should be considered as an intangible benefit and not as a tangible cost savings.

Yet some scholars and practitioners would argue against this position. A counter position is that any consequence of an activity, even if indirect, should be considered a cost of that activity. As one practitioner stated (Conrad, 1999), *"The use of the marginal cost approach can lead to a portfolio of investments which individually meet the criteria but which taken together does not make much sense."* Some opponents of the marginal cost approach argue that use of "overhead" costs is an attempt to capture future costs of project implementation consequences. These opponents argue that there often is a considerable lag between initiating business actions and an associated escalation of organization costs. This also is called *disruption costs*.

Others might argue perhaps that overhead should be used as a "fudge factor" to offset often understated IT department estimates.

Should we include overhead costs in our ROI analyses, or should we adhere to a strict marginal cost posture? The answer to this question relies more on organizational culture and practice than it does on logical truths. A conservative approach would consider overhead costs as appropriate. A more aggressive approach would lean towards marginal costs, ignoring overhead. Perhaps both approaches could be used to provide "worst case" and "best case" scenarios.

INTANGIBLE FACTORS

One reservation by IT managers about using ROI analyses is that there are too many intangibles associated with IT projects. An *Intangible Factor* is a consideration that (a) cannot easily be quantified (e.g., attitudes), or (b) that can be quantified, but not in the dollar metric required of ROI models. It is arguable whether IT projects inherently contain more intangibles than any other business projects. Nevertheless, this section discusses types of IT intangibles and one approach to including them as an adjunct to traditional ROI analysis.

The Benefits Matrix: Intangible factors often are used as "tie-breakers" when ROI analysis of tangible factors is too close to suggest a clear decision. For example, the Payback Periods for

IT alternatives A and B may be 14.2 and 14.5 months respectively. To then select alternative A would be placing a greater degree of accuracy on the ROI model than is warranted by the estimations required. The analyst thus might compare intangible benefits to determine which alternative is the best choice.

The **Benefits Matrix** separates tangible from intangible costs and benefits (Figure 10-9). Benefits (increased revenue) and reduced costs are divided into the top and bottom halves of the matrix. Tangibles (measurable in dollars) and intangible factors are separated into the left and right halves of the matrix. Only tangible factors (left half) would be included in the ROI model.

Types of Intangible Factors: Intangible factors can be divided into two classes: strategic (long term) and tactical (short term)

Strategic Factors: Some strategic intangible factors (all future revenue related) are:

- increase customer satisfaction
- increase sales (if this increase cannot reasonably be measured in dollars)
- increase customer commitment / loyalty
- externally market the proposed new IT system (IT Leveraging)
- increased infrastructure, thereby allowing the firm to seize future business opportunities (IT Staging)

Tactical Factors: Some intra-IT tactical intangible factors are:

- decrease error rate
- decrease time to correct errors
- decrease workstation response time
- decrease report delivery times
- increase level of system security
- increase end-user satisfaction

Note that many of these factors are measurable, but not easily in dollars. However, if the measurement can be converted to dollars, then the intangible factor is converted to a tangible factor and is entered into the ROI model. For example, a consulting client for one of our authors considered decreased workstation response time as leading to increased productivity. The client computed a dollar value for that productivity gain.

Figure 10-9 Benefits Matrix

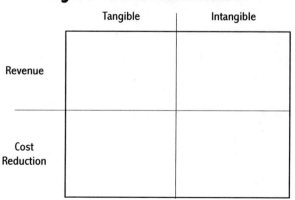

Comparing Intangible Factors: Intangible factors are not included in ROI models because they are too difficult to measure in dollars. One can, however, do a separate analysis of intangible factors and use this analysis in cases of ROI results that are inconclusive. Or, as Foundation Health Corporation did, one could use both ROI and intangible analyses concurrently to make an IT investment decision. We can use the *Alternative Screening Matrix* which weights and analyzes intangible factors (Figure 10-10). Solving this matrix entails the following steps.

- List all intangible factors in the left-most column.

- Determine relative importance weights for each factor (weights should total to 100%).

- List the alternatives being considered across the top row (e.g., proposed new IT system and current IT system).

- For each combination (cell) of alternative and factor, rate the strength of that factor for that alternative. Ratings should be from 1 to at least 5 or more with 1 being worst and 5 being best.

- Multiply each alternative/factor rating by the factor weight giving a weighted rating for each cell.

- Sum the weighted ratings for each alternative.

- The alternative with the highest sum is preferable. However, if the difference in alternative sums is not significant, it is unwise to proclaim a "winner", because that would imply more precision to this approach than it deserves.

The Total figure for the In-house alternative, for example would be computed as:

$$(0.35)(5) + (0.20)(3) + (.20)(5) + (0.15)(5) + (0.10)(4) = 4.5$$

(out of a possible 5 maximum score)

Note that the difference between the totals for the first two alternatives is less than 1.0, but both of these alternatives score much higher that the alternative of retaining the current system. Therefore, the third alternative would be rejected and the other two remaining alternatives studied in more depth (e.g., attempt to convert one or more of the criteria to dollars for ROI analysis).

Intangible factors cannot be ignored. They must be handled by either (a) making the effort to quantify them into dollars so that they fit into ROI analysis, (b) evaluating them in a structured manner (e.g., alternative screening matrix), or (c) assessing them subjectively with no attempt at measurement.

JUSTIFICATION SUCCESS FACTORS

Experiences of many firms in justifying enterprise-level IT systems has led to a collection of factors that appear to be critical.

- The firm must have a deep cost accounting system in order to minimize the number and impact of intangible factors.

- There must be established organization economic justification policies and procedures so that all projects competing for resources use the same methodology so that they can be easily compared.

- Financial and accounting personnel should assist IT personnel in developing business cases.

- There must be incentives for detailed and accurate justification. IT project team bonuses should be tied to ROI performance and sponsoring departments should absorb excess project costs.

- ROI models *"did not come down the mountain with Moses"*; other justification models may be appropriate in certain situations.

- There must be periodic and continuous ROI reporting, not just an initial estimate which then is abandoned.

Figure 10-10 Alternative Screening Matrix

CRITERIA	WEIGHT	ALTERNATIVES		
		IN-HOUSE	OUT-SOURCE	RETAIN CURRENT
Functionality	0.35	5	4	2
Delivery Time	0.20	3	4	5
Upgrade Capability	0.20	5	3	1
Integration Problems	0.15	5	4	5
Scalability	0.10	4	4	1
Total	**1.00**	**4.5**	**3.8**	**2.75**

- Intangible factors must be considered in a planned and structured (weighted) manner; these factors cannot be thrown in as an afterthought.

- Some IT investments are future oriented and are poor candidates for formal ROI analysis. These include infrastructure projects and other IT endeavors that position the organization for agile maneuvering in the difficult-to-predict business future.

Of all of these guidelines, perhaps the most important is establishing organization justification rules and requiring that all departments, even the IT department, abide by these rules. One would hope that such justification rules were flexible enough to handle extraordinary cases, and were easy to modify as the technology and business landscapes continue to change rapidly.

THE WORLD ACCORDING TO ROB

Robert (Rob) Taylor, Senior Financial Officer for Getronics, says:

How do you arrive at the amount that you're going to bid for a technology project?

"We look at certain types of past projects and look for those that were like the one we're bidding on. We see how they worked in the past. We don't use hard statistics, but there are some goals to go in that direction. We have a boiler plate (standard) margin we want to make on the project and we have a boiler plate contingency factor."

What is the contingency factor? How did you arrive at that?

"We use a 15 to 20 percent contingency that we add to our project bids. How much depends on the type of project — you know, the size, the scope, the technology involved. We do pricing reviews; we had one this afternoon. We have a Risk Register where we look what negative things can happen and what the impact would be. We build some rationale for the contingency factor we're going to add to the estimated project cost."

SUMMARY

Justification of enterprise-level IT systems will become increasingly important as such systems become more interactive, complex, and thus more costly. At the same time, such systems that operate across all organization functions and between trading partners will become more difficult to force within the traditional dollar-driven cost-benefit models; there will be too many intangible and future oriented considerations.

Accountants must be flexible enough not to rely on "one-size-fits-all" traditional ROI models. Instead, they must adjust methodologies to the uniqueness of the organization and to the specific technology and business landscape viewed by that organization. Finally, accountants cannot stand by and watch their IT colleagues flounder in this growing morass; we must aid IT professionals in learning to do and in executing this more difficult but more important task of justifying enterprise-level systems.

KEY TERMS

Alternative Screening Matrix	Internal Rate of Return (IRR)	Sensitivity Analysis
Business Case	IT Risk Management	Shared Benefits
Cost Avoidance	IT Risk Matrix	Strategic Intangible Factor
Delayed Benefits	Light ROI	Stratified ROI
Direct Benefits	Marginal Costs	System Portfolio
Discounted Payback Period	Net Present Value (NPV)	Tactical Intangible Factor
Evolving ROI	Opportunity Costs	Technology Leveraging
Full ROI	Project Value	Technology Staging
Intangible Factor		Unexpected Benefits

REVIEW EXERCISES

1. Describe the four (4) risk categories in an IT Risk Matrix.
2. What is the difference between Expected Loss from Threat and IT Risk Value?
3. Management decides to invest in a new IT system rather than a new product marketing campaign. Describe the opportunity costs for this decision.
4. Describe three (3) differences between Light ROI and Full ROI.
5. How is Project Value computed?
6. What is the Return Period? How does it relate to Payoff Period?
7. Compare and contrast Technology Leveraging with Technology Staging.
8. Compare and contrast Discounted Payback Period with Net Present Value.

9. A new IT system will save 50 clerical personnel an average of 10 hours per week. Can we consider this a savings for this new IT system? Why or why not?

10. Give two (2) examples of cost avoidance in a university setting.

11. What is the difference between tangible and intangible factors?

12. Describe three strategic intangible factors.

13. Describe three tactical intangible factors.

14. Describe four critical success factors for IT justification.

CRITICAL THINKING EXERCISES

1. Select five or more medium- to large-sized companies in your geographic area. Compile a survey of these companies' use of ROI analyses using the following questions:

   • Do you use ROI analysis for IT projects? If not, why not?

   • Do you use ROI analysis for all IT projects or only selectively? If selectively, for what type of IT projects do you use ROI analysis?

   • When you use ROI analysis, do you use it continually throughout the project or only at the beginning?

2. The following relates to a recent project involving automation of revenue collection kiosks located at the entrances to California state parks. Reference the data shown in Tables 10-3 through 10-5. Prepare a cost-benefit analysis. State all assumptions and justify your choice of ROI metric(s). Use the following considerations.

   • The system will take 20 months to implement.

   • The system must pay for itself within 5 years.

   • The standard return rate used by the state is 10%.

   • Only the largest 15 parks will be automated; these parks represent 55 percent of total park system revenue.

Table 10-3 Current System Costs:

COST CATEGORY	ANNUAL COSTS (150 PARKS)
Park Level Administrative	$321,200
Entrance Ticket Inventory	56,000
Vendor Discounts Lost / Penalties	7,146
Misappropriation	700,000
Lost Income	236,000
TOTAL	$1,320,346

Table 10-4 Estimated New System Annual Benefits (150 Parks)

COST/REVENUE OBJECTIVE	ESTIMATED SAVINGS ($)
Increase park bank interest income	237,000
Reduce park level administrative hours	240,900
Eliminate entrance ticket inventory	55,000
Eliminate lost purchase discounts	5,000
Decrease park level misappropriation of funds	700,000

Table 10-5 Estimated New System Costs

COST TYPE	AMOUNT	NOTE
Hardware Purchase	$5000	One-time per workstation
Hardware Maintenance	$500	Per workstation per year
Software Development	$500,000	One-time, outsource
Software Upgrades	$40,000	Per year
Telecommunications Enhancements	$100,000	One-time
Telecommunications Maintenance	$8,000	Per year

3. Survey five to ten IT departments in your geographic area and summarize the answers to the following questions:

   a. How do you account for intangible factors when justifying IT projects?

   b. Have you ever used or considered using the Options pricing model?

4. Prepare a Benefits Matrix given the following proposed benefits:

   a. a 15% decrease in error rate

   b. a 20% increase in customer retention

   c. a 10% reduction in inventory

   d. a 12% increase in product sales

   e. a 30% decrease in the risk of data theft or embezzlement

   f. an increase in customer satisfaction

   g. an increase in employee satisfaction

5. Aggie Chocolates is a small firm with cash flow problems. Management is considering whether or to automate its Inventory system by either buying a software package or hiring a group of students from a local university to build an automated inventory system.

   a. What intangible factors should Aggie consider?

   b. What is the relative importance to Aggie of these intangible factors?

   c. What system alternatives does Aggie have?

REFERENCES

Conrad, K.; "*Measuring the Strategic Value of Information Technology Investments*"; **11**[th] **Office Information Technology Conference**; Chicago IL, August 1994

Dickson, G. and J. Wetherbe.; **the Management of Information Systems**; McGraw Hill, 1985

Hackett, G.; *"Why Projects Fail"*; **Internal Auditor**, October 1998.

Martin, M.; **Analysis and Design of Business Information Systems**; Prentice Hall, 1995

Martin, M. *"Intel's Operations Service Center"*; **Intel Corporation**, 2001

Rubash, K.; *"A Study of Options Pricing Models"*; http://bradley.edu/~arr/bsm/pg04.htm

Ruff, F.; *"Factors Underlying Option Prices"*; www.optionetics.com/articles/search/article full.asp?idNo=6161

Strassman, P. *"The Business Value of Computers"*; the **Information Economic Press**, 1990

transaction integrity and asset protection

> "Security is like the apartment doors in New York City. They don't have a lock. The have a slew of locks and chains and even steel bars."
>
> — *Chris Christiansen*

Henry David Thoreau, the 19th century writer and philosopher, made the following entry in his journal on September 8th, 1759.

"I went to the store the other day to buy a bolt for our front door, for as I told the store-keeper, the Governor was coming here. '*Aye,*" said he, "*and the Legislature too.*' "*Then I will take two bolts,*" said I. He said that there had been a steady demand for bolts and locks of late, for our protectors were coming."

Mr. Thoreau obviously had no concept of today's Internet and the e-business transactions that fly through it. Yet he and his neighbors seemed to have grasped the concept that, while we must protect ourselves from external threats, we also must be wary of inside threats – even from our "protectors". A 2000 study showed that 82 percent of computer thefts were perpetrated by employees of which a third of them were managers, half were employees who had been with the company for five years or more, and a quarter were employees who had been with the company ten years or more. You can lock your apartment door, but it won't do much good if the thief lives inside with you. Or, as one of Intel's security principles states, *"Watch the watchers"*.

E-business presents to the accountant different threats and increased risks for old threats. There are now a multitude of electronic doors through which external thieves can slip in and out undetected, and internal thieves can move their embezzled cash outside the firm more quickly and more stealthily than before. We cannot place human guards at each of these cyber-doors, but we can put in their place powerful and intelligent software and biometric sentinels. That is what this chapter is all about.

We will discuss the threats, risks, and techniques used to guard against manipulation of business transactions and invasion of the firm's information assets. The sequence of discussion will be (a) E-security assessment, (b) E-business Threats, (c) Risk Assessment, (d) Security Controls, (e) Intrusion Detection, (f) Authentication, (g) Asset Protection, and (h) Return on Security Investment.

RELEVANCE TO ACCOUNTING

Developing and managing controls to ensure the integrity of business transactions and the protection of organizational assets are not new accounting responsibilities. Our accounting standards have placed these responsibilities upon us for some time. However, the ways and means by which organizations conduct business is changing rapidly. We then must change our methods of control and oversight to counter these new business models. For example, bank reconciliation is still required, but it is not sufficient. It must be bolstered by new technological detection and control techniques that recognize the myriad new ways by which perpetrators can do harm to our business.

There is an essential question that we must ask ourselves. How much technology should the accountant in general, and the auditor in particular, be knowledgeable of? This chapter is replete with technological details. Is there too much detail? We don't think so; we believe that the new accountant should have one foot firmly in traditional accounting principles while the other foot is just as firmly planted in technological know-how.

E-SECURITY ASSESSMENT

There is explosive growth in business and consumer use of the Internet – an open and decentralized communication structure that is increasingly difficult to control. This provides criminals, corporate spies, and other troublemakers increasing opportunities to damage the firm. John Mee, a Web security auditor for KPMG, recently explained to one of our author's classes: *"Is e-business security over-hyped? Probably so. But that shouldn't keep us from recognizing that it's a serious problem that's costing companies millions of dollars in losses and a lot of manpower being diverted from making profits."*

The E-business Security Problem: The FBI conducted a survey of 503 computer security practitioners in 2002. The survey revealed the following facts about the companies for which these practitioners worked.

- 98 percent had web sites.

- 52 percent conducted e-business (e.g., on-line purchasing, on-line customer ordering).

- 38 percent had suffered unauthorized access or misuse of their Web sites during the past 12 months. 30 percent of these firms had experienced 10 or more incidents.

- 22 percent didn't know if their Web sites had been violated or not.

- 90 percent of the security practitioners had detected some computer (Web plus internal) breaches during the past 12 month. 80 percent of these acknowledged financial losses from these breaches.

Other surveys have shown similar results. There is a serious problem with computer security in general and e-business security in particular.

A Security Assessment Model: We propose the following structured approach for assessing the e-business security problem and finding cost-effective solutions (Figure 11-1).

Threats: Determine the specific security threats to which the firm may be exposed.

Exposures (Severity): Quantify (in dollars, if possible) the maximum loss that can result if a particular threat occurs.

Figure 11-1 Security Assessment Model

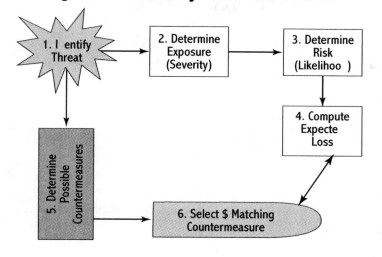

1. I entify Threat
2. Determine Exposure (Severity)
3. Determine Risk (Likelihoo)
4. Compute Expecte Loss
5. Determine Possible Countermeasures
6. Select $ Matching Countermeasure

Risk (Likelihood): Determine the risk of that threat actually occurring. Preferably, this determination should be probability terms (e.g., 12%) although it can be assessed qualitatively (e.g., high low, or as a range).

Expected Losses: Estimate the expected loss from each threat by considering the joint values of exposure and risk. If exposure and risk have been quantified, then the expected loss merely is the product of these two variables.

Search for Countermeasures: Determine all possible countermeasures that will mitigate the threat.

Control Matching: Choose a countermeasure that does not cost more than the expected loss.

This is an iterative model since the countermeasure selected may lower the risk of the threat rather than negate the threat entirely. Still, this simple model will serve as the structure for discussion in the remainder of this chapter.

E-BUSINESS THREATS

The first step in using the model of Figure 11-1 is to assess the threats facing the company using e-business as a means for transacting business. We describe threat assessment in terms of the journalism methodology of asking what, why, who, when, where and how.

What: There are several different types of threats that are new or elevated in an e-business setting.

Data Privacy: The privacy threat involves unauthorized access to employee and customer information. This can result in unwanted traffic (e.g., spam) or even stolen identities. This also can result in long-term loss of customers and employees.

Data Integrity: A message may be intercepted and data fields (e.g., payment address or amount) may be changed.

Authentication: Falsified identity is one of the most prominent e-business threats. You need to ensure that both the sender and receiver are who they say they are. This threat can include the following;

IP Spoofing: A person can change the Internet Provider (IP) address on a message to one which your firewall won't block.

Customer Impersonation: A perpetrator can impersonate a valid customer or vendor and have an order or payment sent to his or her address.

False Web Sites: This threat (also called a ***False Storefront***) involves a perpetrator establishing a false log-in screen that looks identical to your company's Web site home page. Your customers believe that they are doing business with you, but they really are doing business with the perpetrator.

E-mail Hijacking: Here the perpetrator establishes a Web address that is very similar to your company's address. For example, if your address is Aggie.com, the perpetrator might establish an address of Aggie.org. This would divert business (including payments) from your firm to the perpetrator.

Authorization: Unauthorized users should not see information they're not authorized to see. For example, an Accounts Payable clerk probably doesn't need to access the Customer file in order to accomplish his or her job. If a perpetrator breaches your company's firewall, then there should be controls in place to limit which files and programs (s)he can access.

Destructive Code: This includes viruses which can destroy company data. It also can include internally developed hidden code that can be used to perpetrate fraud.

Infrastructure: This threat can take the form of data theft, unauthorized access to passwords, or interception of messages. Another threat of this type is ***Denial of Service***: the overloading of a network system with millions of illegitimate requests.

System Dependencies: A perpetrator may fail to invade your company's Web site due to your high level of security. Yet, if your company is electronically linked to its vendors or business partners, the perpetrator may find a way to broach their systems as a means for "getting in the back door" to your network system.

Who and Why: These threats primarily are coming from five groups; each group has a different motivation for broaching a company's e-business network.

Disgruntled/Former Employees: This group is more interested in damaging the company than in perpetrating fraud. A former employee, however, is knowledgeable of internal company operations and can use that knowledge to commit fraud.

Competitors: Industrial espionage is an old threat now being committed with new technology. For example, a competitor might try to steal your customers' names and addresses.

Hackers: This group considers it a challenge to invade a company's network. Fraud rarely is the motive. A hacker generally is interested in creating enough havoc to demonstrate his or her skills and to be noticed.

Crooks: This group's goal is to commit embezzlement or fraud.

Foreign Governments: This group may be interested in helping businesses in their countries to compete more effectively by stealing your customer and process information.

Where: These threats can emanate on the company's network portals or on the portals of linked networks of subsidiaries, vendors, customers, or business partners.

When: These threats can occur at any time, even when the company is closed for business.

How: There are many methods for breaking into a company's network. Among the more common are the following (RSA Security, 2002):

Password Cracking Tools: There are a variety of available software tools which automate the guessing of passwords. These tools contain extensive dictionaries of frequently used passwords. This approach is facilitated by the fact that many users choose passwords that are predictable, such as "password" or their children's names.

Network Monitoring: Internet messages are routed past individual user nodes which capture only those messages intended for them. In this technique, available software allows a perpetrator to use **Sniffing**: monitoring without detection the contents of any message that streams by and flagging messages based on keywords such as "login" or "password".

Brute Force Dialing: There are programs available which locate modem telephone lines and then repeatedly attempt to sign on to the line with various password combinations.

Abuse of Administrative Tools: Many tools that have been designed to manage networks can be misused for destructive purposes. For example, administrative tools to help managers to detect weaknesses in their networks can be used by hackers for the same purpose.

Social Engineering: Some intruders rely on the fallibility of human beings to steal passwords. For example, a hacker can pose as company IT staffer, call a new employee, and offer to expedite his or her system setup. The naïve new employee volunteers his or her password, thus giving the hacker easy access to the system.

Security Exposures: For each of these potential e-business threats, there is a **Security Exposure**: the maximum amount of company resources (e.g., dollars) that can be lost should that threat actually happen. It is important to estimate that exposure in order to evaluate the proper level of security needed to counter the threat. You can use a qualitative assessment (e.g., high, medium, or low) if actual dollar figures are difficult to attain. Each technology (IT) threat should be equated to a business threat. For example, we might ask, "What are we risking as a business if a perpetrator impersonates one of our customers? How will this affect out financial statements? Table 11-1 shows how KPMG equates IT threat to business (financial) threats.

Stating threats in business rather than technological terms will facilitate the selling of costly security solutions to higher management.

RISK ASSESSMENT

The next step in using the model of Figure 11-1 is to assess the risk (likelihood) of each e-business threat occurring. This is not an easy task, but insurance companies do this regularly in order to determine the amounts to charge for their policies.

Risk Assessment Methods: There are several ways to assess the risks of threats occurring.

Risk Assessment Packages: There are several commercial packages available which help the company assess its risks.

Past Experience: For example, if your network system was unavailable (down) five days out of the 300 customer-available days, the risk of network unavailability can be computed as 5/300, or 1.7 percent.

Table 11-1 KPMG IT to Business Threat Equivalencies

IT THREAT AREA	EQUIVALENT BUSINESS THREAT
Building the System Improperly	Process Control Failure Failed Implementation
Security Breaches	Transaction Alteration Misappropriation of assets Fraud
Privacy Breaches	Legal Exposure Reputation Exposure
System Continuity/Availability	Revenue Loss Business Failure Reputation Exposure

Benchmarking: You can visit similar companies and import their risk estimates.

Outsource: You can buy an insurance policy to protect against a threat or threats. In this case, the difficult task of assessing risk is done by insurance (risk management) experts. Alternately, you can contract with a Risk Management firm to perform risk assessment for your specific setting.

Qualitative Approaches: Risk numbers may be difficult to attain consistently for all e-business threats. In such a case, you may decide to evaluate risks qualitatively – in terms such as high risk, medium risk, or low risk.

A Qualitative Approach: The following qualitative assessment approach is adapted from software testing theory. This approach requires that you (a) list all possible threats; (b) assess the exposure (maximum dollar loss) for each threat in terms of high, medium or low; (c) determine the risk of threat occurrence in terms of high, medium, or low; and (d) array the threats on a graph according to each threat's relative exposure and risk. Table 11-2 demonstrates the first four tasks for Aggie Chocolates.

For example, the threat of a power outage (symbol "O") has a medium exposure but a high risk of occurrence. The threat of sabotage (symbol "S"), on the other hand, has a high exposure, or maximum dollar loss. Yet this threat has a low risk (probability of occurring) because Aggie Chocolates has happy employees and a tight physical security system. The final step in this approach is to array each threat according to its relative exposure and risk. Figure 11-2 does this for Aggie Chocolates based upon the information contained in Table 11-2.

Note the arrow flowing from the upper right to the lower left of Figure 11-2. This indicates the sequence of consideration that Aggie Chocolates should give to solving its security problems. The threat of power outages (symbol "O") is the first encountered along the analysis path. It should be the first threat analyzed and mitigated. Data theft (symbol "D") and human error (symbol "E") are the next threats along the analysis path. They should be attacked next. Aggie Chocolates may run out of money before it can concentrate on the system down threat (symbol "S"). But that threat only has a low exposure and a low risk.

SECURITY CONTROLS

The next step in our model is to find a range of security solutions for each threat. Our goal in selecting a security countermeasure is ensure that all business transactions are secure in that (a) there is limited risk of third-party interception, (b) we can detect when someone has tampered with the transaction message in transit, and (c) the transaction is authenticated by both parties,

Table 11-2 Aggie Chocolates Exposure and Risk Assessment

Possible Threat	Symbol Figure 17-2	Exposure	Risk
Disaster	D	H	L+
Power Outage	O	M	H
System Down	H	L	L
Human Error	E	M	M
Fraud	F	M	L
Data Theft	T	L	M
Sabotage	S	H	L

We will discuss briefly solutions for each of the threats brought forth earlier. We have made no attempt to include the relative prices of each of these solutions since these prices are dynamic and are changing even as we are developing this textbook.

Data Privacy: Some solutions to this threat include employee and customer file encryption and access controls. The greatest protection against this threat is a privacy policy with a long-term perspective. Violations of privacy rarely damage a firm's immediate financial posture; the financial statements are not affected for the short run. In the long run, however, the firm can experience increased turn-over rates for both employees and customers. This can lead to long-term effects upon financial statements in the form of higher employee recruiting/training costs and lost sales revenue.

Data Integrity: Erroneous or incomplete data can lead to file information that cannot be trusted. The problem is that we cannot tell which records have been corrupted by posted data that lacks integrity; therefore we don't trust any of our stored information. The best solution for the data integrity threat is a strong up-front editing system which checks each input transaction for (a) accuracy, (b) reasonableness (e.g., employee working more than 50 hours per week), (c) correct ranges (e.g., month from 01 to 12), and (d) suspicious combinations (e.g., Illinois resident ordering items to be shipped to Mexico).

Authentication: There are two different levels for preventing unauthorized users from accessing our internal business systems. The first level is *Authentication*: the process of assuring that persons attempting to enter the network system really are who they say they are. The second level is *Authorization*: controlling the behavior of those that have been allowed entry into the system.

Authentication can include simply matching the password against a list of authorized passwords. Alternately, it can use a more complex methodology such as *Dynamic Positioning*: a set of rules that users must meet to gain access to the network system. For example, a vendor password being used at three a.m. on a Sunday morning may be denied access to the network system because this time/day pattern is abnormal for this vendor.

Network Security Management Tools attempt to keep unauthorized users from entering the network system. These include firewalls, intrusion detection systems, security probes, and password cracking – most of which will be discussed in detail in the next section.

Authorization: *Application-level Security Tools* manage user behavior within the network system. These include access control, transaction authorization, and threat detection. Access control is restricting password access to specific tasks that can be performed on specific data files or computer programs. Table 11-3 is an example of an Access Control Matrix which allows the security software to automatically grant or deny access to programs or files. If someone tries to access or manipulate a

**Figure 11-2
Aggie Chocolates Risk Assessment Diagram**

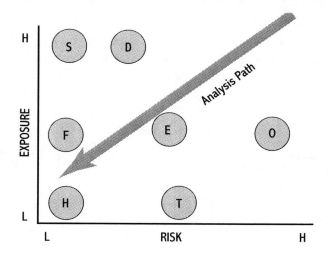

file or program for which he or she is not authorized, then notification of a security threat is sent immediately to management.

Destructive Code: Solutions for this threat include virus detection programs which provide early notification that something is wrong. The firm also can invest in *Program Logic Analyzers* which detects, among other anomalies, (a) program modules not ever or infrequently used, or (b) *Trojan Horses*: imbedded code that only executes at some future time or event.

Infrastructure: Solutions for this threat include:

Continuity Plan: There must be an up-to-date plan to ensure that processing capacity can be restored as smoothly and quickly as possible in event of a major disaster or temporary disruption of processing, The goals of this plan are to (a) minimize disruption, damage, and loss; (b) temporarily establish an alternative means of processing information, (c) resume normal operations as soon as possible, and (d) train and familiarize personnel with emergency operations.

Encryption: This involves the use of cryptography to disguise data being stored or transmitted. *Encryption* is the use of a complex mathematical cryptography algorithm (formula) generated by a computer to jumble the message so that it can only be interpreted by someone possessing the encryption key.

The encryption can be in the form of a *Code*: a symbol used to represent a complete message. Alternately, the encryption can be in the form of a *Cipher*: a one-to-one correspondence (e.g., substitute the letter "X" for each occurrence of the letter "E").

Physical Controls: Only authorized personnel should have access to the network facility and to each computer workstation. This access control can include use of passwords, smart cards (discussed later), or physical identification such as fingerprints.

Password Management: The length and richness of the password is the key to preventing discovery. A 5-number password requires only a maximum of 10 to the 5th power number of combinations for a computer to try to discover ("crack") that password. This is an easy and relatively rapid task for today's computers.

Cracking passwords is facilitated by the human tendency to design a password that can be remembered easily. So we tend to use our birth dates, our social security numbers, and the names of our pet cats so that we can easily remember the password. An effective password is a balance between length and how often a password changes. A 9-digit password might take an average of 180 hours for the computer to discover using the brute force method. If, however, that password is changed weekly (168 hours), then that password is effective because, on the average, it is changed in less time than it takes to crack it.

An effective password is comprised of a mix of letters, numbers and special characters (e.g., "%"). For example, we may use an 8-character password comprised of one upper-case letter, one lower-case letter, one special character, and five interspersed numerals. The use of letters and special characters increases the cracking time from hours to weeks or months. If that 8-character

Table 11-3 Access Control Matrix

PASSWORD	File A	File B	Program 1	Program 2
23A4z2	0	1	0	0
11T8m7	2	0	0	0
76G0t4	3	0	1	0
39S7a6	0	1	0	3

password is changed monthly, this password system would be difficult to solve using the brute-force method.

System Dependencies: There are two basic approaches for protecting a network system against weak security on the part of interlinked vendors, customers and business partners. The first is not to do business with external parties who cannot vouch for the strong security of their systems. The second is to establish agreements with these external parties to ensure timely security auditing by your firm or a trusted third party.

We now will describe in more detail three of the most pressing security problems facing e-business organizations: intrusion detection, user authentication, and asset protection.

INTRUSION DETECTION

Intrusion Detection is the flagging of anomalous transactions as they enter the network system - hopefully before they cause much harm. Hackers and other unwanted visitors will (a) find a way to bypass or fool the firewall, (b) enter the network system, (c) locate and modify administrative files in order to be granted internal access to sensitive files, and (d) modify or steal information from such files. *Intrusion Detection Systems (IDS)* are software designed to detect these intrusions at an early entry stage and notify system administrators of the intrusion. The two types of IDS are knowledge-based and behavior-based.

The Detection Balancing Act: Intrusion detection and authentication (next section) are balancing acts. If your criteria for detecting suspicious transactions or senders are not strict enough, then unwanted and potentially damaging messages will enter your internal system. On the other hand, if your criteria are too strict, then valid messages will be rejected. This leads to additional work associated with the off-line analysis and on-line reentry of these valid transactions. In addition, this can create ill-will on the part of the senders (e.g., customers) of these valid transactions.

Figure 11-3 shows the two different types of errors that exist when using intrusion detection or user authentication techniques.

Ideally, we would like to use an intrusion detection/authentication technique that balances the *Type I (acceptance) Error* against the *Type II (rejection) Error*. IDS can be tailored to the individual user to strike the organization's desired balance between Type I and Type II intrusion detection errors. For example, assume that an organization considers that the costs of invalidly rejecting a valid transaction are twice the costs of accepting an invalid transaction. Then, the IDS can be adjusted to relax the rejection criteria somewhat.

Knowledge-based Tools: *Knowledge-based IDS* uses knowledge of past attacks to assess new messages entering the system. Virus protection software is an example of knowledge-based detection systems. Generally, these tools are reliable and generate few false alarms (Type II er-

Figure 11-3 Intrusion Detection/Authentication Results

Actual Condition	Authentication Result	
	Prevent Access	Allow Access
Invalid Party	Desired Condition	Undetected Fraud Type I Error
Valid Party	False Alarm Type II Error	Desired Condition

rors). These tools, however, only can detect intruders using attack modes already known and incorporated into the IDS. Therefore, knowledge-based IDS must be continually updated with new knowledge about new attacks. The organization is susceptible to new attack modes until these modes have been recognized and the IDS modified accordingly. This weakness can be alleviated by using IDS that are behavior based.

Behavior-Based Tools: *Behavior-based IDS* flags network activities that do not fit expected behavior patterns. This type of IDS has a greater ability to detect previously unreported attacks. However, false alarms (Type II errors) are more common than with knowledge-based IDS. Following are some examples of transactions that behavior-based IDS might flag:

- A customer account never before accessed after normal business hours now is being accessed at 2:53 a.m.
- A transaction is withdrawing 30 percent of a customer's account balance; no prior transaction has used more than three percent.
- There has been an invalid attempt to login to 500 different system accounts in three minutes.
- There have been four attempts to login to the same account within the past two minutes.

Counter Intrusion: Recently developed IDS software is intended to trap intruders rather than just keep them out of the system. A *Honey Pot* is IDS software that offers an attractive target to intruders in order to identify them. Any attacks against the Honey Pot are made to seem successful. This gives system administrators time to mobilize – to log and track the attacker without exposing the organization's internal business systems.

The Bottom Line: Why should accountants be concerned with intrusion detection? This would seem to be a subject more suitable for technical people. There are several reasons why the accountant should have at least a rudimentary knowledge of intrusion detection and authentication threat countermeasures.

First of all, these are a new form of internal control and our accounting standards hold us responsible for internal control activities. Secondly, there are cost differentials between IDS that are knowledge-based, behavior-based, or attack-based (Honey Pot). These cost differentials require some cost-benefit analysis to ensure that the countermeasure selected is consistent with the expected loss resulting from unwanted system intrusion.

Finally, all IDS and authentication techniques are a balance between letting intruders into our system (Type I error) and keeping valid traffic out (false alarms or Type II error). This balance involves the cost assessment associated with each type of error and the striking of a cost-effective organizational balance. This type of cost estimation and balancing lies within the accountant's skill set.

AUTHENTICATION

Authentication is the process of assuring that the person attempting to enter the network system really is who (s)he says (s)he is. Authentication software attempts to answer the questions:

- Who are you?
- How do I know you're who you say you are?
- Do you belong here?
- What rights do you have?

As with IDS, authentication software is a balancing act between letting invalid persons into the system (Type I error) and rejecting valid traffic (Type II error). Authentication software is based on accepting persons into a network system based upon the *Authentication Criteria* of (a) what they know (e.g., password), (b) what they have (e.g., fingerprint), (c) what they are (e.g., laptop computer), and (d) where they are (e.g., GPS positioning). Most authentication techniques are based upon at least two of the above criteria.

There are two categories of authentication tools: biometrics and software.

Biometric Authentication: *Biometric Authentication* is the use of physical characteristics to identify a person. A system user first enrolls in the system by having his or her physical characteristic (e.g., fingerprint) scanned. Key features of that physical characteristic are extracted and converted into a unique, encrypted personal template stored in a database. The user presents that physical characteristic to a scanner each time (s)he desires to enter the system. This then is compared to the database template. If there is a match, the user is allowed into the system. Otherwise, the user is prevented from entering the system.

Matches rarely are perfect; thus rejections can occur for valid users (Type II error). System owners can, however, vary the *Sensitivity Threshold*: the percent of key features that must agree before a match is allowed. Thus the rates of false acceptance (Type I error) and false rejection (Type II error) are within the control of management and should be set based upon the relative costs of false acceptance and false rejection.

Biometrics is an evolving technological field. Authentication accuracy is increasing while device costs are decreasing. There are several biometric authentication media being used today.

These biometric types can be classified into the categories of physical and behavioral.

Physical Biometric Media: This biometric media category relies entirely on the static characteristics of some part of a person's body. These media assume that these physical characteristics will not change over time. They include the following:

Fingerprints: This is the oldest of the physical biometric tools. There are 40 to 50 different key features (points) that can differentiate one person's fingerprint from that of another person. Yet, some fingerprints have proven difficult to convert to an electronic image due to such factors as finger injuries or skin problems. Compaq computers have a relatively inexpensive fingerprint scanner called "Identicator" which can be attached to the keyboard or monitor and recognizes 43 points of identification.

Palm and Hand Geometry: This media measures the geometry and creases of either a person's palm or hand. At present, it is less accurate than fingerprints. Yet it is being used at airports in such locations as JFK in New York City, Toronto, Newark, and Miami.

Face Geometry: There are about 140 key characteristics the can be measured on a person's face. This media even can be used to scan crowds up to 1000 feet away to spot criminals or terrorists. However, some recent experiments by police departments have resulted in far more false than valid recognitions, thereby creating erroneous detainment and ensuing embarrassment to police officials. Still, this biometric media is developing and will become more accurate, thus fulfilling its advocate's boast that *"We look for smiles, not passwords."*

Eye Geometry: This is the fastest growing area of biometric research. There is promise for high scan accuracy for this media. The most prominent use is for retina scanning, although iris scanning devices are in development. There are some 130 different retina characteristics that can be matched as compared to less than 50 with fingerprints. No two human retinas are the same;

even the left and right eye retinas of the same person are different. Yet, eye geometry hardware currently is several times more expensive than for other biometric media. Still, there are some ATMs using retina scanning for identification in cities such as New York, Tokyo and London.

Behavioral Biometric Media: This type of biometric media relies on behavioral characteristics that can change over time. For example, one's voice characteristics can change from childhood to advanced age. The two most commonly used media of this type are keystroke and voice profiles.

Keystroke Profiles: Each of us has a unique pattern for using a keyboard for entering data to a computer system. This uniqueness includes a combination of typing speed and rhythm. One prominent advantage of this media is that your keystroke profile can be captured non-intrusively and transparently without the person having to undertake an enrollment process such as being fingerprinted. Of course, the fact that this keystroke profile can be attained without the user's knowledge raises concern among privacy advocates. Yet, keystroke profiles promise to inexpensively eliminate the need for passwords; there is commercial software available today (e.g., Net Nanny) which uses this biometric media.

Voice Profiles: Voice recognition promises to replace key stroking as the means of entering data to computer systems. Some computer savants predict that key strokes may become obsolete by the year 2010. There are a host of voice recognition programs in use today. Of course, as voice input substitutes for or even replaces key strokes, then keystroke profiles become less viable as an authentication medium. Use of voice profiles will increase. There are unique patterns to each person's voice that can be recognized and captured in a digital profile. Today's voice recognition software sometimes can be fooled by impersonators, but that anomaly will disappear as this technology evolves.

Choosing a Biometric Medium: There are tradeoffs in selecting the biometric medium that is most appropriate for a given situation or organizational profile. Four biometric characteristics that can be used in the selection process are intrusiveness on the user's privacy, the amount of user effort required, the accuracy of properly accepting/rejecting user authenticity, and medium cost.

The reader is cautioned that, for any specific biometric media, some of these characteristics may be changing rapidly. For example, face recognition scanners are becoming more accurate while its costs are decreasing. Therefore, we offer the following exhibit in full recognition that its contents may well be changed by the time this textbook is published. Table 11-4 is merely an example of how the most appropriate biometric media might be selected.

Aggie Chocolates and Biometrics

Aggie Chocolates is a small firm with an average ROI of 13 percent in a very competitive market. It has a comparably low Payment Cycle with only two percent of its accounts receivables in the over-90-days category. Aggie conducted a recent survey of its customer base and found the following customer facts:

- 70 percent had incomes in the upper-middle-class or upper-class categories.
- 40 percent were in the +55 age category
- 55 percent bought Aggie's products because of quality; relative price was not a major concern.
- 85 percent were repeat customers with an average of 4.7 purchases per year.
- The average amount of goods sold per sale was $83.55.

Table 11-4 Biometric Media Comparisons

Biometric Medium	Biometric Goal		Maximum Accuracy	Minimum Cost
	Minimum Intrusiveness	Minimum User Effort		
Fingerprints	Fair	Good	Good	Good
Palm/Hand geometry	Fair	Good	Good	Fair
Face Geometry	Good	Good	Fair	Good
Eye Geometry - Retina	Poor	Poor	Very Good	Fair
Eye Geometry - Iris	Poor	Excellent	Excellent	Poor
Keystroke Profiles	Excellent	Fair	Fair	Excellent
Voice Profiles	Very Good	Poor	Fair	Very Good

Tom Pritchard, Aggie's chief security officer, was interested in improving the authentication process for the company's Web customer ordering system, particularly that portion dealing with access to customer balances and outstanding rewards given to customers through a frequent buyer's incentive program. Tom was considering the use of biometric authentication because he had very little faith in available software solutions. He decided to use a weighted approach to evaluate different biometric media. He selected the following evaluation criteria in the following order of importance (most to least).

Minimum User Effort: (35% subjective weight out of 100%) Aggie had a large number of older customers.

Minimum Intrusiveness: (25%) Aggie's loyal but older and wealthier customer base might resent intrusions on their privacy.

Minimum Cost: (25%) Tom felt that he could sell to management a reasonable but not an outlandish investment in biometrics. The company did not have significant cash resources, but it had enough to finance this level of investment.

Minimum Accuracy: (15%) Tom wanted to keep out unauthorized visitors to these systems, but not to the point of alienating loyal customers.

Tom rated the different biometric alternatives on a scale of 1 to 5 where a "1" indicated poor performance on the criterion and a "5" indicated superior performance. Tom's ratings are shown in Table 11-5. Tom then solved the matrix of Table 11-5 by (a) multiplying each biometric alternative's rating for each criterion (columns 3 through 9) by the criterion's weight (column 2), and (b) summing the weighted rankings for each biometric alternative. Table 11-6 shows the results.

Tom decided to eliminate all of the alternatives except Iris scanning and Keystrokes from consideration. He would study more carefully the characteristics of these biometric methods, particularly as they related to project and ongoing costs.

Software: There are several software approaches to authenticating the validity of network users. New products are entering the market and existing products are changing. We describe the main approaches in this section by emphasizing the approaches rather than specific workings, products or vendors.

SSL: *Secure Socket Layer (SSL)* is software which is interoperable between different hardware platforms. It provides cryptographic security and is scalable to different sizes of network systems. SSL provides the services of (a) server authentication, (b) client authorization, (c) message integrity, and (d) message confidentiality. SSL is comprised of two sub-processes. SSL handshake protocol is used to exchange information about cryptographic capabilities and keys. SSL record protocol is used to exchange the actual data. SSL is supported by most Internet browsers

Table 11-5 Tom Pritchard's Biometric Ratings

(1) Criterion	(2) Weight	(3) Fingerprints	(4) Palm/Hand	(5) Face	(6) Retina	(7) Iris	(8) Keystroke	(9) Voice
Intrusiveness	.25	2	2	3	1	1	5	4
User Effort	.35	3	3	3	1	5	2	1
Accuracy	.15	3	3	2	4	5	2	2
Cost	.25	3	2	3	2	1	5	4

Table 11-6 Tom's Solution to Table 11-4

(1) Criterion	(2) Weight	(3) Fingerprints	(4) Palm/Hand	(5) Face	(6) Retina	(7) Iris	(8) Keystroke	(9) Voice
Intrusiveness	.25	.50 **	.50	.75	.25	.25	1.25	1.00
User Effort	.35	1.05	1.05	1.05	.35	1.75	.70	.35
Accuracy	.15	.45	.45	.30	.60	.75	.30	.30
Cost	.25	.75	.50	.75	.50	.25	1.25	1.00
Total	1.00	2.75	2.50	2.83	1.70	3.00	3.60	2.65

** **Weight (.25) times rating for Fingerprints on Intrusiveness criterion (2 out of 5)**

and is in the process of becoming an Internet Engineering Task Force (IETF) standard under the name *Transport Level Security (TLS)*.

S/HTTP: *Secure HTTP (S/HTTP)* is an alternate approach to SSL that includes the features of (a) authentication, (b) encryption, (c) cryptographic checksums (similar to accounting hash totals), and (d) digital signatures. S/HTTP usage is diminishing as SSL becomes the international standard.

SET: *Secure Electronic Transaction (SET),* developed by two major credit card companies, provides a protocol and infrastructure specification that supports bank payments which can be integrated into any Web site. SET (a) encrypts payment instructions that preclude exposure of a user's credit card number on the network or on the merchant's system, (b) authenticates merchants to users to protect against imposters, and (c) provides authentication of users to protect against unauthorized persons attempting to initiate a bank payment. SET users must obtain a software tool called a "wallet" from their credit card companies. The *Wallet* contains the user's personal certification for entry into SET.

Kerberos: *Kerberos* is a secret-key cryptography system in which communicating parties share encryption keys. It uses a *Key Distribution Center (KDC)* which allows parties to exchange a series of encrypted messages called *Tickets.* These tickets expire after a period of time and must be revalidated. This ticket expiration scheme represents a tradeoff between using a short encryption key and changing it rapidly enough so that the key cannot be solved quickly.

PAM: The *Pluggable Authentication Module (PAM)* is a security technique where the software is not an integrated part of the business application; it is plugged into the application at run (execute) time. It is a software module shared by many applications and is brought into use when called by a specific application.

PKI: The *Public Key Infrastructure (PKI)* is a 3rd-party facilitator that issues, registers and recovers passwords used by business parties for Web communication. It provides a *Certificate Authority (CA)* capability that is a centrally managed directory of registered passwords and the source for the issue of new passwords. Its structure is based upon the use of dual encryption keys: a public key and a private key.

The **Public Key** is an encryption key that is widely distributed and available in public directories. The **Private Key** is an encryption key that is held in privacy by each e-business party. A message coded using a public key can be interpreted only by using the private key.

RADIUS: **Remote Authentication Dial-in Service (RADIUS)** is a protocol for authentication, authorization, and accounting for remote access Internet connections. Communication between sender and receiver are encrypted.

Smart Cards: The **Smart Card** technique requires the insertion of a physical card in conjunction with the user's password. It uses the PKI methodology. Compaq computers now can be equipped with an embedded reader for smart cards.

Security Tokens: A **Security Token** is a time-synchronized identification card with an LCD screen that displays a string of password numbers that change every minute. When logging into a network system, the user types in the user name and the number currently being displayed by the security token. The host network system knows what the number is supposed to be for any specific user at any specific time. It is difficult to crack a password when it changes every minute. In addition, the LCD screen relieves the user from having to memorize the password.

Two-factor Authentication: A higher level of security can be attained if two or three authentication methods are used in combination. For example, an organization can require the use of security tokens that generate one-time passwords *and* some biometric means such as a retina scan. In this way, if one method is broached (e.g., personal identification code stolen), the perpetrator still cannot enter the network system. Of course, two-factor authentication is more costly than using only one medium. This increased expenditure may not be warranted if the expected threat loss is relatively low.

The Bottom Line: By now, you probably are immersed in the alphabet soup that is the current state of e-business authentication. It may get worse until a clear usage standard emerges. As accountants, we need not know the specifics of any one authentication approach or type of software. Yet, we should have a general knowledge of (a) what are these different approaches, and (b) which approach our security managers have chosen, and (c) why that particular approach was selected.

ASSET PROTECTION

In an e-business setting, assets to be protected could include computer hardware, software or information stored in organization databases. We have organized our discussion of asset protection into the three segments of (a) physical asset protection controls, (b) logical asset protection controls, and (c) continuity and contingency planning.

Physical Asset Protection Controls: These are controls that protect hardware such as storage media and software such as archived copies of application programs. These could include:

- placing computer and network equipment in locked rooms and restricting access to authorized personnel
- having only one or two entrances to computer room
- requiring proper employee ID
- requiring visitors to sign log
- installing locks on PCs
- encrypting stored data and archived application programs

Logical Asset Protection Controls: These are controls that prevent access to information stored in data files. They include authentication and authorization techniques already discussed.

Continuity and Contingency Planning: The purpose of this planning is to ensure that transaction processing can be restored as smoothly and quickly as possible in the event of a major disaster. A *Business Continuity and Contingency Plan* is comprised of (a) contingency planning, (b) audit and assurance, and disaster recovery (Figure 11-4).

Contingency Planning: The primary objectives of this element are to plan alternate means of processing information, establish priorities for the recovery process, and train and familiarize personnel with emergency operations. Contingency planning involves (a) assessment of the organizational impact for each type of disruption threat, (b) assessment of the risks attached to each threat, and (c) constructing a plan that provides for cost-effective countermeasures to counter each threat according to the following idealized formula. Some countermeasures that typically are deployed are insurance coverage, periodic back-up of file and transaction data, duplicate WAN/ LAN networks, alternate electric power sources, and alternate processing arrangements. These arrangements can include:

Off-site Data Storage: Periodic backups of file and transaction data are stored at off-site facilities for protection in case the primary site is damaged or destroyed by disasters such as fire or floods. The State of Alaska, for instance, requires all state agencies to (a) back up files daily onto an auxiliary storage device such as magnetic tape, and (b) transport the back ups to another state facility at least 10 miles away in order to protect against Alaska's higher than normal risks of earthquake occurrences.

Reciprocal Agreements: The organization can fashion agreements with other companies to use their computing/network facilities in case of outage. For example, Foundation Health Corporation of Ranch Cordoba, California provides backup processing for many other health management organizations (HMO) in the greater Sacramento area.

Alternate Processing Sites: Alternate physical processing facilities are rented or purchased so that the IT department can move its operations there in case of an emergency such as flooded facilities. A *Hot Site* includes pre-positioned hardware, software, and networking so that this alternate site can be operational in a matter of hours. The less expensive *Cold Site* contains bare essentials such as lighting and electricity and requires hardware movement and installation; it takes days rather than hours to bring the system back into operation as an alternate site.

Shadow Mode is the most expensive alternate processing mode. This involves running systems in parallel at the main and an alternate site. When the main site is threatened, processing can be switched to the alternate site in a matter of minutes.

Audit and Assurance: The Continuity/Contingency plan is not

Figure 11-4
Continuity and Contingency Planning

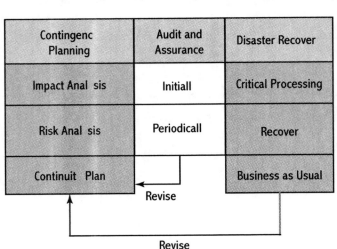

Contingenc Planning	Audit and Assurance	Disaster Recover
Impact Anal sis	Initiall	Critical Processing
Risk Anal sis	Periodicall	Recover
Continuit Plan		Business as Usual

Revise

Revise

viable until it is tested by simulating the disasters (threats) facing the organization. The plan also should be audited and assured by an outside agency at the initial formulation stage and periodically thereafter. This may lead to plan revisions.

Disaster Recovery: If a threat does occur, then the disaster recovery segment of the plan must be implemented quickly. The typical recovery sequence is as follows:

Movement to Alternate Processing Site: If required, IT operations are relocated to the hot or cold site. If shadow mode is used, the alternate site is switched on.

Critical Processing: Transaction processing at the alternate site generally is restricted to critical systems such as customer ordering and inventory. A **Critical Process** is defined as a process which, if shut down, will cause the company to discontinue operations. Restriction to critical processing (a) frees personnel for the recovery process, and (b) reduces the number of transactions that must be processed against recovered data files.

File Recovery: The process of recovering the system back to its original state begins (Figure 11-5).

The file and transaction data stored off-site are retrieved. The backup file data is first loaded onto the computer system. Then all transaction data since the last file save date is processed one transaction at a time until the newly recreated files are complete as of the current date.

Business as Usual: Once all data files have been posted with all transaction data up to the moment, the organization can resume normal operations. A debriefing session is held with all recovery personnel to determine what changes should be made to the Continuity/Contingency plan.

Diversified Asset Protection: It is unwise to base the organization's e-business security posture upon only one type of asset protection. Concentration on one is less expensive and easier to manage. However, if that measure doesn't work, the organization is in trouble.

The goal of diversified security is to quickly recover or even seamlessly continue doing business when disaster strikes. There are several approaches being used by major companies.

Multiple Routing: United Airlines has an on-line customer service unit which it duplicates at two physical centers connected through a Metropolitan-area Network (MAN). Both centers have identical Web servers, application programs, and databases. United uses multiple internet routes leased from different providers. There may be as many as eight routes being used at any one time. Files at both centers are updated simultaneously and identically for each customer transaction (Shadow Mode). If there is a catastrophic failure at one center, the other center assumes the first center's traffic without interruption or manual intervention.

Outsourced Hot Sites: BNP Paribas is a financial services organization. It contracts with Schlumberger-Sema to provide hot sites. Duplicate parts of the company's technology applications are stored securely in buildings that

Figure 11-5 File Recovery Process

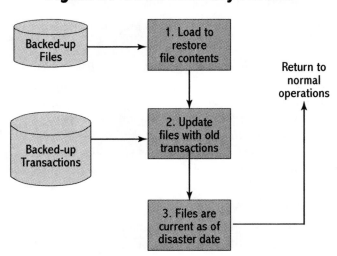

are miles away from operational sites. IT personnel travel to these hot sites to initiate recovery operations.

Internal/External Blends: Hot site providers often are expensive. Therefore, some companies have been moving in the direction of internalizing disaster recovery. Boeing Corporation, for example, uses a mix of multiple in-house recovery centers and mirrored hot sites. This lowers the expense of using only off-line recovery centers.

Satellite Backup: The United States Post Office (USPC) has used land lines as its primary connection between post offices. Yet, spurred by the 9/11 terrorist attack, USPC now has built a network of 11,000 VSAT satellite installations. The switch-over from land line to satellite communication is automatic and transparent to local post offices.

Diversified security is more expensive than use of a single technique. That increased expense can be justified only by matching it to the expected amount to be lost should a threat (e.g., disaster) occur. That matching is the subject of the next section of this chapter.

RETURN ON SECURITY INVESTMENTS

Security professionals today have a difficult job selling security needs to top management, despite increased levels of appreciation for security threats following the 9/11 terrorist attacks. These security professionals must (a) provide high-level data protection, (b) ensure privacy, (c) manage user access, (d) stay within reduced budgets, and (e) justify security project investments to money-oriented executives.

Economically justifying security investments would seem to be a simple matter if you use the model suggested in this chapter. You determine the maximum amount (exposure) that you could lose if a potential threat should occur. Then you determine the risk of that threat occurring – a probability value between zero and 1.0. When you multiply the exposure by the risk, you arrive at the expected dollar loss from that threat. You then select from a list of security countermeasures those that have costs less than or equal to your expected loss.

While this approach seems conceptually sound, it rarely can be used so simply in today's complex e-business setting. The reasons for this are (a) it is difficult to place dollar values on the exposure and risk variables, (b) threat risks are changing constantly as countermeasures become better but potential perpetrators become more knowledgeable of invasion methods, and (c) there are hidden risks in security products that are not designed correctly or comprehensively.

Security savants have suggested that an approach different from traditional return-on-investment should be used for justifying investment on e-business security.

Justifying Security: The approach suggested by many security analysts is *Return on Security Investment (ROSI)*: determining the maximum security value that an organization can attain for a given amount of dollars that inevitably will *have* to be spent. This approach considers that security is a strategic investment rather than just another expense. It is analogous to saying, *"We have to build a warehouse. What's the least dollar amount that it will take to build that warehouse and what's the best warehouse we can get for that price?"* ROSI does not ignore reduction of operating expense. It just considers the fact that, after all the possible cost-shaving is done, the security project still may not pay for itself under traditional ROI guidelines. Efforts can be made to reduce security costs to a minimum by tactics such as the following.

Future Planning: Prepare networks and support systems to take advantage of future security investments. For example, you may choose to spend a little more now on security software

Intel Security Principles

Intel uses 13 universal security principles. As stated on its Web site, "*These are basic assumptions (rules) when formulating security strategy and policy and when analyzing security solutions.*" Following are Intel's security principles.

- *Be Vigilant:* Security requires continuous monitoring.

- *Enlist the Users:* Security can't work if the users don't consider security to be important.

- *Embrace Simplicity:* Simplicity means fewer links.

- *Evaluate the Whole System:* Your security structure is only as secure as the weakest link.

- *Close the Big Holes:* Spend your security budget securing the biggest problems and the largest vulnerabilities.

- *Fail Securely:* Design your security so that, when products fail, they fail in a secure manner.

- *Detect and Respond to Attacks:* Respond promptly. Use an alert triage system. Close vulnerabilities when attackers find them.

- *Assume Ignorance:* Protect against user error as well as active hostility.

- *Watch the Watchers:* Audit your own processes regularly.

- *Limit Privileges:* Restrict access according to business needs and acceptable business risk.

- *Use Choke Points:* Minimize access points (e.g., through firewalls). Then you can secure these few points more carefully.

- *Provide Defense in Depth:* Use multiple, complementary security products so that a failure in one does not mean total insecurity.

- *Protect Assets at the Source:* Use an appropriate level of protection as close to the resource (e.g., file) as possible.

that has open-system architecture. In this way, future security products or enhancements can be "plugged in" at minimum conversion costs.

Look for New Security Products: Adopt new products aimed at reducing security costs. Look for **Security Suites**: packages that include multiple rather than a single security countermeasure.

Build Security into New Applications: There are examples of engineering new software that have saved security management operating costs by as much as 20 percent. Security analysts should be members of all e-business development project teams.

Consider Insurance: The costs of disaster insurance have been climbing. Still, the insurance industry has a long and largely successful history in placing dollar values on variables such as exposure or risk.

Benchmark: Learn how other companies of similar size and mission are "solving" their security investment problems.

Outsource Security Management: Portions of your security management can be outsourced.

Outsourcing Security: A B2B market largely is a provider and aggregator of services for which an organization may not have the resources to support itself. Using an application service provider (ASP) or security service provider (SSP) might prove cost-effective. Yet, security problems are replete with intangible variables that defy the quantification required of traditional ROI justification models. Costs are easier to state in dollars than are security impacts and risks.

You should expect key security services from any prospective outsource security provider.

- Documented information security policies and procedures
- Redundancy for security-critical elements such as firewalls and authentication systems
- Clearly defined procedures for response to security incidents
- Strong authentication and encryption for administrative access to security infrastructure
- Background checks for personnel with access to client data or administrative access to systems and applications
- Documented security audits performed at least annually
- Client data isolated from that of other clients, with sensitive data encrypted
- Intrusion detection at the application level to find transaction anomalies
- A formal Service-level Agreement (SLA) which ensures that the provider meets the availability and performance standards suitable to your organization

An organization without much security expertise might consider contracting with a public accounting firm to search for, evaluate and recommend an outsource security provide. The upfront additional expenditure may well prove cost-beneficial for ensuing operational costs and security quality.

SUMMARY

Our accounting standards specify that we are responsible for transaction integrity and asset protection. Yet these topics have become increasingly complex and difficult to master. They probably won't prove to be much easier in the years to come. How then can we fulfill the responsibilities thrust upon us? We offer the following suggestions.

Keep up with the evolving methodologies and techniques at a general level of knowledge. Establish an ongoing trust relationship with technical people responsible for e-business security. Ensure that the organization is aware of, practicing, and actively reviewing general security principles as demonstrated in the boxed entry "Intel Security Principles". Use the outsource provider checklist of the previous section as an audit checklist for security practices in your organization.

Our traditional accounting responsibilities are not easy to accomplish in the ever changing and more technical e-business world. We must change with this world and keep one eye on the horizon to spot emerging changes that will affect us.

KEY TERMS

Application-level Security Tools

Authentication

Authentication Criteria

Authorization

Behavior-based IDS

Biometric Authentication

Business Continuity and Contingency Plan

Certificate Authority (CA)

Cipher

Code

Cold Site

Critical Process

Data Integrity

Data Privacy

Denial of Service

Dynamic Positioning

E-mail High-jacking

Encryption

False Storefront

File Recovery

Honey Pot

Hot Site

Intrusion Detection

Intrusion Detection Systems (IDS)

IP Spoofing

Kerberos

Key Distribution Center (KDC)

Knowledge-based IDS

Network Security Tools

Pluggable Authentication Module (PAM)

Private Key

Program Logic Analyzer

Public Key

Public Key Infrastructure (PKI)

Remote Authentication Dial-in Service (RADIUS)

Return on Security Investment (ROSI)

Secure Electronic Transaction (SET)

Secure HTTP (S/HTTP)

Secure Socket Layer (SSL)

Security Exposure

Security Suite

Security Token

Sensitivity Threshold

Shadow Mode

Smart Card

Sniffing

Ticket

Transport Level Security (TLS)

Trojan Horse

Type I Error

Type II Error

Wallet

REVIEW EXERCISES

1. State two reasons why e-business security is important to accountants.
2. Describe the differences between data privacy and data integrity.
3. Describe three authentication threats.
4. What are the System Dependency threats?
5. Who are the parties posing e-business threats? Why are they doing it?
6. Describe three methods used to break into a company's network.
7. How can threat risk assessment be outsourced?
8. How do privacy violations affect the company's financial statements?
9. Describe three countermeasures to data integrity threats.
10. Compare and contrast authentication with authorization.
11. What does a Program Logic Analyzer do?
12. What is encryption? Why is it important for asset protection?

13. What is the difference between Type I and Type II detection errors?

14. Compare and contrast Knowledge-based with Behavior-based IDS.

15. What is a Honey Pot?

16. What is a Sensitivity Threshold? Why is it important?

17. Why is it forecast that Keystroke Signatures will decrease in usage?

18. Compare and contrast SSL with SET.

19. Compare and contrast Kerberos with RADIUS.

20. What is the difference between Private and Public keys?

21. How does a Security Token work?

22. What are the components of a Business Continuity and Contingency Plan?

23. What are the differences between a hot site, a cold site, and shadow mode?

24. Describe the disaster recovery process.

25. What makes a particular process "critical"? Describe two critical processes for a:

   a. university
   b. manufacturing company

26. What is ROSI? Why is it important?

CRITICAL THINKING OPPORTUNITIES

1. Survey three to five e-business companies in your geographic area to determine how they determine their threats, exposures and risk. Prepare PowerPoint slides for your survey results.

2. Analyze a password that you use to enter a workplace or university network. How could that password be improved? Why?

3. What type of IDS does your university use? Why was this IDS selected?

4. What type of biometric device(s) would seem appropriate for student access to individual grade and financial aid information? Why?

5. Research the Internet to find high, average, and low product prices for all of the authentication techniques described in this chapter. Write a memorandum to the IT Manager explaining the results of your research.

6. Your IT Manager is proposing the use of two-factor authentication for your Web customer ordering system. Develop a detailed outline (don't do the work) for determining the economic feasibility of this proposal.

7. Interview your university's IT Manager to determine his or her department's procedures for:

   a. developing a Business Continuity and Contingency plan
   b. security audit and assurance
   c. contingency planning
   d. disaster recovery

8. Survey three to five e-business companies in your geographic area to determine how they economically justify investments in network security.

9. Compare your plan in exercise 8 with your results in exercise 11. How do they differ?

10. One of Intel's security principles is "Enlist the Users". Compose a memorandum to Intel's

Vice President of IT explaining how you believe that Intel's security principles could be clarified and improved in order to make them clearer to (and thus elicit support from) users.

11. Consider the arguments for using ROSI rather than traditional ROI. Are these arguments valid? Why should security investments be treated differently than other IT investments in infrastructure (e.g., databases) or applications (e.g., inventory system)?

REFERENCES

CERT Coordination Center; *"Configure the Web Server to Use Authentication and Encryption Technologies";* **Security Improvement Modules**, July

CSI/FBI; **2002 Computer Crime and Security Survey**; June 2003

Fratto, M.; *"Security Tokens"*; **Network Computing**, August 20th, 2001

RSA Security Inc; **E-security: Do You Know Who You're Doing Business With**"; June, 2002

Glover, S., S. Liddle, and D. Prawitt; **E-business: Principles and Strategies for Accountants**; Prentice Hall, 2001

Intel; *"Universal Information Security Principles"*; Intel Web Site, 6/27/02

Karofsky, E.; *"Insight into Return on Security Investment"*; **Secure Business Quarterly**, 4Q 2001

Paul, B.; *"Opening Your E-business Perimeter";* **Network Computing**; 1/8/03

Salmonson, C. and J. Mee; *"E-business Security"*; KPMG presentation at California State University Sacramento, 12/2/03

the future

> — "The art of progress is to preserve order amid change and change amid order."
>
> — *Alfred North Whitehead*

There are some technology futurists who are predicting that computers will surpass humans as the dominant life form. As one such (unnamed) savant said, *"Why would you think that a carbon life form would be superior to a silicon life form?"* There also are some business futurists who are predicting that the accounting profession will become as extinct as the dinosaur. We don't believe either of these predictions. At the same time, we do believe that humans in general and accountants in particular must change their ways if their species are to survive. This is a time of change. If we do not change as well, our traditions and skills will age faster and faster until we are old and the world about us is young.

How well prepared are you for this future? Let's borrow a futures planning exercise that the Information Technology Group at Intel uses to encourage executives to develop a forward-looking perspective towards technology. This exercise can be done individually or in small groups of two or three persons who report their results to the group at large.

Future of Society: First develop scenarios for what society will look like 15 years from now. Prepare three such scenarios: an optimistic view, a pessimistic view, and a most likely view.

Future of Accountancy: For each of these three scenarios, develop what you think will be the roles of accountants including the knowledge and skills that they must possess.

Your Goals: Where do you want to be 15 years from now? What do you see yourself doing in the accounting profession? What skills and knowledge will you need by then?

Personal Inventory: Where are you now? What skills and knowledge do you possess?

Personal Gap: What additional skills and knowledge must you acquire in order to attain your goals 15 years from now? How will you prepare? Can you handle great change in your profession? How will you adapt?

As Robert (Rob) Taylor of Getronics noted, *"The one thing I see more and more every day is our change in viewpoint. Over the years, accountants have looked at the past. Now, with current accounting systems and tools, we're able to get a better picture of what you're going to do in the future."* We must look to the future more than our traditional past. We believe that this future will be exciting for the accounting profession and that we will master the technological forces that we will face. We believe that our profession best exemplifies Alfred North Whitehead's quote beginning this Epilogue – we *can* be the agents of orderly change.

In that vein, we will end this book the same way we started it – with a quote from Nikos Kazantzakis honoring the uniqueness of man as compared to machine.

"What a strange machine man is.
You fill him with bread, wine,
fish and radishes, and out come
sighs, laughter, and dreams."

index